Television, Tabloids, and Tears

Television, Tabloids, and Tears

Fassbinder and Popular Culture

Jane Shattuc

University of Minnesota Press

Minneapolis

London

Chapter 3 first appeared as "R. W. Fassbinder as Popular Auteur: The Making of an Authorial Legend," *Journal of Film and Video* 45 (Spring 1993), reprinted by permission; chapter 4 first appeared as "*Contra* Brecht: R. W. Fassbinder and Pop Culture in the Sixties," *Cinema Journal* (Fall 1993), reprinted by permission.

Published by the University of Minnesota Press
111 Third Avenue South, Suite 290, Minneapolis, MN 55401-2520
Printed in the United States of America on acid-free paper

Library of Congress Cataloging-in-Publication Data
Shattuc, Jane.
    Television, tabloids, and tears : Fassbinder and popular culture /
Jane Shattuc.
        p.   cm.
    Includes bibliographical references and index.
    ISBN 0-8166-2454-2 (alk. paper). — ISBN 0-8166-2455-0 (pbk. :
alk. paper)
    1. Fassbinder, Rainer Werner, 1946–   — Criticism and
interpretation.   2. Berlin Alexanderplatz (Television program)
I. Title.
PN1998.3.F37S52   1994
791.43'0233'092 — dc20   94-30357

The University of Minnesota is an equal-opportunity educator and employer.

Contents

Acknowledgments

It is now my turn to debunk the myth of my authorship. This book results from the ideas of hundreds of people who have shaped the work in its ten-year evolution. First, I owe a great debt to my teachers. Claudia Gorbman's sly humor made learning about film such a pleasure. Tino Balio taught me the importance of clear and precise historical thinking. David Bathrick inspired my interest in the contradictions of German culture and shaped much of the politics of the book. James Steakley offered me a model in his dedication to the history of marginalized culture. Tom Streeter and John Fiske influenced the book more than they realize; they introduced me to cultural studies.

But only with the help of friends and colleagues did I write this book. I must recognize Henry Jenkins—my best critic and tenant—who swallowed his resistance to high culture to read numerous drafts and to give extensive comments. The book was also helped by the generous encouragement of Timothy Corrigan, Virginia Wright-Wexman, and Marcia Landy. Ed Larkin refined my translations. My colleagues Michael Selig and Donald Fry lent me their intelligence and savvy about the intricacies of academic publishing. The commentary, political commitment, and friendship of Jackie Byars, Nancy Ciezki, Jackie Joyce, Diane Kostecke, Mary Rhiel, Laura Thielen, Robyn Warhol, Rose Ann Wasserman, and Patty Zimmermann made writing this book a pleasure. Misha Bogdanov offered me not only emotional support but also insight into the practical implications of my political theories. My family, Rick Shattuc, Helen Bloch, Mary Stanton, and Will Shattuc, gave me a sense of perspective.

This book also benefited from the support of a number of institutions. First, I need to thank the University of Bonn and the German Exchange Service for two years of financial support in West Germany. Additionally, I owe a debt of gratitude to Westdeutscher Rundfunk and Frau Hannah Sell of the Fernsehspiel Abteilung for opening the doors to their Fassbinder holdings and archive. And I must recognize Janaki Bakhle and Rob

Mosimann of the University of Minnesota Press for their enthusiastic and highly professional support of this project.

Finally, I want to dedicate this book to my parents, Loretta and Frederic Shattuc, who tempered my radicalism with their Midwest populism and humor, inspiring the idealism of the book.

1 / The Melodrama of Fassbinder's Reception

Mechanical reproduction of art changes the reaction of the masses towards art. The reactionary attitude toward a Picasso painting changes into a progressive reaction towards a Chaplin movie. This progressive reaction is characterized by the direct, intimate fusion of visual and emotional enjoyment with the orientation of an expert. Such fusion is of great social significance. The greater the decrease in the social significance of an art form, the sharper the distinction between criticism and enjoyment. With regard to the screen, the critical and the receptive attitudes of the public coincide.

Walter Benjamin, "Art in the Age of Mechanical Reproduction"[1]

As of 1980, Rainer Werner Fassbinder's epic television adaptation of Alfred Döblin's novel *Berlin Alexanderplatz* was the longest (sixteen hours), most expensive ($6 million), and most widely seen television project in German media history. It was seen by 20 million West Germans—an unprecedented viewership for a New German Cinema film. Although the expense and length of the series have since been exceeded,[2] Fassbinder's production engendered the longest and fiercest controversy to date. Not only the press but also the broad West German public participated in this debate. Through letters and petitions to the producing station, magazines, and newspapers, thousands of viewers expressed their support of and anger at the series.

1

Interestingly, the debate was not just about the filmmaker's radical politics; it encompassed the role of filmic form and popular reception, the role of the state in the production of an inherently *German* filmic form, and, importantly, the unexamined status of the film director or the author (*Autor*) as an anointed cultural representative.

How can we account for this unusual controversy? Could the film's premiere on the popular medium of television be a logical extension of Benjamin's claim: with its ability to reach a broad audience, mass-produced art breaks through the aura traditionally associated with the work of art and engenders a critical attitude toward a work? Or did the uproar result from the public's supposed traditional antagonism toward the avant-garde and the overtly political? And, ultimately, we must ask: Given Fassbinder's controversial public history, how and why was he chosen to create Germany's most costly and possibly most widely seen art film?

The purpose of this book is to unravel this seeming contradiction. To do so, it is necessary to examine Fassbinder's form of "politicized melodrama" within the history of auteurism or *Autorenfilme* (the German counterpart) in West German television, the institution for which he produced nearly half of his works. By analyzing Fassbinder's art film form within the institution of West German television — two histories that culminate in the production of *Berlin Alexanderplatz* — the book questions the possibilities and limitations of Fassbinder's radical ideology within West German television. More generally, it examines the role of critical filmmaking in relation to twentieth-century popular culture.

Contrary to expectations, Fassbinder received the sustained support of West German television despite the fact that their ten-year relationship was marked by continuous controversy, originating in both the television industry and the West German public. The problems began with the refusal of Westdeutscher Rundfunk (Cologne's ARD affiliate)[3] to produce the last segments of Fassbinder's television worker series, *Eight Hours Are Not a Day* (*Acht Stunden sind kein Tag*), in 1972. Then the station, after an initial financial pledge, refused in 1976 to support Fassbinder's adaptation of Gustav Freytag's *Credit and Debit* (*Soll und Haben*) because of the novel's alleged anti-Semitism. And in 1978 it withdrew promised financial support for Fassbinder's *Third Generation* (*Die dritte Generation*), a film connecting the rise of terrorism to West German capitalism.

The controversies surrounding Fassbinder's television work came to a head in 1980 when Westdeutscher Rundfunk (the institutional producer) disavowed content responsibility for *Berlin Alexanderplatz* and rescheduled the mammoth production to the less-viewed late night hours. The most obvious question is this: Why would West German television as an agency of the state risk its financial stability by supporting Fassbinder's productions, whose controversial nature went beyond just these four incidents? Indeed, he was gay, a drug user, and a leftist with terrorist affiliations. One possible answer is that the state, and West German television in particular, were able to contain and appropriate Fassbinder's radical reputation by controlling the presentation and the public discussion surrounding the various films' television broadcast. Another likely answer is that Fassbinder's television work in general was not *that* radical, which is why public television could ride out each crisis. But these answers are too simple.

West German television's tolerance of Fassbinder's productions was built around a series of contradictory determinants: (1) television's needs, stemming from its antifascist founding principles; (2) television's ability (as a state monopoly) to control the discourse surrounding its presentations; and (3) the limited radical nature of Fassbinder's films. But this view does not account for the degree of public outcry and unprecedented political pressure against Fassbinder's productions. To understand this incongruity, it is necessary to analyze the unique authority of an "auteur" or *Autor* in West German television.

Fassbinder's oeuvre stands as a fascinating stepchild of the self-conscious manipulation of a genre's mass appeal and the high-culture connotations of the auteur theory. Fassbinder and his institutional supporters were able to combine this high-cultural concept of authorship with popular culture's interest in emotion and genre, or what I have termed Fassbinder's confessional melodrama. The discursive play of these two often-opposing concepts was never resolved. When one charts the various contradictions and tensions of West German television's institutional needs against Fassbinder's critical filmmaking, one begins to see how West German television has institutionalized ideological controversy. Its conception and use of "auteurs" remain pivotal to an understanding of the "radicalness" of Fassbinder's television work. He was canonized, however, not for his radicalness but for his artistry.

This history cannot be easily explained by any simple determinism, be it economic, aesthetic, or political. Instead, West German television's support of Fassbinder's "radical" television works was a response to the contradictory pressures and needs of West Germany in the 1970s — a period marked by rapid inflation, massive student unrest, and terrorism. Although Fassbinder's films have been labeled "radical" as part of the German New Left, there was nothing *essentially* radical about them. Tony Bennett argues similarly against an essential text: "The *text* must be replaced by the concept of the concrete and varying, historically specific functions and effect which accrue to 'the text' as a result of the different determinations to which it is subjected during the history of its appropriation."[4] To argue that they were in any sense subversive, Fassbinder's television works must be understood through an analysis of the role of their form and content in history.

Fassbinder and Melodrama: Historicizing Text-Based Criticism

The majority of analyses of Fassbinder and his work have concentrated on the films themselves. Central to most criticism of Fassbinder is the argument that he adapted the melodrama form after discovering the Hollywood melodramas of the 1940s and 1950s, and in particular the work of Douglas Sirk. This appropriation of generic convention allowed Fassbinder to work within a traditional popular form while subversively undercutting the ideology of that medium; he utilized the stylistic devices of melodrama to contradict the narrative's overt social morality. In her article on Fassbinder's *Ali/Fear Eats the Soul* (1973), Judith Mayne exemplifies this position on Fassbinder and melodrama:

> While *Ali* is not strictly a genre film, it relies heavily on conventions of the Hollywood melodrama perfected in the 1940s and 1950s. It is tempting to refer to Fassbinder's use of genre as a politicizing of the melodrama. Certainly *Ali* reflects upon the social reality of West Germany and modern capitalism. Those political realities so often repressed in mainstream cinema appear to surface in the film, creating a confrontation between melodrama and politics.[5]

Other commentators on Fassbinder's use of melodrama have ranged widely in the degree to which they are willing to establish *direct* relationships between the melodrama form and an ideologically critical effect. In homage to Fassbinder in his survey on New German Cinema, John Sandford allows only an ambiguous relation between politics and form when he describes Fassbinder's melodramas as "a host of uncomfortably self-conscious domestic melodramas that have for many become the epitome of his work."[6]

Although it is not directly stated, Sandford is alluding to the critical stance that melodrama is an ideologically subversive form.

The "discomforting" quality of Fassbinder's melodramas takes on explicitness when Tim Corrigan argues in his reading of Fassbinder's *The Bitter Tears of Petra von Kant* that

> Fassbinder came gradually to this awareness that good politics are incident without effective avenues of communication, his strategies moving through intellectual phases associated with Straub, the "anti-theater," and the French New Wave. Yet ultimately, with the assistance of his extraordinary cameraman Michael Ballhaus, he allied himself with the American cinema so that they could use his highly developed and proficient syntax to subvert its ideologically unsuspecting perspective.[7]

Here Corrigan establishes a fundamental division between the stylistic and the narrative/thematic levels; that it subverts the opposition makes Fassbinder's melodrama so ideologically effective. This theory of form as a kind of political commentary on the ideology of the Fassbinder media text is echoed in Eric Rentschler's discussion of Douglas Sirk's influence on Fassbinder:

> The fact is ... that Fassbinder's major lesson from Sirk was one of strategy, not of style. From films like *All that Heaven Allows* and *Written on the Wind* he learned how a popular form could be recast to appeal to audience expectations while simultaneously subverting them, calling movie derived reactions into question as well as the social structures traditional narratives have affirmed.[8]

Three important assumptions underlie this "critical melodrama" perspective: (1) as a Hollywood genre convention, melodrama breaks from the realist codes that dominate classic Hollywood films and therefore disrupts the ideology that informs them; (2) spectators can be "distanced" from their ideological positions by the operations of the film or television production; (3) most essentially, the ideology can be defined through analysis of film.

The view that the Hollywood melodrama of the 1940s and 1950s inherently has a critical potential stems from many sources.[9] In film studies, Thomas Elsaesser's influential article "Tales of Sound and Fury: Observations on the Family Melodrama" established many of the theoretical parameters for a film's political potential.[10] In his admittedly provocative and speculative essay, Elsaesser outlines what specifically constitutes film melodrama, namely, the Hollywood family melodrama of the 1940s through

1963. And he argues that melodrama's defining characteristic is its creation of an ideologically open text whose authority can be questioned.

Tracing the complicated network of historical antecedents from the medieval morality play to the sentimental novel of the eighteenth century and the *Baenkellied* or popular ballads of German *Volk* culture, Elsaesser argues that what unites these diverse cultural forms with the Hollywood melodrama of the 1950s is the tension between the story's overt moral content and its stylistics or expressive mise-en-scène. The story is always of a "moral/moralistic" character; broad, nonpsychologically motivated actions such as victimization and class conflicts form the principal structuring devices. It is, however, the stylistics of these melodramas that have served as either an "ironic" counterstatement by giving "false emphasis to the extreme morality of the story" or a distancing effect in which "the rhythm of experience often establishes itself against its value (moral, intellectual)."[11]

Elsaesser examines the work of Douglas Sirk as the central example of a director who exploited the inherent self-consciousness of melodrama. For example, in *Written on the Wind* (1956), a scene after the funeral of Hadley Sr. that has no apparent plot significance is read by Elsaesser as having this "ironic commentary" significance. An extremely *black* servant is seen removing a wreath from a door. A *black* ribbon falls off the wreath and its movement along the ground is traced by the camera dissolving and dollying on to Lauren Bacall's striking *green* dress. Given the unnatural intensity of the mise-en-scène's color scheme, the scene takes on a disquieting aura. It also destroys any sense of optimism in the film, echoing the obvious fatalism of the title. Paul Willemen, Jon Halliday, and Steve Neale have also suggested similar readings of how Sirk undermined his films' ideological coherence.[12] As a result, they all have made claims for melodrama as having a special status as either a progressive or a modernist genre.

Although these analyses of Fassbinder, Sirk, and melodrama have contributed a great deal to the understanding of the text and ideology, they have failed to provide a historical account of the "progressive text." Elsaesser never elaborates on the historical circumstance for Sirk's modernist form within Hollywood other than to indicate Sirk's origins in Weimar theater. Nor does he explain what led to a politicized use of the genre or why the film viewer abandoned the usual apolitical generic understanding of melodrama as a heightened emotional arena. In fact, Laura Mulvey points out that to argue that melodrama is an inherently ironic or distancing form leads to a potentially misogynist position given that women and their domestic experiences tend to be the subject of melodrama generally and Sirk's films specifically.[13]

One answer to the question of why these films are distancing for Elsaesser as well as critics who have applied his Sirkean analysis to Fassbinder's films may lie in the director's intentionality or "self-consciousness." Since the codes of censorship and the necessities of commercial success in the classical Hollywood cinema precluded overt political content, melodrama provided directors a chance to manipulate the form/content dichotomy to produce a critical form of filmmaking. But authorial intentionality does not suffice to create an ideologically aware spectator when the film viewer again has been historically conditioned to read commercial film and television as a sourceless authority. For years women have been emotionally involved in the content of film melodramas. This is not to argue that the Hollywood films or even Fassbinder's television programs can or could contain no fissures in their closed texts. But these fissures, contradictions, or ruptures in ideology must be understood as a condition not only of the text but also of the historically informed spectator who is open to such a reading.[14]

Yet genre criticism still remains a prime method for a historically specific analysis of Fassbinder's ideology and a textual analysis of his use of melodrama. But the emphasis must be shifted from film form and content to the historical culture that provided meaning and political significance to a genre. On one level, genre as a critical concept allows us to situate Fassbinder's melodramas in relation to the social context and the immediate historical situation within which they arose and were interpreted.

A genre film is simply a type of popular film that is constructed around familiar narrative conventions that both audiences and filmmaker recognize. As a product of capitalist filmmaking or even ratings-conscious state television, the melodrama genre is based on popular appeal through a repetition of a successful formula. Its conventions are rooted in the historical norms and expectations of the culture from which the film emanates. In his comparable analysis of Hitchcock's use of the generic form, Fredric Jameson argues that genre studies allow one to "examine generic traditions, constraints and raw materials out of which alone, at a specific moment of their historical evolution, that unique and nongeneric thing called 'the Hitchcock film' was able to emerge."[15] And therefore a historical analysis of Fassbinder's use of this "broad" form on German television will allow us to understand the connection of the "Fassbinder film" with the social context of his popular appeal.

Political Modernism

To begin to historicize Fassbinder and his films, one needs to acknowledge that Fassbinder cannot be separated from the rise of film studies; they have had a symbiotic relationship as film theory and film practice became aware of each other by the 1960s. The academic interest in isolating Fassbinder's form as politically progressive originates in the debate about the relationship of culture to historical materialism. It began in mid-1960s media studies, fueled to a large degree by the political unrest surrounding the role of the United States in Vietnam, Godard's ongoing experiment in radical film aesthetic, and, most important theoretically, the French Marxist cultural writings of Roland Barthes, Jacques Lacan, Louis Althusser, and others. The central media issue revolved around the question of whether an adequate radical film/media aesthetic practice could be designed to mesh with the extensive aesthetic and ideological analysis that was being produced by such journals as *Cahiers du Cinéma, Screen,* and *Media, Culture and Society*: Could film form effect positive political change? Sylvia Harvey designates this historical trend in media scholarship as "political modernism" and defines it as "the long dream of unifying or relating semiotic and ideological analysis together with a desire on the part of some practitioners to combine a radical aesthetic practice with radical social effects." This controversy continued what she sees as "the aesthetic quarrel of the century" between modernism and realism.[16]

Broadly stated, the debate was an attack on the conventions of "realism" as represented by the dominant classical Hollywood film and the dominant capitalist ideology for which the films and conventions served as a vehicle. The debate evolved out of the argument that any break in capitalist ideology should, to a large degree, start with a labor on the dominant forms of representation of capitalism (i.e., the Hollywood realist film). On a textual level, this argument was taken up by the aesthetically and politically leftist films of Nagusa Oshima, Jean-Luc Godard, and Jean-Marie Straub, all of whom attempted to question the "realist" ideology in which they as filmmakers operated.

French film critics such as Jean-Luc Comolli and Jean Narboni extended the debate to whether this progressive text could be found in Hollywood or popular film. It was within this vein that Fassbinder's films have generally inherited the political modernist label. His filmmaking was first heralded as directly descended from and influenced by Godard's political project.[17] But political interest in Fassbinder's work grew as a possible unification of the two strains of the debate: his self-conscious melodramas seemed to mix popular accessibility with modernist estrangement.

Ostensibly, many of these theoretical writings, especially those applied to Fassbinder's films, were guided by an appropriation of the writings of German theater theorist Bertolt Brecht, who was seen as the forefather of the "form as political" debate.[18] The revival of Brecht's theories for the majority of these political modernists was predicated on his statements on epic theater. Brecht emphasized the role of technique (or "signifying practices" in the terminology of political modernism) in the production of the spectator's awareness of his/her role as subject of the play's ideology. This "self-awareness through technique" fits comfortably within the modernist sensibility of foregrounding the process of representation. And for numerous 1970s theorists of political modernism in film and media studies, the devices of "distanciation" became central to the production of politically radical texts.

The techniques of Brecht's distanciation—acting, episodic plot construction, and mechanics of representation—were all to be foregrounded, leading the spectator to an awareness of the play as one possible account of reality. Film theorists argued that this form of decentered representation does not fall into the traditional modernist notion of recognition for recognition's sake, but rather is created with the distinct intention of causing the spectator to second-guess the ideological completeness of the aesthetic object. Here, critics argued that Fassbinder's form moved beyond the ambiguous dissonance of melodrama to an overt engagement with political issues and a visual form that systematically distanced the viewer.

Yet political modernism has always been based on a logical impossibility: any aesthetic is based on idealist suppositions in that it searches for the specific nature of an aesthetic object that transcends history. Any attempt to reconcile historical materialism and aesthetics is destined to fail. Tony Bennett argues that this problem results from the formalist sensibility that has dominated recent ideological analyses of culture that try to reconcile two sets of concerns:

> the one consistent with the historical and materialist premises of Marxism and with its political motivation, and the other textual criticism coming out of bourgeois aesthetics.... The crucial theoretical break lies in the recognition that, instead of "Marxism *and* aesthetics," the real concerns sit uncomfortably with one another.[19]

A central example of this problem is the continuing interpretation of Fassbinder's works as "films" when nearly half were made for television.

This seemingly simple change in medium alters radically how we are to understand the political role of Fassbinder's work. First, it changes the formal considerations based on the smaller screen and the constraints of length of television programming. Second, it calls into question traditional film theories of theatrical spectatorship and the ensuing voyeurism. Most importantly for this book, television reaches a broad range of people — a popular audience — beyond the rarefied audience of the art cinema. This has had specific political consequences for West German television as a public medium balancing dependence on a taxpaying public and its role in the production of the works of such a problematic figure as Fassbinder.

Contemporary European Film and Political Economy Criticism

According to Richard Dyer and Ginette Vincendeau, traditional histories of European cinema align around the binary opposition of American entertainment film and European art cinema.[20] In fact, the traditional materialist account of postwar European film makes this opposition rather disquieting: after the physical and economic devastation of Europe in World War II, Europe's industries rose unprotected economically from the ashes of war as undercapitalized infant industries. They stood as easy prey for the major American film companies whose strong domestic hold was unaffected by the ravages of the European war. With the U.S. government's Marshall Plan to reinstate capitalism in economically and politically weak Europe, multinational Hollywood firms were able to reassert their dominance in a Europe starved for dollars and productivity. The postwar European film industry resulted from the ever tightening grip of American monopoly capitalism and its multinational style.

The art cinema of the late 1950s and early 1960s rose as the last major gasp of a nationally identifiable "art" film movement. Thomas Guback argues that even though the war had enhanced the position of the American film industry, budding postwar European filmmakers were able to take advantage of a temporary weakening of the American hold on the European market. The "weakening" was the result of two crises that hit in the American home market: the Paramount decrees of 1948 forcing divorcement of the exhibition branch from the distribution and production branches of the vertically integrated domestic structure of the American studio system and the rise of television in the United States in the 1950s.[21]

During this all too brief period of monopoly breakdown and transition for the major American film companies, foreign film companies, it is argued, were allowed to enter a previously impenetrable American film market. These nonindustrial, "rough-hewn" European films offered a markedly different and viable product in a 1950s moviegoing America dominated by wide-screen Hollywood spectacles such as *Bridge over the River Kwai* (1958), *Ben-Hur* (1959), and *Cleopatra* (1963).

Although the European "art film" incursion was to some degree institutionalized through an art house circuit, the phenomenon as a whole was short-lived. After a temporary economic upheaval, the American film firms returned economically stronger and more diversified.[22] Learning from the relative success of the art cinema in America, Hollywood films adapted some art film characteristics: a nonfactory look and more "realistic" content (on-location shooting, sexual explicitness, and topics dealing with contemporary "problems"). Mimicking the Europeans, the major studios moved their filmmaking abroad in search of authentic locales and the greater economies of a nonunionized, undercapitalized postwar Europe.

Central to the American move into European production was the fact that these so-called runaway productions were able to subvert most attempts at governmental barriers to entry. By registering as local firms, American film subsidiaries were able to take advantage of European government-sponsored production subsidies. European governments provided monies to fledgling film companies to aid their domestic markets in order to stimulate prospective national film industries and protect them against the ever present specter of American domination. But with greater capital and a supportive U.S. government, American film concerns have inevitably destroyed all corporate and governmental opposition to their world film domination. Thomas Guback argues that "in reality these programs served limited purposes and only managed to postpone for a couple of decades the coming to grips with the commercial aspect that dominates film-making in capitalist market-oriented economics."[23]

In this scenario the major American film companies have been so successful in their ability to subvert government attempts to bar the entrance of American films into other countries that by the late 1960s European film had become virtually indistinguishable from the American product. In today's market, the argument goes, if an American multinational does not finance or produce a European film, there is a 90 percent chance that it will be distributed and/or exhibited theatrically by an American firm in

Europe. Joseph Phillips echoes this political economy position: "When they finance production by foreign filmmakers, the product may tend to have a somewhat more local theme, but in most cases, they will choose projects that seem to have audience potential in the United States."[24]

To conclude this abbreviated description of contemporary filmmaking history, the central theme running through these various histories can be generalized thus: against the onslaught of monopoly capitalism in the culture industry, there can be no effective resistance. Furthermore, because of its large domestic market advantage, the Moloch of American film industry had moved by the 1970s toward total domination of European and then Third World financing. As a result, it is argued, such incursion should be classified not only as an economic imperative but also as a form of cultural imperialism in which there no longer exists an identifiable cultural, political, or artistic alternative to the bland, homogenized product of the conglomerate filmmaking of the 1970s and 1980s.

This highly structured version of contemporary film history does not do justice to the complexities of Fassbinder's history and modern filmmaking. Admittedly, I agree and sympathize with the general historical directions that Guback and similar political economy historians have taken. Capitalism has lessened the political and artistic heterogeneity — an important facet of a cultural democracy — of recent filmmaking. But the general application of political economy theory to film history has more often than not resulted in an economic determinism that has emphasized the totality of monopoly capitalism and its control of the culture industries.

These histories often neglected oppositional or even slightly different filmmaking in contemporary film and television. More importantly, they have failed to recognize how European state television by the 1970s had become the vehicle for the production of film or a visual nationalism based on national art histories. An examination of the television work of Fassbinder provides an example of this strange mixture of nationalism, oppositional culture, and regional diversity within the German media world.

Indeed, the traditionally conceived postwar German commercial film industry waned not only as a result of economic invasion from Hollywood multinationals but also, and more importantly, because of the anomalous political situation of Germany as an occupied country. The occupation allowed for what was arguably the first systematic use of the "media" as a method of political reeducation of a conquered people. Because the Allies conceived of film as a commercial entertainment medium and broadcasting as a tool for public education, film played a less pivotal role in the "reeducation" and "democratization" of a fascist Germany than did German broad-casting, which was defined as being in the public interest. And since Fass-binder (as well as the majority of independent German filmmakers) depended throughout his career on West German public television's financial support, given the weakness of the commercial film market, the Allied-imposed ide-ological difference between film and broadcasting had important conse-quences for the construction and reception of Fassbinder's films.

Neoclassical and Political Economic Theories of State, Nationalism, and Media Culture

Broad economic histories of European media—based on either traditional neoclassical or Marxist economic theories—have a difficult time explain-ing the contradictory history of West German state television and its sup-port of an explicitly plural German culture. The role of the state from a neoclassical liberal perspective is to promote the interests of society as a whole and to mediate and reconcile the antagonisms that arise from social existence. At its most basic, the neoclassical economic view envisions the state as a mechanism of regulating competition and allowing the market-place to remain open.[25]

Orthodox economic historians can comfortably accept government re-strictions when the state intervenes in order to protect its industries through tariffs, quotas, and trade agreements—all limitations based on future growth and increased economic power. But the neoclassical model reveals its limi-tations when one adds the issue of change and history. It assumes a static worldview in which economic sufficiency is the central goal of govern-ment interests. Such a model cannot subsume issues of a purely political nature—Nazi and American imperialism or even the Allied postwar de-nazification program, for example. The history of the German media and their interaction with the West German government as a purely eco-nomic protector has been fraught with contradictions stemming from Ger-many's anomalous political history of a fascist, a communist (East Ger-many), and a capitalist government in the past fifty years. In fact, economic historians of Western Europe have generally agreed that what distinguishes Germany's economic history from that of other West European nations is the degree to which "politics at the highest level" has been a determining factor.[26] Although they are deeply intertwined in the economic history of German media, such "political" considerations are outside the neoclassical model.

In many ways, the traditional Marxist economic position offers an alternative to the ahistorical neoclassical view. The state and its political considerations are central. The government is a product of the interests of a particular class and, therefore, promotes not competition but rather monopoly. Within traditional Marxist economics, imperialism, war, and cartelization come to center stage in the rise of German capitalism in the twentieth century. In this theoretical frame, Nazi German history becomes a stage of capitalist development as German economic history moved from free trade, or limited protection, to unlimited protection; from free to cutthroat competition in the world market; and finally from mercantilism to the colonialism of fascism.

From this economic standpoint, the postwar occupation of Germany functions as a reassertion of the ruling capitalist bourgeois class back into the position of governing power as in the "democratic" Weimar era. After the errant rise of petit-bourgeois rule under Hitler (which political theorist Nicos Poulantzas argues characterizes the aberrant nature of the fascist class system), the Allied occupation returned the old German bourgeois elite to positions of power through the process of denazification.[27] Although the goal officially was to contain fascism, the ultimate purpose of the American move into postwar Germany was to bring stability to American international markets and continue expansionist multinational policies. Major American film companies, within this model, are among the many multinationals that used the occupation to gain an even stronger market control in an unprotected Germany.

No historian would question the fact that the film industries in both the United States and West Germany are examples of the economic systems that their respective governments wish to promote. But the problem with highly generalized Marxist analysis is the complexities of problem solving in the modern state. On a purely economic level of analysis, "it is the nature of capitalism to change but ... because the different parts of world economy change at varying tempos ... their positions relative to one another are ... unstable."[28] For example, in the postwar expansion the West Germans created a social market economy (*soziale Marktwirtschaft*) in which the state functioned as a much more central regulator of the economy than in the neoclassical American system that backed its renaissance. The West German market economy capitalist system developed with greater intervention on the part of a planned economy and social welfare system than in a neoclassical, relatively unrestrained economy, which has led to greater state intervention in the media.

But in the case of Fassbinder and his work for public television, economic histories need to acknowledge that the product's purpose moves beyond profit into the realm of culture and nationalism. Not only is the concept of an explicitly *German* culture historically problematic after the rise of Nazism, the concept of culture itself cannot easily be separated from a concept of nationalism in general. Nationalism has been defined by Ephraim Nimni as "a political and ideological movement whose main concern is the well-being of a national community, be it real or fictitious."[29] Therefore we must consider how the West German state has engineered the course of growing media economy as well as a "healthy" nationalism, of which Fassbinder was, oddly, a leading ambassador.

Indeed, the tendency of recent German histories to chronicle art cinema and not popular cinema stems from the fact that the German government, like that of most European countries, has tended to support what Dyer and Vincendeau call the "high white traditions" as emblems of national identity as German export culture.[30] Only recently has there been a concerted effort in film criticism to break down this opposition of high European and popular American as film critics have sought a European popular cinema. This book searches for the popular response to Fassbinder's television work, but in West Germany the manufacture of high culture was much more self-conscious than in other European countries and became synonymous with the *Autor* (the author) — the central discourse of the German state and its cultural arm of public television to legitimize their production of German culture and in particular Fassbinder's work.

The *Autor* and Cultural Capital

A Fassbinder film can be understood without knowledge of his biography, but such a reading is naive. Biographical reading is a result of how films of the European art cinema were promoted in criticism and in the popular press as the personal statements of their directors in the 1960s and 1970s. These statements have had real and historical "objective" status in the reception of Fassbinder's films within his own country. Although the Fassbinder myth involved both his filmic form and the changing history of film in West Germany in the 1970s, this book limits itself to examining Fassbinder the historical being in order to understand "the Fassbinder film."

Oddly enough, while the West Germans were innocently debating the relationship of Fassbinder's films to his life, an increasing number of theoretically inclined film historians chose to disregard the role of director as a

meaningful element in the reception of a film. Since Roland Barthes's proclamation of "the death of [the] author," film studies have refused more and
more to analyze the role of the director, preferring to show that the category is, in Barthes's words, "an empty process, functioning prefectly without there being any need for it to be filled with the person of the inter-
locutor."[31] The influence of structuralism and poststructuralism on film
historians for the most part resulted in the belief that a director such as
Fassbinder was either a "subject" of a complicated web of ideological operations or, at best, an effect of the filmic text.

On the one hand, we should welcome this reaction to the simple ahistorical and apolitical idealism of the theory of the auteur as the creative
center of a film. But on the other hand, we have fallen into a contradictory
position: we have reduced the director to an ahistorical "given" of the
film, but he or she is nevertheless still publicly received as an active individual who created the film's meaning. As John Caughie argues, this contradictory about-face resulted from the discipline's attempt "to deny its former attachment by leaving the author (or auteur, or director) without an
adequate place in theory: if the author is not at the centre, he is nowhere;
if the romance is over, I will reject him utterly."[32]

"Fassbinder" as an artistic figure was not only a creation of the director's own making, but also the result of prevailing discourses on the role of
the artist or *Autor* and the media in West Germany in the 1970s. Thomas
Elsaesser's *New German Cinema: A History* reveals how the concept of the
Autor's creative role differs from the French auteur and Hollywood director.
In contrast to *Cahiers du Cinéma*'s egalitarian belief that the auteur could
flower in a popular and commercial setting such as Hollywood, the discourse of the German *Autor* stands as an angry reaction against the growing
commodification of German film in the 1960s and 1970s.[33]

The *Autor* comes closest to the role that the European art cinema director played, functioning as the director, writer, and editor constrained by a
small state-supported or commercial budget. But the German independent
filmmaker demanded total autonomy from aesthetic and economic constraint.
In 1962 the founding document of New German Cinema, the Oberhausen
Manifesto, argued repeatedly that the director must be free of "the usual
conventions of the established industry," of the "restrictive influence of commercial partners," and of the "tutelage of the other vested interests."[34] The
call for unusual artistic privileges for the German director was repeated in
the official history of the Kuratorium (the first state-supported film school):
"The filmmaker should have autonomy in giving shape to his film without

having to take legal and financial risk."[35] According to Elsaesser, such demands were ultimately for a state-supported avant-garde that had no direct responsibility to its audience.[36]

Autorenfilm evolved as a central ideology by which the state created and protected a national film and media culture. Here the *Autor* represented the "author as a public institution"; the director's individual expressivity in a film fulfilled the state's mandate to produce a plurality of political points of view after the univocal culture of fascism.[37] Nevertheless, the West German state engendered a legitimization crisis in that it set up a class conflict around who determined *German* artists and culture. The amorphous nature of the assignation of *Autor* status helped deflect the unequal privilege of awarding public monies to one individual based on bourgeois notions of aesthetic individualism. Elsaesser argues that the *Autor* became "a euphemistic way of classifying the unclassifiable."[38] With the *Autor* discourse, film aesthetics became film politics.

Television, Tabloids, and Tears breaks with a high-culture emphasis on the form and the artist in Fassbinder criticism; it investigates Fassbinder and popular culture—what he and his works meant to the "average" German. State television's support of Fassbinder on a public medium offers a chance to look at the cultural class divisions in Germany. Here Pierre Bourdieu's concepts of cultural capital and competence are relevant. Aesthetic norms are a form of domination; they result from the ability of the educated bourgeoisie to impose their cultural standards on others through such distinctions as "good taste" and "vulgar taste" and "artisan" and "artist." Created by the "high-born" or the well-educated, these cultural oppositions perpetuate the myth of "naturally given" standards or what Bourdieu calls "a new mystery of immaculate conception."[39] Bourdieu writes that taste "owes its plausibility and its efficacy to the fact that, like all ideological strategies generated in everyday class struggle, it *naturalizes* real differences of nature."[40] Fassbinder, as the most renowned *Autor*, reveals the triumph and failure of bourgeois cultural domination in postwar West Germany.

This book charts the emergence of two different Fassbinder genres based on melodrama: the melodramatic adaptation for television and the confessional melodrama for his privately produced and theatrically released German films. These two spheres of exhibition created two separate audiences and sets of expectations for Fassbinder's films. In the 1970s Fassbinder's success was built on two separate images of the director: the faithful adapter and the underground star/director.

With the television film *Berlin Alexanderplatz* these two heretofore separate Fassbinder genres come together explosively. The ideological estrangement in *Berlin Alexanderplatz* stems not from the heightened expressive elements or the mise-en-scène, but rather from the extent to which Fassbinder stretches the plausibility of narrative causality and the method with which he breaks social codes and taboos. Although these breaks with dominant film narrative traditions are a striking element in Fassbinder's film, they are to a degree controlled and read in relation to an auteur narrative or Fassbinder's authorial point of view as presented within the film and in the extratextual history of Fassbinder's work in television.

This book shifts the debate from these textual considerations to the historical contradictions inherent in a particular bourgeois discourse on the *Autor.* West German support of Fassbinder was based on institutional discourses that accorded him the status of an individual artist whose work was nonetheless representative of German culture. But what does it mean to be both exemplary as an artist and representative as a German? It is this contradiction that made Fassbinder a potentially disruptive figure. Fassbinder more than any recent German director explored the limits of the *Autor* discourse; his anomalous life was the subject not only of his work, but also of the West German tabloids. And when he declared "I am Biberkopf"—the protagonist of *Berlin Alexanderplatz*—he engendered an unprecedented national debate on what constitutes an acceptable *German* artist and who has the power to determine art.

2 / Engineering a Democracy through *Autorenfilm*: The Political Context of Television's Support of Fassbinder

In relation to the political decontamination of our public life, the government will embark upon a systematic campaign to restore the nation's moral and material health. The whole educational system, theater, film, literature, the press, and broadcasting—all these will be used as a means to this end. They will be harnessed to help preserve the eternal values which are part of the integral nature of our people. Adolf Hitler, 1933, in one of his first radio addresses[1]

The primary purpose of the occupation was to disarm and to demilitarise Germany and uproot the Nazi party, not to promote Anglo-German friendship.... There was no reason why the German people should not in the future take a worthy place among the peoples of Europe, but it would be for the Germans to deserve such a place, perhaps by long apprenticeship.
From the 1956 memoirs of Lord William Strang, political adviser to the British Occupational Military Government[2]

The hallmark of the rise of Rainer Werner Fassbinder on television is his status as an *Autor*: a director who has creative control of a film similar to the control an author has over a literary work. But this description belies the complexity of the cultural and historical connotations that surround the application of the high-culture term of *Autor* to a film director. The political underpinnings of television's support of Fassbinder as an *Autor* and his *Fernsehspiele* (made-for-TV movies) can be traced to television's institutional foundation: the Allied reeducation program to de-Nazify the Germans.

Allied postwar philosophy was that the Germans had to be "raised up" culturally from the depths of Nazi mass culture to democratic individualism. This program was to be no traditional education process. Rather, as Lord Strang's high-minded statement indicates, the Germans were to be reeducated through an "apprenticeship" to the more "democratic" values of the Allies, most particularly the British. The rise of Fassbinder as an *Autor* or a struggling individual German artist is by far a more self-consciously created and problematic discourse than art cinema historians have suggested. This high-culture discourse resulted from a historical fear of mass culture and its association with the lower classes in Germany, whether it came in the guise of American film and dime novels at the turn of the century, Nazi propaganda, or American cultural imperialism in the postwar period. We need to consider how "democratic" media became aligned with the aesthetic individualism of high-culture traditions as a defense against what was seen as the "deindividualizing" nature of mass culture.

In tracing the origins of the concept of "mass" in relation to the media's effect, Raymond Williams argues that it was during the Nazi period that the term became infused with connotations of political control. He writes: "It is interesting that the only developed 'mass' use of the radio was in Nazi Germany, where under Goebbels' orders the party organized compulsory public listening groups and the receivers were in the street."[3] This association of mass media with control engendered a conflict between the Allied occupation plans and the postwar German bourgeoisie. The Allies wanted to use the media to exert control and for reeducation, whereas the German middle class saw mass culture as a central challenge to the return of its cultural authority.

British Broadcasting, the State, and Education

Both his birth in 1945 and his adult status as an *Autor* made Fassbinder a child of the occupation. Although "JCS 1076"—the generally agreed upon position statement of the Allies in 1945—said that Germany was "not to be occupied for the purpose of liberation but as a defeated enemy nation," the British disregarded the punitive tone of this directive after the Allied zones were created.[4] With their long experience in foreign occupation during the imperial period of the nineteenth century, the British brought a keen sense of the role that high culture and the media could play as a form of indirect but effective control of an occupied nation.

In the eyes of the British, Anglo-American concepts of democracy and liberal political thought could not be physically forced on a people as proposed in the American Morgenthau plan.[5] Rather, "democratic" values were to be substituted for the militaristic and authoritarian values of German fascism. This could be accomplished through a reeducation process and new institutional structures for a "democratic" German culture that would continue long after the occupation. In his analysis of the political underpinnings of this reeducation program, British historian Nicholas Pronay argues that the British notion of "pluralism" went beyond changing German opinion; it involved restructuring the entire institution of media: "By remaking and as far as possible re-staffing the educational system and reorienting the curricular and scholarly vehicles for attitude formation—including the rewriting of the nation's history, that perhaps most powerful formulator of basic attitudes—a long term change of outlook and attitudes would be secured." For Pronay this plan ultimately demanded that the Germans look to the English-speaking people as their "exemplar."[6]

As opposed to the commercialization of the postwar German film industry and press by the American occupational authorities, the decision to nationalize broadcasting indicates the degree of importance the Allies attached to the political influence of broadcasting. As stated in one official U.S. military journal in the beginning of 1946, the Allied broadcasting policy was:

> a) To make use of the information media in bringing home to the Germans the objectives of the occupation, and to reconstitute German informational services in such a manner that they assist in the democratic reorientation of the people; and
> b) The establishment of a free German media of expression, cleansed of Nazi and militarist influence.[7]

Even though television was not to arrive for another six years, the Western Allies' public broadcasting decision set the stage for television to become the single most important mass medium for one of the most audacious intellectual and political projects of the twentieth century: the cultural engineering of a German democracy.

On one level, one can argue that the two Allied countries' redirection of the German media was a "natural" extension of the strengths of their own domestic media. The American authorities commercialized the film industry when it reappeared after the war. As a result, the postwar American military decision indirectly helped reassert American prewar industrial control of the German film industry. The Americans believed in a rather naive (and self-serving) Adam Smith-derived correlation between democracy and free enterprise.[8] The British, with one of the most sophisticated and extensive world broadcasting systems — the British Broadcasting Corporation (BBC) World Service — took over postwar German broadcasting as a public institution continuing the English tradition of social welfare.

Some historians of the German postwar period, however, have suggested that the Allies did not introduce American-style commercial broadcasting "because of the derelict state of the German economy at the time."[9] The decision did stem partially from a lack of consumer goods to advertise, but the commercialization of the postwar German film industry (an even more capital-intensive industry than radio) speaks against such a simple economic argument. In addition, broadcasting had always been a public concern in Germany since its inception in the 1920s when the Bundespost regulated the Reichsrundfunkgesellschaft (the state broadcasting company). The Telegraphenregel (telegraph law) of 1892 established the post's control over the technical facilities and the right to collect user fees for radio broadcasting. Regular radio service had begun in October 1923. The 1928 Telecommunications Law reaffirmed the post's sovereignty over radio broadcasting, and this law was still in effect when the Allies occupied Germany in 1945. On this level, the British model of the BBC should be seen as partially the Allies' attempt to create the smoothest transition between what was perceived as the authoritarian use of a public medium under the Nazis and the "democratic" use of state-run media during the Weimar period.[10]

On a more important level, however, the different directions taken by the film and broadcasting industries emanated from strong social and political differences between the British and the Americans over the creation of "democratic" or "pluralistic" values within a culture. A member of the reeducation team, the British Public Relations and Informational Services Control, in occupied Germany, Michael Balfour later echoed England's relative disinterest in film's reeducation possibilities. He reminisced in 1985:

> Of the media, the press and radio were by a long way the most important.... I'm afraid that I attached — and still attach — little importance to films. New German features were in the nature of things slow to emerge. A selection of old German features was admitted on sufferance because of the need to reduce German boredom by having something to show in the cinemas.[11]

The British concept of broadcasting and democratic pluralism stemmed from the rather benevolent but hierarchical tradition of state control and broadcast management by the educated elite within Great Britain. The Americans, on the other hand, carried out a much more complicated relationship with state control and socialism: at first they tolerated their Soviet ally; after the war that tolerance evolved into distrust as the spread of communism loomed. Unlike their transatlantic cousins, the English were never as daunted by the growing "socialist menace" of Soviet-style state broadcasting. While the U.S. secretary of state was complaining to the Soviets at the Moscow Conference of spring 1947 that "there is a vital connection between modern democracy and a free press and radio," the English were quietly grooming former German resistance members, often socialists and communists, to run their zone's radio station.[12] Socialist-leaning political affiliation did not offend the English as long as it did not interfere with their less than egalitarian system of top-down broadcasting governance. They were also much more comfortable with socially "managed" broadcasting than with the Americans' marketplace management style.[13]

Historically, the English concepts of character formation and parliamentary rule lay in educating the ruling elite of a subjugated people. In this way the British had sought to maintain their empire through an inexpensive but highly effective form of indirect control throughout the nineteenth century, as exemplified by their rule of India and South Africa.[14] The British saw democracy as a result not only of socioeconomic rule, but also of mental and psychological makeup.

Democracy was to emerge from imbuing Germans with British educational values and the social distinctions that come with educated discernment. Unlike any other system, the English concept of "education" emphasized values, soundness, and breeding more than the scientific or intellectual matters that were central to the American and German systems.[15] One of few methods for a low-born person to attain upper-class status in British culture was through a "proper" education. This Pygmalion tradition demanded not only attendance at the "right" schools (Oxford or Cambridge), but also the process of molding—or as some have described it, indoctrination—that comes with a class transformation. The success of this educational and cultural tradition both internally and in the empire led the English to believe that even the much distrusted post-Nazi Germans could be transformed. Nicholas Pronay argues that "no matter how distant or alien or deep-rooted the political tradition or culture of another society might be, it was always possible to bring about a change of attitudes in depth through a combination of occupation and 'education.' "[16] And what better agency to inculcate English cultural and educational values in postwar Germany than that bastion of high culture, the BBC?

The Founding of West German Broadcasting: The Search for a Pluralistic Institutional Structure

In his influential history of the founding of West German broadcasting, *Broadcasting and Democracy in West Germany* British historian Arthur Williams refers to West German broadcast media as "a fundamental vehicle of democracy."[17] But he fails to state that his concept of democracy in broadcasting assumes that the BBC, the prototype for the present West German television, *is* a "democratic" institution. Without delving into a debate on the BBC's class bias, one can examine the British reeducation program and see the cultural and class biases that the British implanted in their reconstruction of German broadcasting.

Founded in 1927 to replace a short-lived commercial company, the BBC derives its funds from an annual fee that the British must pay for a license to own television sets. The BBC has been run by a board appointed by the British government, which traditionally has not interfered in the board's governance. Sidney Head's introductory text, *Broadcasting in America,* describes it as a "paternalistic system"; the board's members are drawn from leading members of the British community (the landed gentry, elected lords, and company presidents for its first board).[18]

The BBC has by design limited the production of popular programming as an antidote to the dominance of American popular culture in Britain. Although the programming philosophy is not as simplistic as Sidney Head's statement that government-sponsored television "hold[s] that popular tastes tend to be frivolous," the BBC has a rigid philosophy of "public service."[19] This ambiguous phrase translates into a sense of the British educated class disseminating cultural competence for those less fortunate. Sir John Reith, the BBC's first and most influential director general, replied to the accusation of elitism in British public television that "few knew what they wanted, fewer what they needed." As a result, the BBC evolved into an educated and sophisticated world broadcast system disseminating high culture as a whole country's "culture." Indicative of this class-down system is the fact that the BBC refused to do systematic research into the preferences of their British audience until the 1970s. BBC historian Asa Briggs quotes one official's reaction to audience wishes in the late 1960s:

The real degradation of the BBC started with the invention of the hellish department which is called "listener research." That Abominable Statistic is supposed to show "what the listeners like" — and, of course, what they like is the red-nosed comedian and the Wurlitzer organ.[20]

The British brought this political and class-based sense of education and broadcasting with them in their reeducation plans for the lowest of classes: the Germans. If the mandate of the Allies was to create a form of cultural pluralism to substitute for the monologic ideology of the Nazis, using the BBC as a model of "democratic" culture was contradictory: it replaced fascist culture with high culture.

Although each of the Allied zones created its own internal broadcasting system, the British, as the major architects of the reeducation, had the most long-range constitutional effect on programming.[21] Because broadcasting was seen as a central agency of attitude formation under the Nazis, the planning of its public role initially was taken over in the postwar period by an elite corp of imported Oxbridge-trained policy makers from both the BBC and the Political Warfare division of the British military. During the war the British had developed a highly sophisticated counterpropaganda unit. Working through the Foreign Office, this unit used the BBC and the extensive governmental agencies devoted to the relatively new science of propaganda. Reorienting the Germans through culture and education after the war was based on a programmatic method of inculcation learned through wartime propaganda; it seemed to be a most rational and enlightened (although somewhat sinister) method.[22] Where the Americans (and to a lesser degree the French) wanted a decentralized broadcast system of many semiautonomous stations in order to ensure a plurality of institutional and regional voices, the British fought for centralization based on the BBC's London-dominated system that would allow them to carry out systematically their broad cultural policies.

The "democracy" created by these cultural policies was to be individual, intellectual, and ethical, not a geographical phenomenon based on regional and ethnic differences. Some historians have disdainfully labeled it brainwashing.[23] The British argued that the occupying authorities' mission should be twofold: selecting an elite corps of "suitable" Germans and apprenticing them in the English method of controlled democratic broadcasting; and establishing a constitution based on an independent state-run broadcasting system. With these structural mechanisms in place, the British would not need to fear the return of fascist propaganda under German control.

Major General Alex Bishop, the commander in charge of the re-creation of the informational media for the British zone, echoed reticence to impose overt British reeducation through programming at the British station Nordwestdeutscher Rundfunk (NWDR) in Hamburg. Bishop's public position was that the role of British occupational broadcasting should be

> to provide for the BZ [British zone] of Germany a Home Service on the lines of the BBC Home Service. . . . To retain its audience and to build effectively a new tradition in German broadcasting, NWDR must not be too obviously concerned with the re-education of the audience, or even with any obvious attempt to raise its cultural standards. Entertainment will not be too obviously edifying, and information not too obviously instructional. Excessive attention by NWDR to the political and historical re-education of the Germans will destroy its credibility, and it follows that the overt presentation of 'world' or 'British' views of current and past events should be conveyed to the German public mainly by other means.[24]

The British contribution to German reeducation was distinguished by these "other means," which were to be built into the institutional fabric of German broadcasting.

A Managed Democracy: The Selection of the Administrator

True to promise, an elite of highly educated "good" Germans continued to program the "right" spectrum of culturally pluralistic voices as guaranteed by their constitutional mandate. But these questions still remain: By what criteria were these German policy makers chosen? What constitutes a plurality of voices in West German broadcast programming?

No one better exemplified benevolent, patriarchal English broadcast management than Sir Hugh Greene, who originated the British zone's broadcasting constitution at NWDR. He is still considered the father of West German broadcasting by many Germans today.[25] Brother of novelist Graham Greene and head of the BBC's German Service during the war, Oxford-educated Hugh Greene symbolized administration by an educated liberal patrician. According to one of Greene's German "protégé" broadcasters, Greene allowed

> every ideology, every opinion, and we all learnt what it means [to have] a free press, freedom of opinion, of expression and to make programmes with a high degree of information and were very de-

pressed that with the going home of Greene, went out of German radio this special integration of being correct in information but at the same time being interesting.[26]

Greene's influence on German broadcasting was twofold. First, he established the prototype for the benevolent but strong administrator—the model for the West German broadcast *Intendant,* or director general of the German broadcast stations. There was a liberal spirit at NWDR under Greene, but the power structure was decidedly authoritarian. It is often pointed out that the British under Greene were the first to turn over their broadcasting rights to the Germans, but this fact does not speak to the careful selection of management that allowed an early transition. According to Michael Tracey, it was always a "cardinal principle" of the BBC's employment procedures that "political ideas and affiliations are irrelevant ... [until they] begin to feed and affect [a person's] work."[27] But what constitutes "political ideas" is relative.

Second, Greene was known for hiring and firing a series of top administrators based on their "communist" sympathies (Cologne *Intendant* Burghardt and political commentator Karl von Schnitzler, among others) while allegedly allowing many former Nazis to remain for want of other "reliable" personnel.[28] Greene maintained British authority through his careful choice of personnel who would carry out reeducation of the Germans as defined by the English.[29] But what constituted "correct" British values were class and cultural traditions, not an overt political point of view.

Although the Germans remain nostalgic for the "independent" status of broadcasting in the early days of Greene, those liberal British ideals should be regarded, as Tom Streeter points out, as "more a calculated illusion than a reality."[30] In his dissertation on Greene's work, Michael Tracey unwittingly reproduces the subtle elitism built into the British concept of broadcasting when he bemoans German broadcasting after Greene's departure:

> There were no liberal traditions, no public-school trained, well-meaning, intelligent public servants whose commitment is to a sense of the totality rather than the partiality of things. There were none of the symbolic and emotional continuities without which the model, British society and culture, would itself collapse into chaos. In Britain the position of the BBC was accepted as an amusing, not overly consequential indulgence in tolerance and democracy by a self-assured ruling class.[31]

Greene left a West German broadcast system where powerful administrators, producers, and programming decisions were insulated because of their status as "educated" employees of *public* broadcasting. Perhaps the best example of this tradition is the choice of Klaus von Bismarck—great-nephew of the nineteenth-century "Iron Chancellor" Otto von Bismarck—to head Westdeutscher Rundfunk in its most controversial days during the 1960s and 1970s when the station produced its most radical programming and supported Fassbinder's work. Given the missionary zeal of the origin of West German broadcasting and the independence of its patriarchal management, a broadcast station was able to distance itself not only from direct government control, but also from the public's programming preferences. The role of this top-down management style was further strengthened by Greene's second major influence: the ARD constitution.

The Definition of "Democratic" Programming in the West German Broadcasting Constitutions

The political power of the German broadcasting system in the 1970s—the richest and most powerful in Western Europe—was responsible for orchestrating almost all of the explicitly German television and film production in that period. The German system encompassed two networks (ARD and ZDF) and a regional third network devoted to explicitly local educational issues. The German system is still funded publicly through a monthly television tax payable to the post office—a system similar to that of the BBC. The ARD was made up of eleven locally administered regional stations that contributed all the programming in proportion to the amount of income from viewer fees. The Zweites Deutsches Fernsehen network (ZDF), on the other hand, was a national network that broadcast continuously to all of Germany. Only in the past decade, with the rise of new technology such as cable and satellite, has the ARD and ZDF hold on German television begun to weaken. This exceptionally long domination of the airwaves by West German public television stems from the reeducational role that German television was mandated to play.

In the initial construction of West German broadcasting, the Allies translated their sense of broadcast democracy structurally based on regional and geographical differences stemming from the occupational zone system. Although the British wanted a centralized model, American paranoia over the possible resurgence of government influence over broadcasting (and commerce) in postfascist Germany prevailed at Potsdam in 1945. The original stations established in the three zones at the beginning of the occupation remained separate.[32] And with the division of the all-powerful British NWDR into Sender Freies Berlin (SFB), WDR in Cologne, and NDR Hamburg in 1953, the first German network evolved into its present decentralized nine-station system by the late 1950s.[33]

In the early 1950s these stations set up a loose confederation called the Arbeitsgemeinschaft der öffentlichrechtlichen Rundfunkanstalten der Bundesrepublik Deutschland (ARD). The original ARD structure was outlined by the leading figures at the British NWDR in 1950.[34] The network's title translates roughly as "the joint association of public corporations for broadcasting in the Federal Republic of Germany."[35] The stations simply "agreed" to broadcast together. Based on a common license fee, each station broadcast its own regional programming until eight o'clock in the evening. After that, the different ARD stations broadcast common programs that were provided to each station in proportion to its income.

The Basic Law of 1949, which established the federal constitutional parameters of broadcasting, is important for this study for two reasons. First, it laid out the basis for freedom of expression for the support of controversial programming (such as Fassbinder's) in Article 5:

> Everyone shall have the right freely to express and disseminate his opinion by speech, writing and pictures and freely to inform himself from generally accessible sources. Freedom of the press and freedom of reporting by means of broadcasts and films are guaranteed. There shall be no censorship.

And second, with the exception of this one statement, the law made no reference to who or what is "responsible" in broadcasting. Since the individual lands (*Länder*) were given the prerogative to create any legislation that did not infringe on the constitutional rights of the Basic Law, they and their individual broadcast stations chose how "democratic pluralism" was to be defined. This distinction became important in that the lands differ measurably in their politics. Westdeutscher Rundfunk (Fassbinder's patron station) represents a social-democratic land and therefore can have more radical programming. In the 1960s and 1970s, WDR was known as *Rotfunk* (red broadcasting).

Further, the British were able to exercise extensive influence over the course of broadcast constitutional law. Their role exceeded that of the other Allies for two reasons. First, the British zone's power came from sheer size: it extended from the Danish border to the industrial center of Germany, the Ruhr valley. More importantly, this area contained the largest population. Sheer numbers gave the British more authority than the economically and politically stronger Americans. As a result, the British zone's NWDR, with 3.5 million license holders, in 1948 ranked as the third-largest broadcasting organization in Europe after the BBC and Radio Diffusion Française.[36]

Second, the British wrote (in 1947) the first NWDR broadcast constitution, which served as a prototype for the other stations. With a characteristically English sensibility, they built democratic pluralism into the NWDR constitution through a political and cultural spectrum of administrators, not through the programming. The originators of this concept (primarily Greene and Adolf Grimm) established a series of representative governing councils to ensure diversity of opinion, distance broadcasting from state interference, and make the station answerable to "public" opinion. Not surprisingly, their model was the BBC.[37]

To counter imbalances, a system of proportional representation (*Proporz*) was created throughout the three tiers to stem partisan politics in the stations of each *Land*. The remedy apportioned the representation on the broadcasting council of each station according to the elected percentages that the political parties held in the *Land*'s parliament. This form of "democratic" broadcast management engendered a whole set of problems: first, the intervention of the political parties into broadcasting ran counter to its founding principle that broadcasting should be independent of the state; second, even though the council was constructed around an unusual democratic impulse of drawing citizens from the community (from churches, unions, and arts management), these groups were highly select, established, and ultimately safe; and finally, as even Williams points out, these public representatives were drawn from the bourgeoisie or upper classes: "They will all be leaders in their particular areas of activity, and this presupposes a certain level of education and, possibly, of income."[38] In other words, plurality resulted in a highly select broadcast governance group.

In the absence of commercial broadcasting's reliance on profitability and audience size (the lowest common denominators) to validate programming decisions, West German television has substituted a "public" educational system. Programming decisions are not broad-based, but are arrived at through class-based and political party affiliations. The individuals who are appointed to these boards, and most particularly the program producers, become paramount. WDR selected left-leaning intellectuals to be its powerful television film producers, and their tastes were central to the rise of New German Cinema in the 1960s and 1970s.

On this level, West German broadcasting lived up to the hierarchical model of the BBC: a public broadcasting system that generally allows for

diverse points of view, but whose form and content remain resolutely defined by an educated elite who disseminate their cultural competence with
little regard for class and educational differences. German television has taken
its educational mandate with even greater missionary zeal than the "benevolent" cultural authority of the BBC in Britain. But it is the British influence in those years of reeducation that created the current contradictory
mixture of public medium and high culture.

The German Intellectual Reception of Popular
Mass-Produced Culture

For all their integration of German intellectuals into the reeducation process,
the British were nevertheless stymied by German pessimism about the
social reception of mass media, and in particular the American and Nazi
mass cultures. Hostile, century-long debates about the popular status of low-
grade, mass-produced fiction, or *Schund* (trash), shifted in the first part of the
twentieth century into a discussion of the then newly popular phenomenon of film.

German expressionist artists—the last major gasp of German romanti-
cism—reacted in horror to the mass production of visual images. Franz
Pfemfert decried the popularity of film in the first issue of the expressionist
journal *Die Aktion*: "Edison is the slaughterer's cry of a culture murdering
era. The battle cry of non-culture."[39] Censorial debate about the ill effects
of "low" but popular forms led to growing dissatisfaction in the German
working class. American mass culture was often seen as more "liberating"
in that it emanated from broad and accessible nineteenth-century theatrical
melodrama traditions. "Movies" (*Kino*) stood as a radical challenge to the
"refined" Wilhelmian literature that dominated late nineteenth-century German culture. According to Anton Kaes, by the 1920s the introduction of
American film as a mass medium had cut into the educated bourgeoisie's
"intellectual leadership" as books and literature lost their prestige. He argues:

> This new traditionless mass public was skeptical about a culture
> which was associated with edification and instruction and which
> presumed a classical education. It turned instead to the products
> of industrial mass culture, most imported from America, to satisfy
> the need for distraction.[40]

The cultural leaders of the German bourgeoisie, seeing mass-produced
popular culture as a threat to their hold on culture, attempted to legislate

against the production of "popular" literature through censorship laws in 1874 and 1913.[41] Still, the cinema survived as a refuge for popular culture and outlasted the Nazis' denigration of the "outsider" influence of film and their own propagandist use of it under the Reichsfilmkammer. When television appeared in 1950, the educated middle class once again attempted to reassert its power to define culture as the new electronic medium became the latest form of popular mass media that they mistrusted.

Coming from a different political and intellectual point of view, the influential Marxist theorists of the Frankfurt school exhibited a similar prejudice against mass-produced popular culture. The mass media were seen as contributing to the "massification" of the German people; the resulting deindividualized anonymity was pivotal in the rise of national socialism. The 1947 publication of Siegfried Kracauer's influential *From Caligari to Hitler: A Psychological History of the German Film* increased the postwar German educated middle class's distrust of the mass media as a vehicle for positive political and intellectual change.[42]

In his Freudian-Marxist study, Kracauer argues that because of its mass exhibition form, the cinema had a specific utility for creating a mass disposition, or in his words "a collective mentality." But in Kracauer's view, it was the middle class that led to the rise of fascism through its domination of German ideology in the 1920s, and since it controlled Germany as well as the film industry in the Weimar period, the bourgeoisie was able to disseminate its ideas and neuroses in visual and narrative motifs. Collectively, it created the unified consciousness or mass sensibility that led to the rise of Hitler and fascism: "In pre-Nazi Germany, middle class penchants penetrated all strata," a situation that resulted in "the nation-wide appeal of the German film—a cinema firmly rooted in middle-class mentality."[43] From the expressive art films to the mass entertainment films, Weimar film should be read as the state of mind of all Germans who "acted as if under the influence of a terrific shock which upset normal relations between their outer and inner existence."[44] The mass medium of film stood as both an instigator and a sign of a fascist mentality.

Kracauer's film theories exerted a strong influence on the postwar writings of Max Horkheimer and Theodor Adorno, who had returned to West Germany in the 1950s from exile in America. Kracauer's critical view of the film industry's complicity in the rise of fascism augmented the critical theory of the "culture industry" in Horkheimer and Adorno's 1944 study *Dialectic of Enlightenment*.[45] In fact, their theories of mass culture were first published in West Germany in 1958 in *Film 58* and later in the pages of the leading film journal of the 1950s, *Filmkritik*.[46]

German left-leaning sociological analysis of the mass media was universally pessimistic after Nazi use of film and radio as vehicles for fascist ideology. Thomas Elsaesser argues that this cultural negativism was particularly strong among all the Frankfurt school members who had emigrated to America. For them, however, the problem lay with how easily film lent itself to melodramatic content and moved political issues from the socioeconomic into the emotional realm. These émigrés "regarded the emphasis on psychological and emotional conflict in mass-cultural products itself as a typically bourgeois and petit-bourgeois displacement of political and social problems and anxieties."[47] The German intelligentsia—on both sides of the political spectrum—viewed mass culture as an assault on German individualism. The optimism expressed by Walter Benjamin as he heralded the revolutionary potential of mass-produced film remained a rare exception to general distrust of mass media. This pessimism only grew when mass culture extended its hold on the German working classes by entering their homes in the guise of television.

German television became the newest focal point for the persistent German intellectual bias against the mass media's political potential. The analysis of television's role in German society continued in a highly speculative sociopsychological vein about the mass media's reification of the thinking "individual." The medium was commonly typed as either "auraless" or "enslaving."[48] One writer (ironically, the future head of the second television network) typified the general distrust of television when he wrote in 1951 that

> the flickering restlessness fills our vision with billions of images, most of which are seen by a few viewers. As a result, our vision is also turned inward. It irritates the unrest in us when there is nothing more happening; the majority of us cannot bear to be alone because our imaginations are dead.[49]

His discussion of television's specific influence depended on an analysis of content and reception without any mention of form.

Such skepticism—bordering on an expressionist nightmare—has pervaded political, aesthetic, and psychological discussions of German television throughout its nearly forty-year history. As a result, German television has lived a constant legitimization crisis as it has sought to prove that it can be a medium of democratic individualism as well as of aesthetic merit. The history of the television drama, or *Fernsehspiel,* results from the intertwining of two contradictory views of fascism and the mass media: the Allied positivist view of broadcasting as a constructive instrument of German reeducation and a German liberal-to-Marxist intellectual tradition of distrusting the media's ability to create the individualism of democratic thought.

Competition for the West German Film Viewer: West German Television Comes of Age

The problem of reconciling these two conflicting attitudes about television was not an issue until West German television began to be taken seriously as a potentially influential mass medium in the late 1940s.[50] At first the Germans seemed to be hesitant about the new medium. In 1957 only 6 percent of German households—and 76 percent of American households—had television sets.[51] The general lack of consumer goods in the still recovering postwar German economy partially accounts for this disparity. After 1957 the numbers grew relatively rapidly, increasing a million yearly until the 1970s, when licenses for television sets reached the saturation point.[52]

In these early years of German broadcasting, when Fassbinder and his counterculture generation were children, film and television competed as furiously as they did in America. The beginning of network broadcasting in 1954 and the phenomenal growth of television licenses after 1957 created a corresponding need for programs to fill the schedule. Given the limited funds resulting from a small viewership, television producers preferred to show films previously proven to be popular to fill their schedules. ARD was showing eighty films per year by 1959–60, when German television was broadcasting only four hours and fifty-three minutes per day. Only one-fourth of these films were of German origin.[53] Since at the same time a record number of film theaters (577) failed, the weakening commercial film industry could not help but perceive television as a major competitor. Television was vying for the cinemagoer's leisure time as well as patronage. In the beginning, the American-dominated film industry reacted angrily to the growing economic threat of television and proclaimed polemically through SPIO, its trade organization, in the early 1950s: "Not one meter of film for German television."[54] Film distributors and exhibitors chose to ignore the possibility that German television could strengthen film economics and refused to rent films to the emerging stations.[55]

In 1956 the West German film industry began a steady decline in attendance, while in 1957 television reached its first benchmark: one million viewers. In the years between 1956 and 1964, film attendance would drop from 800 million to 300 million while television viewership would increase from 1.5 million to 10 million.[56] The writing was on the wall, but the waning industry responded not with competitive strategies, but with demands for federal subsidy. In the face of television competition, the American film industry experimented with competitive technological innovations such as wide-screen processes, 3-D films, and drive-in theaters, whereas the German industry responded passively. The commercial filmmakers wanted what was to become their ultimate downfall as a competitive industry: television must pay for the profits that, as a state-run agency, it took from the private (or quasi-private, given its dependence on state aid by the mid-1950s) film industry. This demand was made even before West Germany had a second network.

Fernsehspiele and Adaptations in the Adenauer Era: The Production of High Culture in the Face of a Waning Film Industry

While the German film industry was producing the infamous "quota quickies" of the 1950s and 1960s, German television was creating a new filmic form — *Fernsehspiel,* the major indigenous genre of West Germany. Instead of the American diet of weekly sitcoms and hour-long dramas, West German television has depended on one- to two-hour made-for-TV movies as its central fictional form. The high-culture connotations of these "television dramas" were perpetuated by the fact that they were produced under the stewardship of some of Germany's most renowned intellectuals. In the early 1950s, influenced by the BBC tradition, NWDR had attracted all the antifascist intellectuals and artists it could. According to Richard Collins and Vincent Porter, NWDR's broadcast of "the readings of poetry, new German prose, radio drama and programmes on the other artistic events and happenings" became not only a "focus" but a central "source of patronage" for young postwar artists and intellectuals.[57]

The British attempted to reconcile the growing conflict between the Allied view of the positivist use and the German distrust of the mass medium even before the medium was turned over to the Germans. Their answer was to produce established culture written by canonized authors whose work at some level highlighted the individual as opposed to the mass. In

March 1951 NWDR produced the first *Fernsehspiel,* Goethe's *Prelude in the Theater* (*Vorspiel auf dem Theater*).[58] Comparisons of the German television drama with the first live American television drama, *Requiem for a Heavyweight* (1956), illustrates a significant difference in literary pretensions.

Constrained by the "live" three-electronic-camera setup of early television technology, German producers chose to produce stagy adaptations, particularly from the theater, in the 1950s. Taking on the classical Hollywood narrational procedures, West German television producers taped their works as filmed theater. They strove for clarity of space and time based on the logic of narrative continuity; a limited number of shifts in time and space made for less editing. The introduction of magnetic videotape in 1957 allowed the *Fernsehspiel* to move technically and formally one step closer to the sophisticated editing and camera movement of film, but it was still dependent on a protagonist and a clear cause and effect logic associated with Hollywood narrational practice.

In terms of subject matter, such freedom did not spur the production of original made-for-TV films. What distinguishes German television even up to today (although decreasingly so) is dependence on the adaptation of well-known literary works for its made-for-TV films. Through this form, Fassbinder as well as most of what we know as New German Cinema would gain public recognition. The primary mission of German public television was to be "educational," and filming these works offered television's mass audience complex literary works made accessible by classical Hollywood methods.

Appropriately enough, the first West German *Fernsehspiel* was an adaptation of a play by Johann Wolfgang von Goethe, perhaps Germany's most canonized literary figure. Television drama served as the medium to expose the "mass" of Germans to the liberal cultural values of canonized literature. If a cultural pluralist democracy did exist on television, it was found in the diversity of individual authors represented. In 1953 E. M. Berger, then the leading producer of made-for-TV films, expressed the official position of NWDR as follows:

> It is good to recall that the dramaturgy of the theater and film, not to mention that of radio, is still not too old. Fortunately, television at first followed the theory of these media quite purposefully, before it strove to develop its own unique forms.... With the strengthening perimeters of television, television like film will have to fall back on the firmly established area of theater.[59]

A look at the actual number of *Fernsehspiel* productions in the 1950s reveals how much this conservative bias toward "established" forms had taken hold. Of the 564 *Fernsehspiele* produced from 1951 to 1959, 81 percent (459) were adaptations (see Appendix B). Of these adaptations, nearly 80 percent came from theater, 13 percent from novels (or other nontheater sources), and 6 percent from radio plays (*Horspiele*) (*see* Appendix B).

Like Fassbinder's work, these television adaptations were based on the literature of the nineteenth and twentieth centuries (most particularly, the literature of the 1920s). Not surprisingly, the adaptations were credited to the literary authors as their artistic source; rarely was either the television adapter or the television director mentioned.[60] Some of the German-language playwrights produced most commonly were Gerhart Hauptmann, Arthur Schnitzler, Ferdinand Bruckner, and Carl Zuckmayer. The major writers of nontheatrical works were Stefan Zweig, Franz Kafka, Franz Werfel, and Ernst Penzoldt. The lion's share of foreign works came, again not surprisingly, from the Allied countries. Although the overwhelming majority of the adaptations emanated from the sanctioned literary canon, some of the more left-leaning stations (particularly NWDR) did attempt a limited number of popular productions of comedies (*Lustspiele*) and works by what are known as the "boulevard authors" (*Boulevard-Autoren*) such as Curt Goetz, who wrote popular sex comedies.[61]

Beyond the German theatrical tradition of middle-class edification (*Bildungsbürgertum*) in theater, there are other economic, technological, and political reasons for the predominance of adaptations in the 1950s. Beyond the ease of the stage productions, adaptations were less expensive to produce than original films. By using canonized literary sources that had already gained an audience, television had a tried and true basis for potential broadcasting success. Original television films, on the other hand, had the unpredictable variable of audience reception.

But these economic arguments belie the political influence of the Adenauer years and the cold war. One of the major television taboos of this period was discussion of the German Democratic Republic (East Germany).[62] By producing only authors from the literary canon, television avoided political problems in two ways. First, it did not have to legitimize its choice; history had already canonized these authors. Second, producing works by "classic" writers avoided not only contemporary cold war issues, but also depiction of the still highly sensitive Nazi period.

The Creation of a Native German Televisual Form:
The Original *Fernsehspiel*

Only when established writers began to accept television's potential for depicting contemporary reality did the *Fernsehspiel* lose its dependence on adaptation. In 1961 some of Germany's best-known literary authors (Heinrich Böll, Günter Grass, and Martin Walser) — "Gruppe 47" — met to discuss the difficulties of independent authors (*freie Schriftsteller*) in postwar West Germany and the possibilities for writing truly original *Fernsehspiele* within a state-controlled medium.[63] A slow consensus evolved: What differentiated the television play from fiction was television's journalistic engagement with contemporary "reality" (*Realität*). But the visual form this realism was to take never was developed.

In the ensuing thirty years this discourse on the television's inherent "realism" has taken a number of thematic turns, but strong agreement that the virtue of the made-for-TV film lies its photographic realism has remained. If any other medium influenced this discussion, it was photojournalism. It is no coincidence that interest in the critical documentary came after the West German Constitutional Court established television's paramount political importance.

Additionally, one must point to the growing liberalization of West Germany and its media after the *Der Spiegel* affair of 1962. The federal government under Chancellor Konrad Adenauer had illegally seized the records of West Germany's major news magazine, *Der Spiegel,* after the magazine published information that Adenauer perceived as "top secret."[64] Along with the government's misuse of power over the *Länder* in the case of the creation of a second network, such authoritarian abuses prompted Adenauer's resignation in October 1963.[65] The end of Adenauer's rule symbolized the end of capitulation to American political and economic demands. The media took on a somewhat oppositional role, signalling a growing political liberalization and even rising nationalism in the early 1960s in West Germany. These changes led directly to the resurgence of the left by the mid-1960s — a political climate that no one could have imagined when the Allied occupation armies rolled into a defeated post-Nazi Germany.

The everyday quality of television became an attractive vehicle for the rising interest in socially conscious drama and political change. In his history of the *Fernsehspiel,* Knut Hickethier argues that the growing "critical realism" in made-for-TV films was a result of an increasing awareness in German television of "how to form artistically the realism which is handled daily in the other program forms of this medium."[66] Martin Walser, writing in 1959, concurred: "One cannot find formal laws for television. It belongs to reality. Like a business street, a plane, or a newspaper, its primary aim is to transport us into the interior nature of reality."[67] Egon Monk, director of NDR's film and television film department (Film und Fernsehspiel Abteilung), created an influential series in the early 1960s based on the average German's existence during the Nazi period. This series was famed for its documentary portrayal of "everyday life" (*Alltag*). Of this growing interest in the critical docudrama view of *Fernsehspiele,* Monk would later argue that the political engagement of television films in the 1960s was a "prerequisite" for television production in order "to shake the trust in the correctness of the directives of those in power at that time, and to convince our viewers it is better to doubt twice than accept something once on faith."[68]

This journalistic view of *Fernsehspiele* was still in operation in 1970s criticism when Fassbinder made the majority of his television films. Influential critic Hans Blumenberg proclaimed in *Die Zeit* in 1978 that television was a "journalistic not an artistic medium." Ultimately, according to Blumenberg, there are two basic forms of made-for-TV films: the literary adaptation and the theme film, which he argued dealt with "socially relevant present-day problems." Fassbinder's television work supports this claim in that he primarily produced adaptations, with an excursion into a series of melodramas about repression in the West German bourgeois family. Blumenberg argued further that television can take up "present social problems under which we suffer ... in a much more direct, exact, expansive and realistic manner than the cinema film."[69] This prejudice toward television as a journalistic, "realistic" medium resulted from the evolution of one of German television's central fictional genres of the 1960s and the early 1970s—the socially conscious docudrama. But once again, the actual form, style, and narrational process of the docudramas never developed. Somehow the reliance on contemporary reality presupposed a certain heretofore unarticulated "objective" form. From the perspective of recent Anglo-American film criticism, the German docudrama's form aligns with the classical Hollywood film. Only the content—contemporary German culture—made the docudrama a *German* form.

By 1960, the two major networks began to make a concerted effort to search for authors (*Autoren*) who would write exclusively for television. Yet these authors remained only scriptwriters; they did not direct their made-for-TV films, nor, on the whole, did they have any background in television or film production. This emphasis on the written process of television film portrays a major bias toward not only the imposed literary basis of television film, but also the perceived importance of the word over the visual portion of the work in this early period of production. Even though original television films began to increase, adaptations dominated the television screen until 1970, when they dropped for the first time to less than half (41.6 percent) of all made-for-TV films (see Appendix B).[70]

Although such well-known *Autoren* as Christian Geissler, Franz Hiesel, Günter Herburger, Manfred Bieler, and Dieter Waldmann all wrote original television scripts, there still remained a distinction between those who were "true" writers (*Schriftsteller*) and those who wrote as a "job" (*Autoren*). The evolving 1960s television concept of authorial drama production (*Autorendramaturgie*) reveals the degree to which authors participated in early 1960s television films, even though they came out of the written media and did not see television as a technologically and formally different medium. The so-called objective techniques of Hollywood classical films and filmed theater remained the vehicle for their scripts. Although in the 1960s the number of original television films (*Autorenfilme*) did increase to 720 from 105 in the 1950s, only 22 percent came from "known" literary authors.

Ultimately, the period also saw a tremendous growth in made-for-TV films—from 548 in the 1950s to 2,070 in the 1960s.[71] The *Fernsehspiel* had become West Germany's major indigenous televisual form. It rivaled the feature film for audience attention by 1968 as the film industry sank into its last and final crisis. In that year, 434 films premiered in German cinemas while 277 feature films and 211 made-for-TV films were broadcast.[72] By 1968 the television and film industries were antagonistic rivals not only as similar audiovisual media, but also as media that produced and exhibited rival narrative forms of filmmaking.

But still, these battling filmmaking industries had strong content and formal differences, mainly as a result of television's preoccupation with legitimating itself through the sanctioned world of literature, but also of television's economic dependence on inexpensive videotape production. It would take outside forces—the rise of the French auteur theory and independent filmmaking in West Germany—to create the necessary discourse and freelance labor pool for television to support a truly filmic, not theatrical, form.

The Influence of the Auteur Theory and the Oberhausen Manifesto on the German *Fernsehspiele*

To understand Rainer Werner Fassbinder's success as an *Autor,* one needs to separate the German concept from its French counterpart, the auteur. The centrality of "authors" (*Autoren*) in the television production of filmic art was established long before the auteur theory appeared in the late 1950s. Nevertheless, the precedent of the French New Wave (1959–64) and the rhetorical emphasis that it placed on film as a specific art form separate from and equal to literature exerted a strong influence on the late-budding German independent film movement.

In France, as early as 1948 Alexandre Astruc had proclaimed the specificity of cinema:

> The cinema is quite simply becoming a means of expression, just as all the arts have been before it, and in particular painting and the novel. After having been successfully a fairground theatre, or a means of preserving the images of an era, it is gradually becoming a language. By language, I mean a form in which and by which an artist can express his thoughts, however abstract they may be, or translate his obsessions exactly as he does in the contemporary essay or novel. That is why I would like to call this new age of cinema the age of *camera-stylo.*[73]

As a declaration of artistic independence, Astruc's plea for film as a form of individual expression became the basis of the auteur theory in the *Cahiers du Cinéma* in the mid-fifties. In 1954 François Truffaut attacked the French film industry's dependence on adaptation and literary canon in *Cahiers du Cinéma,* arguing in the usual polemical style of the French New Wave: "I consider an adaptation of value only when written by a *man of the cinema.* Aurenche and Bost are essentially literary men and I reproach them here for being contemptuous of the cinema by underestimating it."[74] And Jean-Luc Godard admonished the French film establishment with even greater vituperation: "Your camera movements are ugly because your subjects are bad, your casts act badly because your scripts are worthless; in a word, you do not create cinema because you no longer know what it is."[75]

Combining filmmaking and criticism, these writer/directors of the budding French New Wave championed certain directors—auteurs—who by sheer strength of their personality were able to put their expressive stamp on the products of commercial film industries. This emphasis on a form of expressive individualism in filmmaking that is able to shine through the anonymous nature of a mass medium is the unifying theory throughout the various *Cahiers* auteur writings. It was the approach that was most attractive to German television producers in search of a telefilmic art.

The more problematic issue was the unwillingness of young West German filmmakers, as represented by the Oberhausen group, to work with the film industry or even the burgeoning public television system, which they perceived as an interfering, bureaucratic extension of the state. The Oberhausen Manifesto demanded total independence from government and industrial interference in filmmaking. On one hand, the German filmmakers were fascinated with the French interest in individual expression. As German author Wolfgang Köppen put it, "in France one hands the poet the camera."[76] But unlike the French New Wave directors, the Oberhausen group did not see the possibility of their conception of the "art" film being realized in a commercial world, let alone in a mass medium such as television. German film historian Andreas Meyer concurs that these young German filmmakers had none of the dedication to "popular" film that the French critics at *Cahiers du Cinéma* had: "In contrast, economics, capital, box office, old producers, old lines of business, old film, etc. would be exorcised; totemic curses were also directed against the public's sentimental needs, which did not correspond to their own [the directors']." Meyer argues that the filmmakers "mistrusted" the German public for their lowbrow tastes. "The 'young filmmakers,'" he writes, "wanted to become authors [*Autoren*], publicists, messengers, prophets (similarities can be found to the virulent student movement five years later). Films should originate as diaries, poems, personal reflections, and private obsessions."[77]

Even the official history of the Kuratorium junger deutscher Film argues that the Oberhausen Manifesto's claims to economic independence were rather unusual given the period:

> The *Autor* film was henceforth to make history.... The fundamental principle ... was that the filmmaker should have autonomy in giving shape to his film ideas without having to take legal or financial risks. He was to retain control over the direction and the entire production process including the commercial exploitation of his film. This concept was clear, but in the situation of the German film at the time, highly unorthodox.[78]

Alexander Kluge, the central author of the Oberhausen Manifesto, exerted the greatest influence on this generation of young filmmakers. Kluge was a filmmaker in his own right and an outspoken theoretician for the rising generation of filmmakers in the mid-1960s. Although Kluge's filmic method was openly Brechtian—fusing Marxist theory and a formal challenge to convention—he never denied the complexity of his work and that of the other New German filmmakers for the "average" German spectator. But more than that of the other independent films by the Oberhausen signatories, the difficulty of his films has always been posed as a form of ideological and aesthetic opposition to the domination of American capitalist culture in the guise of Hollywood filmmaking.

In his theoretical writings, Kluge attributed Germany's problems of filmic identity to his country's assimilation of the more popular international formal conventions of Hollywood films. In his collaborative work with Michael Dost and Florian Hopf, Kluge responded to problems of New German film's failure within Germany by asking: "Should German cinema refine itself into an abstract, finally self-annihilating, international standard, or could it succeed in developing its own particular, language-bound basis of production and reception in our own country?"[79] Kluge's search for an explicitly *German* cinema with its nationalist rhetoric played comfortably into the growing nationalist mandate of German television in the late 1960s.

Yet for all Kluge's attempts to infuse this young generation of filmmakers with political awareness, their main concern was self-expression. Their anticapitalism stemmed more from their interest in an anti-industrial form of filmmaking, as opposed to the mass culture present in the guise of a foreign intruder—Hollywood. Günter Rohrbach, a television executive producer for Fassbinder in the 1970s, surmises that the French New Wave had a strong influence on these early filmmakers' desire for "film as an expression of personal experience, feeling, and attitude." He argues that film for them "was a different type of literature. In the *Autorenfilm,* the director rightly has absolute control; it is his idea which becomes the film, his script, his characters. He is the creator. The formula or concept—'a film by . . . '—is quite legitimate here." In Rohrbach's eyes the Oberhausen Manifesto was ultimately a declaration for "the ominous position of the film *Autor.*"[80]

Given this emphasis on directorial control, the burgeoning bureaucratic world of television seemed too foreign and inhospitable a haven at that time for a preindustrial romantic outlook on the creative process. The federal government acquiesced to the Oberhausen demands with the creation in 1965 of the Kuratorium junger deutscher Film, an independent funding agency; the action testifies to the growing recognition that independent art film culture was gaining by the mid-1960s. By 1967, the first Kuratorium generation of young German filmmakers or what has since been labeled "young German film" produced a significant number of independent films.

But German public television was changing. A 1963 federal Constitutional Court decision mandated ideological balance to be carried out through "democratic pluralism" at the programming level. The court argued that broadcasting must provide a forum for "all socially relevant groups"[81] on all forms of television programming. It allowed WDR's Film und Fernsehspiel (film and television play) department to extend the mandate to fictional programming.

Given the predominance of American mainstream television and film programming on German television, this federal decision for balance allowed television producers, especially at Westdeutscher Rundfunk, to counter-program these "dominant ideology" programs with works of nondominant or independent filmmakers. By 1977, 47.3 percent of the films shown on West German television were of American origin.[82] WDR's bold decision was to produce and program German films that revealed a form of personal expression as a counterweight to the highly popular but anonymous mass entertainment programs such as *Bonanza, Dallas,* and *Father Knows Best* and the countless Hollywood film classics that filled the West German airwaves in the 1960s and 1970s.[83] Here, the ideological distinctions became even more controversial when it was public monies that funded the less popular German films and *Fernsehspiele.*

Indeed, the court's decision signified the increasing West German awareness of the political and cultural importance of television. It resulted in an evolving contradiction that pervaded the growing sense of visual nationalism in the German public television system of the 1960s and 1970s: difference in textual complexity in what was televised as native "German" programs and as "non-German" (most usually American) fictional programs. The spectrum of relevant voices enforced the already accepted use of known authors through adaptation or individual expressivity as a form of "democratic" programming. In the end, German television had been given a difficult state mandate to produce individualist films on a mass medium. It has translated into the state's support of the "relevant voices" of young German individualists of the Oberhausen Manifesto and the *Autoren* of New German Cinema — even when the films did not have broad appeal.

West German Television and the Rise of an "Alternative" Film Culture

Given the growing centrality of German television in the production, finance, and exhibition of German film, how can one speak of Fassbinder as an independent filmmaker? There was no such thing as a truly independent film as demanded by the Oberhausen Manifesto, except possibly through the Kuratorium's support. There was an endless maze of tax shelters, prizes, and state subsidies at the federal and state level. In 1967 the government enacted the Film Promotion Act (Filmförderungsgesetz)—the mainstay of government subsidization—which awarded approximately $37,000 to 65 films in 1969.[84]

A filmmaker could put together a number of these sources, produce a film, and distribute it under his or her production company, as Fassbinder did through antiteater-X-film and later Tango Films. Since Fassbinder created low-budget films as an extension of his theater group in the late 1960s and 1970s, he was able to finance his films privately and through his actors' working for a percentage of the profits. Of Fassbinder's first twenty films, he submitted only the screenplay to *Effi Briest* (1974)—his critically acclaimed "refined" adaptation of Theodor Fontane's novel—to the state subsidy board. In the late 1960s these films could be exhibited in the independent art cinemas and university film clubs without television intervention.

It was no accident that in 1968, during the height of the antiwar movement, the government shifted financial support for independent film from the Kuratorium, a semi-autonomous institution, to the state film funding board and public television—both quasi-governmental regulatory bodies. Without funding from the Kuratorium, young German filmmakers felt that their only chance at substantial financing was to exploit the author-oriented made-for-TV films.[85]

Both the growing West German television industry and the film industry were hit by the economic recession of 1966–67. The number of *Fernsehspiele* declined from 1967 onward, dropping from 248 in 1967 to 211 in 1968, the most drastic one-year decline of their history. On the other hand, the percentage of *Originalfernsehspiele* increased and continued to do so until the 1973–74 season.[86] During this time of extreme West German financial crisis, public television was aided by its ability to use freelance or independent filmmakers for its less pretentious in-house productions. Fassbinder's early television work revolved around commissioned studio tapings of productions from the Action Theater/antiteater. He directed videotaped versions of *The Coffeehouse* (*Das Kaffeehaus,* 1970) for WDR and *Bremen Freedom* (*Bremer Freiheit,* 1972) and *Nora Helmer* (1973) for Saarländischer Rundfunk.

By conceiving of these films within the institution of state television and then having them produced by independent filmmakers, television officials were able to create an aura of multiple points of view while retaining tight control of what was produced. According to Zweites Deutsches Fernsehen's legal adviser, freelance workers were "the means of guaranteeing the principle laid down in its broadcasting charters, that socially relevant groups and their varying shades of opinion shall receive due expression in varying ways." But they also represented an economic savings as "an efficient reservoir, well capable of self renewal, which can be called upon whenever, to meet varying requirements, it is desired to screen to programmes of a particular color."[87]

Television producers all too willingly labeled (or mislabeled) these freelance laborers as artists (*Autoren*) in order to mask television's essentially exploitative relationship with them. For their part, the young German filmmakers were desperate for financing in a country without a viable film industry. The producers argued that the lack of economic guarantees allowed these artists the necessary distance for their creative "freedom."[88] By the end of the 1960s television was slowly increasing its role not only in the production of film, but also in those films that were considered "high art" by creating artistic oeuvres through repeated support of freelance artists.

By the late 1960s cinema culture had found its friendliest institutional supporters in the highly educated and cultured West German television producers. In 1970 Frieda Grafe and Enno Patalas argued that television had become the home of "the premier theaters," the "studio theaters," and the "film clubs." Looking back on the 1960s, they pointed to the "educated" German television film programmers as the catalyst for film art culture in West Germany in that they "would demonstrate some measure of film form consciousness and the capacity to differentiate in their productions."[89]

But not all television stations were capable of supporting a filmmaker beyond one film or through a series of films or the necessary oeuvre that defined an *Autor,* nor were many stations able to foot the production costs necessary to produce a feature film. The two central producing television agencies of New German Cinema were Zweites Deutsches Fernsehen (ZDF) in Mainz and the ARD's Westdeutscher Rundfunk (WDR) in Cologne. ZDF and WDR were the German equivalents of the major American film studios because they financed, coproduced, or distributed almost all of West Germany's feature films of the 1970s. Between them, they "created" the Fassbinder film seen by the broad West German public.

Zweites Deutsches Fernsehen

In an attempt to differentiate its film programming from that of the ARD stations, the first ZDF *Intendant* created a central film division (Die Hauptredaktion Fernsehspiel und Film) and appointed established film critics (as opposed to ARD's use of personnel from its entertainment divisions) as its film programmers in the late sixties. The expressed purpose was "to come to the aid of television with film and to come to the aid of film with television."

To fulfill these plans, Heinz Urgureit, a longtime critic with West Germany's most prestigious film journal, *Filmkritik,* was appointed to head the department. By 1967, over 20 percent of ZDF's programming came from films and made-for-TV films. This percentage resulted from the increasing number of commercial feature films (and a declining number of *Fernsehspiele*) shown on the network as it attempted to increase its audience.[90] To that end, ZDF broadcast 2,200 feature films (not including repetitions) between 1963 and 1980. These films included approximately 600 German premieres of foreign films that could not find theatrical release in West Germany's conglomerate-controlled venues. Of ZDF's own productions, 60 percent came from commissioned or freelance labor in the 1970s.[91]

In this twenty-year period, ZDF broadcast films on history, politics, and popular German subjects[92] along with network-broadcast works by contemporary art film directors including such difficult and controversial directors as Pier Paolo Pasolini, Luis Buñuel, and Robert Bresson. In an attempt to educate the public about this rising art cinema, ZDF pioneered a series of film education programs on commercial films.[93]

For ZDF the division between the feature film and the made-for-TV film remained quite strong in these years. In both its feature film selection and its film commissioning, ZDF was more ideologically balanced and cautious than the political party-dominated regional ARD stations. Therefore ZDF developed the work of the more "intellectual" Werner Herzog and Alexander Kluge. Fassbinder's reputation and more plebeian productions remained too radical for this national network.

"The Little Television Drama" (*Das kleine Fernsehspiel*) was the only ZDF program to offer Fassbinder support in the early 1970s. Begun in

1970, the program is still devoted to productions that fit into its half-hour time slot. This time constraint ensures that the films remain marginalized from the culturally more significant feature-length film. The program runs after 11:00 p.m. and as a result has not attracted a working-class audience. Nor does it compete with the more "popular" prime-time programming. But it does provide aspiring filmmakers with national exposure, largely to the professional and educated classes. With its relatively low budget, it was able to finance only one short film of an aspiring filmmaker or part of a larger film: Fassbinder's 1971 *Der Händler der vier Jahreszeiten* (*The Merchant of the Four Seasons*).[94]

The producer legitimized such choices as Fassbinder's work based on television's potential to placate the growing politicization of filmmaking through institutional support: "The young television producers do not want to storm the barricades, but rather help with finding a better, more unique style for television. Film has its own art houses, its cineaste, and clubs. What we need is a community for *Teleasten.*"[95] Although this support of experimental film might be seen as radical, the rationale for the use of films was still based on what one recent *Screen* writer called the German tradition of "personal expression and individual vision. There is no orthodoxy of form against which the film is typed."[96]

Westdeutscher Rundfunk

Westdeutscher Rundfunk stands as Fassbinder's central producing institution. For WDR he produced eight *Fernsehspiele* or *Fernsehfilme.*[97] As the richest and most radical station in the ARD representing a social-democratic land, WDR was able to insulate itself from much of the controversy surrounding Fassbinder's television work. In general, WDR served as a lightning rod that attracted the most radical and experimental directors of the New German Cinema. If ZDF was responsible for development of Kluge's and Herzog's careers, WDR was responsible for Fassbinder's and Wim Wenders's.[98]

Burdened with the huge need for programming for both the First Network Program (WDR) and its regional Third Program or channel (Westdeutsches Fernsehen, or WDF, which was created in 1965), WDR's Film und Fernsehspiel Abteilung (film and television drama department) became a central production house for German fictional film and television programming in the mid-1960s. Under the benevolent social-democratic authority of *Intendant* Klaus von Bismarck and Dr. Hans-Geert Falkenberg, head of cultural programming, the department carried on the British high-culture tradition of center-to-left cultural programming even in its support of Fassbinder.

While ZDF used film critics as producers, WDR's film dramaturges (*Redakteuren*) came from producing made-for-TV plays, movies, or German theater.[99] As a result, WDR's film and drama department did not develop the concept, which was given to the filmmaker to produce. Rather, the producers at WDR, like patrons in the high arts, treated the filmmakers as already established *Autoren* and encouraged them to develop their own ideas.

This unusual sensibility emanated from the department's now famous head, Dr. Günter Rohrbach (now director of the huge film studio Bavaria Atelier). Rohrbach differed from his predecessors (such as Egon Monk) in that he was not a practitioner but rather a manager who wanted to attract authors and directors and provide them with patronage, not direction. It is no coincidence that Rohrbach's ideas came at a time when West Germany was developing not only its first generation of independent filmmakers but also a cultural revolution in the irreverent and politicized atmosphere of the late sixties.

Rohrbach had the economic foresight to blur the distinction between *Fernsehspiel* and *Film*. For him, the difference between the two was only technical — a difference in transmission. To improve the quality of WDR's television film output, he concentrated film financing on three well-made films a year. At the same time, he upgraded the quality of the *Fernsehspiele* by decreasing their number and by hiring film directors to work on videotape with higher production values such as Fassbinder's taped versions of his antiteater work. Rohrbach and fellow WDR producer Günther Witte argued that the collective effort of their television co-workers at the time was to "return the trust in the German film market through quality to the public." As a result, WDR began to move toward using film in the 1970s; Fassbinder's 1972 worker series, *Eight Hours Are Not a Day*, was shot on sixteen-millimeter film.

More centrally, Rohrbach gathered together well-educated and left-leaning producers or dramaturges (*Redakteuren*) to administer WDR's dramatic work.[100] Peter Märthesheimer, a television drama producer, was assigned to Fassbinder as his WDR producer beginning with *The Niklashaus Trip* in 1970 and ending with *Berlin Alexanderplatz* in 1980. Märthesheimer attained his doctorate at the University of Frankfurt studying sociology under members of the Frankfurt school in the 1960s. He coproduced and cowrote with Pea Fröhlich and Fassbinder *The Marriage of Maria Braun* (*Die Ehe der Maria Braun*, 1978) — a WDR coproduction. The Märthesheimer/

Fröhlich team also cowrote the two other films of Fassbinder's trilogy chronicling postwar Germany: *Lola* (1981) and *Veronika Voss* (*Die Sehnsucht der
Veronika Voss*, 1981). Märthesheimer was also responsible for the highly controversial 1979 German broadcast of the American series *Holocaust*, which
helped revive the debate about German responsibility for the Holocaust.[101]
His written defenses of his history of controversial television productions
are a fascinating hybrid of academic thinking, left-wing politics, and man-
agerial logic — a far cry from the American model of television producer as
deal maker.[102]

Märthesheimer and the other *Redakteuren* acted as unusually enlightened business agents whose job it was to find and employ independent *Autoren*
and *Regisseure* and insulate them from the bureaucratic problems endemic
to noncommercial and state-run television. Through this WDR-inspired
process of establishing relatively unknown filmmakers through ongoing financial support and national exposure, television was able to create a group of
"known" *Autoren*.

Although I will argue in chapter 5 that Fassbinder's work offered a formal challenge on some levels, his television work was pronouncedly more
dependent on Hollywood narrative forms than his independent work at
this time. He functioned as a popularizer of high culture, whether it was
adapting canonized works or his own plays from the Action Theater and
antiteater. His work for television was constrained by limited budgets, the
clear logic of cause and effect continuity editing, and adaptation.

Fassbinder's engagement with the "everyday reality" of middle-class
Germans distinguishes his work for WDR more than his adaptations.
WDR produced his *Fernsehspiel* studies of the repressive nature of the German bourgeois family: *Martha* (1973), *Fear of Fear* (*Angst vor der Angst*,
1975), and *I Only Want You to Love Me* (*Ich will doch nur, dass Ihr mich liebt*,
1976). WDR supported a number of filmmakers willing to work in this
docudrama genre of the *Fernsehspiel*, including less stellar but now well-
known "politicized" *Autoren* of the then mounting phenomenon of New
German Cinema: Wolfgang Menge, Reinhard Hauff, Helma Sanders, Peer
Raben, Volker Vogeler, Rosa von Praunheim, Peter Zadek, Chris Ziewer,
and Erika Runge, to name a few. Nevertheless, these films still remained
few (with the look of television stamped on them) and noncompetitive. It
would take a financial investment way beyond WDR's, let alone West German television's, capability to create the international phenomenon of New
German Cinema (*Neues Deutsches Kino*) in the 1970s.

The Internationalization of *Neues Deutsches Kino*: The *Tendenzwende* and the Film/TV Agreement

Much of Fassbinder's success in television and in the German state subsidy system had to do with the timing of his generation of filmmakers' arrival on the cultural scene. In 1972, in a major conservative political swing, the West German government under Willy Brandt reversed its previously liberal policies toward the student movement, issuing a series of radical decrees that suspended due process and initiated massive security checks. Soon the state enacted a law (the Berufsverbot) forbidding anyone who had been documented as demonstrating against the West German government to ever work for the federal government (the future employer of the majority of educated middle-class German students).

This law helped to initiate the *Tendenzwende* (the change of tendency) as the West German political climate swung from critical opposition to state intervention in order to control this new generation of politics and culture.[103] Spurred on by the worldwide recession of the 1973–74 "oil crisis," this swing marked the end of West Germany's postwar experiment in personal freedom and government nonintervention. Nowhere was the *Tendenzwende* felt more profoundly than in public television's production of *Autorenfilm*.

The West German film industry never recovered from the 1967 Subsidy Law, and German television became central in the production and exhibition of film by the 1970s. The number of films broadcast on the two main television networks rose to a high of 346 in 1975; the Third Program averaged another 137 films on its five regional stations (see Appendix D). Separate from television-produced films, feature films constituted just over 8 percent of the main networks' programming. By the mid-1970s, two-thirds of all West Germans were acquainted with films only through the medium of television.[104]

Given this drastic change in economic power and media popularity, the West German government used this moment to move in and exert greater control of the independent film movement. It finally chose to recognize the full extent of public television's role in West German film. When the Bundestag went to renew the Film Promotion Law (Filmförderungsgesetz) of 1967 in 1974, it passed a companion law, the Film and Television Agreement (Film/Fernsehen Abkommen).[105] Significantly, this law would not drastically change the American-dominated German film industry's downward roll, but rather increased the length and scope of the films that television had been producing. The bill was designed to require television to share its film successes with the dying film theater market.

The new law solidified West German television's role as the state's protector of an explicitly German film culture. Television was promoted as the enlightened and benevolent noncommercial producer of German film, the final barrier to the ever growing menace of American conglomerate filmmaking. These "independent" or commissioned films would be given greater financial support and therefore be able to compete theatrically. In other words, the socially critical and personal-expression television films of the independent *Autoren* filmmakers were now going to get the financial boost they needed. Because these films were produced independently, they were allowed greater formal play than was previously allowed for television release. As a result, German film finally entered the international realm of auteur or art films. "Name" television directors such as Fassbinder were rewarded with large feature budgets for the international export market.

The 1974 Abkommen basically required the ARD and ZDF to spend 44 million marks ($10.3 million) over the next five years on either "high quality" coproductions with the German film industry or prebuying before the films were produced. The central stipulation was that the films play first in movie theaters; two years later they could be broadcast. Given that the television networks had no say in the content or form of the films, this agreement marked a new relationship between the networks and the independent filmmakers they had helped to establish. The networks moved from commissioning films to financing them.[106]

The different film and television film departments continued to have the power to decide which films they wanted to finance or buy. To that end, the television networks set up together the Achter Commission (Kommission für Gemeinschaftsproduktionen) in order to choose which films would be the five per year they would fund with the film industry. The films in the first five years of the agreement tended to have low budgets (200,000 marks or $62,000) by American standards, but because they had access to the huge television-owned Bavaria Atelier—Europe's largest film production studio—they had a gloss that gave them greater theatrical potential (*Berlin Alexanderplatz,* for example, was filmed there in 1980). In the case of a film financed and promoted by the ARD network, a member station would stand as the producer. Nevertheless, the amount of money spent was more than for most previous television films. More importantly, the arrangement allowed independent filmmakers who were financed by the

Abkommen a chance at theatrical release and, ultimately, a chance for international distribution.[107]

This system was created to finance "small" films by aspiring *Autoren* in the mid 1970s.[108] The 1974 Abkommen established guidelines for prepurchasing films. The television network paid approximately the same amount (200,000 marks or $62,000 per film) as for a coproduction with the film industry. But because the television stations did not have much say in the course of the films, they tended to favor directors with whom they already had a working relationship and a proven success record. Since all that a director submitted to the commission was a final script, the tendency was to fund only *Autoren* who had worked with them before 1974, and only experienced directors. This had a cooling effect on the support of unknown filmmakers and increased television's willingness to fund Fassbinder — their most prolific known director.

From 1974 until the end of this first agreement in 1979, the two networks coproduced more than fifty films and purchased the television licensing rights to twenty. Under this agreement, WDR coproduced Fassbinder's *Despair* (1977) and *The Marriage of Maria Braun* (1978) — two of his internationally recognized films. The ARD coproduced or prepurchased the rights to other films under the 1974 Film and Television Agreement (see Appendix E). As a result of this agreement, West German television was involved in the production of a quarter of all West German features by the mid-1970s.[109]

Der Filmverlag der Autoren: Television Coproduction and the Independent Film Industry

To understand television's influence on Fassbinder's career, we need to examine its powerful but indirect influence on the central independent distributor of the 1970s, the Filmverlag der Autoren (film publisher of authors). The possibility of relatively interference-free television support did spur on successful independent film distribution companies. Among the small, "alternative" distributors of the 1970s, the Filmverlag der Autoren, of which Fassbinder was to become a pivotal member, stands out as a symbol of the strength of independent *Autoren* and one of the most successful counterdistribution agencies of this period.[110]

Founded in 1971 by thirteen filmmakers other than Fassbinder, the distribution company assumed that the personal nature of their films conferred on its directors the status of "authors" and that their films should be accorded a different form of treatment (note the use of *Verlag* [publisher] instead of *Verleih* [distributor]).[111] The political objective of the firm was stated thus:

> Point number one is the abolition of the old status of producers [*Produzentenstatus*]. A cooperative has come into being, one that is based on partnership and in which the normal master-slave relationship of many companies is no longer in operation. That means: the responsibility for the film product is a total, collective responsibility; it is not hierarchical or divided into set jobs. The control of the single productions of the maker is mutual, as is the assistance in the collective.[112]

Five years earlier, the Oberhausen Manifesto declared aesthetic individualism; this document speaks to a greater degree of political commitment.

Although Fassbinder was not yet a member, he distributed some of his early successes with the Filmverlag, whose agreement stipulated that the creator and the firm split profits fifty-fifty; the Filmverlag's portion was then reinvested in the next productions. In its early years, before 1975, the collective coproduced almost exclusively with television *Fernsehspiel* departments. Its output represented not only its own films but also those of others.[113] During this period (1971–74), the Filmverlag invested 500,000 marks ($156,000) in the distribution of its own films as well as those of other *Autoren* (Herzog and Kluge). Fassbinder's *Effi Briest* and *Ali/Fear Eats the Soul,* distributed in 1974, brought the Filmverlag's largest return: 1.1 million marks ($343,000). The Kuratorium lent an additional 150,000 marks ($49,000) to the Filmverlag's productions.

Enactment of the film/television Abkommen was a setback for the Filmverlag in that its production possibilities were reduced. The agreement also lowered the number of television coproductions by consolidating the interests of the two networks. The Filmverlag began to lose money in the second half of 1974 and lost approximately 500,000 marks ($156,000) by the end of the year. Interestingly, the Marxist director Lauren Straub had taken over as business director of the collective in August 1972, implementing a more hierarchical business structure. Even with the more classically conceived business structure, the firm could not make up for its losses through either in-kind credit or distribution.

As a result of these losses and the Abkommen, the Filmverlag dissolved and reemerged in 1974 as Filmverlag der Autoren GmbH. Each of the original members paid in 20,000 marks ($6,200); Fassbinder and Uwe Brandner joined the collective and each contributed 10,000 marks ($3,100). Given the ongoing losses, by 1976 Straub attempted to change the "small, individual film" orientation of the Filmverlag to meet the needs of a larger, more diverse international film market for German films. In an attempt to double the distribution offering, Herzog, Siskel/Brustellin, and Schlöndorff became members in that year.[114]

The year that German film broke through into the international market, 1975, is the year that marks the definite hierarchy of film authorship. A split began to develop in the Filmverlag. A hierarchy was created from the rising support of "name" directors from outside the Filmverlag. By 1975 West Germany had established *Autoren* who were "bankable" through name recognition and the consistency of their style. Because the Filmverlag depended on its directors being financed primarily from outside (which translated most often into television support), it was more difficult for the newer or less proven directors to gain support in the conservative post-Abkommen years. With Werner Herzog and Volker Schlöndorff added to the list of Fassbinder, Hark Bohm, Wenders, and Hans Geissendörfer, the Filmverlag represented a majority of the most successful West German *Autoren* and by 1976 had evolved into the second-largest film distributor in West Germany while television remained its central producer.[115]

Perceiving the company as a lucrative venture, Rudolf Augstein, publisher of *Der Spiegel,* in 1977 offered to buy into the Filmverlag with the stipulation that the nonproductive filmmakers be jettisoned. The directors acceded, paid in 600,000 marks ($200,000) each, and took over 55 percent of the firm; each filmmaker (Fassbinder, Herzog, Wenders, and Brandner) received 6.5 percent. The Film/Fernsehen Abkommen of 1974 had contributed unwittingly to the death of the small film that by definition distinguished the personal-expression work of the German *Autoren,* in which television production had played so central a part. Now an *Autorenfilm* was a much larger budgeted, potentially international phenomenon; it had broken through the "ghetto" of the small, low-budgeted television film that helped to spawn the quirkiness of the early *Autorenfilme.*

The Filmverlag's history portrays the price in rise of name directors such as Fassbinder within the capital-intensive film industry: independent filmmakers lost the radical impulse to control all phases of their films' release and foster aspiring filmmakers. Fassbinder, as the leading name director, in 1970 became the Achilles heel of their original countercultural impulse. Even Fassbinder himself by 1977 admitted the growing difference between established *Autoren* and new filmmakers in the Filmverlag: "Sad for people who are doing their first films, which they can't place with any distributor and then can't place with the Filmverlag either. And people who aren't doing their first film are looked over for their marketability nowadays."[116]

In seven years, *Autor* had evolved into the mark of profitability as the work so labeled became publicly recognized and salable. In many ways, 1975 was the year that German film broke through, but it was also the year that the effect of the Abkommen's raising of the financial stakes and international audience potential was first felt across a wide group of German independent filmmakers. *Autorenfilme* had by 1977 evolved to what the Filmverlag was initially conceived in reaction against: *Produzentenfilme* (producer films).[117]

Der amphibische Film: The Collapse of the Distinction between the West German Feature Film and Television Film

The coproductions of the Film/Fernsehen Abkommen did not exhaust television's support of independent filmmakers. Made-for-TV films were still a powerful but much more limited force in the development of the New German Cinema in the 1970s, but the formal and content differences between the two kinds of film were rapidly breaking down. In May 1977, Günter Rohrbach made the now famous statement that differences between the feature film and the television film should be eliminated: "The single-medium forms are disappearing, the amphibian films [those suitable to both media] are in a boom period. We, the television producers, are interested in the fact that it remains that way."[118]

Although it was vilified in the popular press, Rohrbach's plea for the "amphibian film" gained acceptance as a pragmatic point of view. As German television became ever more central in the finance and production of feature films in the 1970s, there was a marked growth in the feature films of the established television *Autoren* but a corresponding decline in the number of made-for-TV films. Two important outcomes of the concept of the amphibian film can be seen in the television coproductions with Fassbinder: ZDF's *Bolwieser* (*The Stationmaster's Wife*) in 1977 and WDR's *Berlin Alexanderplatz* in 1980. Both works were to be filmed in two versions—one for television and one for theatrical release—yet the theatrical versions were delayed or never made because of financial and legal problems.

Bolwieser was edited down from a two-part, 201-minute television film to 122 minutes and blown up from sixteen to thirty-five millimeter for theatrical release several years later, and *Berlin Alexanderplatz* became an export theatrical film simply by virtue of being shown in a theater.

In the process of becoming the film production power brokers for West German independent film in the early and mid-1970s, West German television, especially WDR, experienced a series of financial setbacks. The most serious for WDR revolved around the backlash against their exploitation of the freelance or independent film production workers in the name of artistic or *Autoren* freedom. The rise of television films had depended on using freelance workers as if they were regular employees, but with the inflation of the mid-1970s, television stopped providing steady employment. At the same time, the state's distinction between freelance workers and successful filmmakers — between *Autoren* who were being regularly underwritten by the Abkommenkommission and those who were not — became doubly apparent. As Sheila Johnston points out, this antagonism can be traced back to the "unresolved and explosive tension" behind the original film *Autoren* concept as conceived in the Oberhausen Manifesto, which called for the *Autor* to work and to be supported in an environment "immune from the very forces that had created it."[119]

The inflation of 1973–74 brought to the surface the economic system that had been obscured by the financially strong years of West German television in the 1960s and early 1970s. As a result of a court decision on the freelance union's demands, WDR was forced to take on 400 employees by 1977; because WDR employed the greatest number of independent film industry workers, it was the hardest hit. The German independent filmmakers were searching for institutional economic security. No longer were the artistic individualism and independence that originally defined them as *Autoren* in the Oberhausen Manifesto so important.

One can also see the influence on *Fernsehspiele* of these economic and political changes brought about by the general malaise of the *Tendenzwende*. The *Fernsehspiel* had reached its postwar production high of 243 in 1970. By the time of Rohrbach's call for the "amphibian film" in 1977, the number of television films had declined to 218, the lowest number produced since 1963. Not only did the overall number decline, the number of television films based on adaptation rose. An original *Fernsehspiel* by the mid-1970s cost between 500,000 and 1 million marks ($156,000 to $312,000). Responding not only to the financial crises but also to the Abkommen and

the *Tendenzwende,* the percentage of inexpensive and less politically problematic noncontemporary adaptations began to grow from 36.8 percent in
1972 — their lowest year in the history of postwar broadcasting.[120]

In addition to more adaptations, there was growing financial pressure
to move away from the less popular German personal *Autoren* made-for-
TV films toward entertainment programming. By the mid-1970s one can
see the established cultural divisions: "German" entertainment or popular
programing surrounded the production of cabaret and variety traditions of
German culture, but in relation to film and popular fictional entertainment,
American film still represented the majority of popular films on German
television.

Fassbinder weathered this period for a number of reasons. He was *the*
name *Autor* by the time of this conservative wave. More importantly, his
early work for television was never extremely radical in that he tended toward adaptation — he popularized established literary work for a broad audience as the German "Hollywood" director — so by the mid-1970s television's move toward popular programming did not necessarily exclude his
work. It did mean that a good half of the larger television stations' film
schedule by 1975 emanated from the cheaper imports from foreign countries, especially the United States.[121]

As cheap (one-ninth the cost of a self-produced film) and popular entertainment, broadcast feature films once again began to increase by the mid-
1970s.[122] WDR and NDR, the two largest and most politically and aesthetically progressive stations, had to struggle to keep some semblance of a
television-produced and controlled film alive. During these "reform-oriented
years" (as they are euphemistically referred to in WDR journals), WDR's
Fernsehspiel productions became less individualistic and politically less critical.[123]

By 1977 the importance of WDR's as well as all stations' *Fernsehspiele*
was clouded by the success of the large coproductions. In 1977 WDR internationally coproduced Fassbinder's *Despair (Eine Reise ins Licht — A Jour-
ney into Light)* and Peter Handke's *Die linkshändige Frau (The Left-handed
Woman),* both of which were shown at Cannes. The station also coproduced
Margaretha von Trotta's first large-scale film, *Das zweite Erwachen der Christa
I (The Second Awaking of Christa I),* Robert van Ackeren's *Das andere Lächeln
(The Other Smile),* and Hans Jürgen Syberberg's *Hitler, ein Film aus Deutschland (Hitler, A Film from Germany),* which was shown that year at the London Film Festival.[124] By 1977 WDR was West Germany's single major patron
of theatrically released German feature films that were shown in German

art cinemas and exported internationally as New German Cinema, but were not seen by the broad West German public.

How was this division between high and low film culture created by a public institution? Ultimately, the concept of *Autor* allowed German television to appease both its British founders and the postwar German bourgeoisie; it asserted the values of bourgeois education and traditions as "German culture." But it was at the problematic loss of the production of a popular culture on a state-supported medium. As a result, the state lived with a constant legitimation crisis as a state medium producing a culture that the majority of its public did not participate in or enjoy. Although the *Autor* discourse pervaded all of postwar German culture, television gave it its most public exposure as a mass medium. What started out as an exercise in democratic culture ended up asserting a new hierarchy dependent on bourgeois tastes. But of all the *Autoren,* it would be Rainer Werner Fassbinder—the director who gained the most from this culture—who turned on it. The state had produced "the aesthetic Fassbinder" or the *Autor.* But through his own work, he unmasked the class and aesthetic assumptions of his status as an *Autor.* Fassbinder made himself the object of public scrutiny through either the popular idiom of his film melodrama or the theater of the tabloids as the absent star. This contradiction is the subject of the rest of this book.

3 / Fassbinder as a Popular Auteur: The Making of an Authorial Legend

I discovered a way to approach autobiography less onanistically, less as an end in itself, and possibly to find out what I could say about myself that would be more universally valid.   Rainer Werner Fassbinder[1]

People like F. [Fassbinder] are totally not suitable for a positive cultural and media scene. Away with F.

Letter to *Der Spiegel* after broadcast of
initial episodes of *Berlin Alexanderplatz*[2]

Fassbinder always had all the prerequisites to become a legend. The image of this provocative character moved the imagination of human beings. And it served the demands of publicity for the artist perfectly: the artist himself was a part of his art.
                    Günter Rohrbach[3]

The *Autor* discourse was the construction of a growing German cultural nationalism of the 1960s, and Rainer Werner Fassbinder was its most prolific, well known, and "notorious" example as a filmmaker. The state's support of Fassbinder offers a seeming contradiction in that he received more support from German television than any other of the New German Cinema television directors, yet the mere mention of his name would raise eyebrows by the mid-1970s. The art cinema elicits biographical readings because art films are promoted as the personal statement of the director; Fassbinder openly connected his life to his films. We need to look at Fassbinder the historical being for an understanding of the "Fassbinder film."

Precedent exists for discursive analysis of the director's "biographical legend." In his study of the films of Carl Dreyer, David Bordwell revived this Boris Tomashevsky term in order to come to a historical understanding of the way that "authorship significantly shapes our perception of the work."[4] Bordwell quotes Tomashevsky: "The biography that is useful to the literary historian is not the author's curriculum vitae or the investigator's account of his life. What the literary historian really needs is the biographical legend created by himself [the artist]. Only such a legend is a literary fact."[5]

This type of analysis goes beyond the career studies and biographies to show how a director creates a persona in public utterances, writings, and interaction with the film world. Bordwell argues: "However subjective, however self-centered, such a legend may appear, that legend has an objective function in a historical situation." In many ways the biographical legend establishes the preferred reading of the text: "Created by the filmmaker and other forces (the press, cinephiles), the biographical legend can determine how we 'should' read the films and career. We do not come innocent to the films."[6] As much as the auteur theory purported to examine the sociohistorical intersection of directors and their styles, it functioned more often to mystify the director's role by canonizing the director through association with other "great" artists or by labeling the director a "genius" who defies historical explanation.

Although I am in agreement with the general direction of the Tomashevsky/Bordwell project, I take my analysis of the Fassbinder biographical legend one step further: I argue that it is not exclusively the product of the director's self-conscious manipulations of his public image, as Tomashevsky suggested. Rather, it is the result of a number of competing and often contradictory discourses that evolved out of state-regulated capitalism and culture in West Germany. We need to look at the various participants with a vested interest in the phenomenon known as a Fassbinder film, and the clearest way to analyze these competing positions is to analyze the concept of *Autor* or authorship as it is applied to Fassbinder.

Three major competing forces constructed the Fassbinder legend of a popular as well as a high-culture filmmaker: the television industry, the press (which I subdivide into the German film/media journals; the bourgeois "cultural" press; and the mass-circulated boulevard organs, mainly of the Springer Press), and Fassbinder himself. I have further subdivided the cultural press along class and political alignments.

In West Germany there is a clear distinction between the bourgeois and popular newspapers, and their respective readership is divided by class. Although various classes have access to and read bourgeois newspapers and magazines, one can categorize them based on which class constitutes the majority of their audience. Among the major "bourgeois" or "cultural" organs are *Der Spiegel, Die Frankfurter Allgemeine Zeitung, Die Frankfurter Rundschau, Die Zeit, Die Süddeutsche Zeitung,* teleschau, and *Die Stuttgarter Zeitung.* I have also included the more professional television journals and newsletters (*Fernseh Information* and *Kirche und Rundfunk*) as part of the cultural press. The popular press encompasses the conservative Springer tabloids *Die Welt* and *Das Bild* (the most widely read dailies) and the popular television magazines such as *Hör zu, Funk Uhr,* and *TV Hören + Sehen,* which range from a liberal to a conservative bias.[7]

I base this history on statements published between 1967 (when Fassbinder's name first appeared in the press) and 1982 (the year of his death) by the three major discourses—public television, the press, and Fassbinder—as they competed to construct Fassbinders of their own. This history is garnered from reading fifty-two West German journals, newspapers, and magazines in order to discern a pattern—what Michel Foucault calls a "regularity (an order, correlations, positions and functions, transformations)"—that we call "the Fassbinder legend."[8] Although this analysis does not attempt a systematic mapping of a biography, the discussion does present the most common "regularities" of what was written about the director.

Whereas the American and British academic reception of Fassbinder's work was primarily Sirkean, the German reception was more often related to his life. More than other directors, Fassbinder attempted to create a popular public persona in order to appeal to the public base of state-supported *Autorenfilm.* German accounts of the director and the "notorious" sexual politics of his films as well as his life filled the pages not only of the "cultural" press but also of the mass "boulevard" press. Fassbinder's status as West Germany's leading director added a new dimension to film reception: the director's biography as the text.

The central argument of this chapter is that since the art cinema foregrounds the director as the primary unifying structure, whether formal or biographical, in the art film, the director replaces the Hollywood star as the major means of spectator identification. When Fassbinder became a television auteur, he fell victim to conditions of public consumption similar to those suffered by such Hollywood stars as Bette Davis and Clark Gable. Because of the unusual conflation of directorial and star functions in popular and high-culture media, Fassbinder benefited from and was victimized by the *Autor* discourse.

Not only Fassbinder's homosexuality, class, education, and political allegiance were debated publicly, but also his suitability as an artist and the "originality" of his films—the hallmark of bourgeois creativity. The method of this analysis of Fassbinder's image is derived from Richard Dyer's analysis of Jane Fonda in *Stars*,[9] but the Hollywood division of labor between star, scriptwriter, and director collapsed with Fassbinder, an art cinema director. At issue was not only Fassbinder's ability to represent German culture, but also the myth of aesthetic individualism.

The Theater Fassbinder: The Collective as a Challenge to the *Autor*

In the case of Fassbinder, the discourse of *Autor* revolved first around his work within the avant-garde/leftist theater of the late 1960s, of which he was a central practitioner. It is paradoxical that the critics chose to nominate him as an *Autor* even when his work in a collective began as a challenge to this bourgeois tradition. In theater (and literature) there was a growing related dissatisfaction with the dominance of the "author" as a singular authority within postwar German society. Theater troupes in Berlin, Munich, and Stuttgart challenged the power of the theater *Intendant* (the administrator) to define the canon of "producible" drama.

Attracted to the immediacy of the theater and its potential for "direct" action, leftist playwrights and novelists rewrote the traditional theater classics (e.g., Peter Weiss's *The Investigation,* Martin Walser's *Child's Play,* and Peter Zadek's *Measure for Measure*). They altered not only the content but also the form of these sacrosanct works, in part to play havoc with the respect traditionally accorded the original authors' intentions. Many of these plays were (re)written to fit new priorities: politics and student activism. The staging was constructed around sit-ins on stage, interruption with banners, and leafleting.

They took their theater to the streets and to bars frequented by the lower classes in an attempt to create a "popular" theater. Theater collectives sprang up in basements (*Kellertheater*) and on the street (*Strassentheater*) in the mid- to late 1960s and challenged the primacy of the author's position in the interpretation or production of his or her work.[10] Modeled on the long tradition of socialist theater stemming from Weimar experiments such as the *Volksbühne* (people's theater), these groups deemphasized hierarchical control and middle-class notions of aesthetic individualism. The German theater was challenged for its bourgeois underpinnings. "Zerschlagt das bürgerliche Theater!" (Destroy the bourgeois theater) ran the title of a February 1969 guest editorial in the culturally powerful journal *Theater heute*.[11] In this milieu Fassbinder first appeared as a *member* of a theater collective in 1967.

Action Theater (1967–68)

Beginning in October 1967, the Munich-based theater collective Action Theater represented an iconoclastic attempt to turn German theatrical tradition upon itself. This leftist group was communally controlled by approximately seven members.[12] The group adapted canonical works such as *Antigone, Leonce and Lena,* and *Iphigenile,* investigating their intrinsic value by brazenly substituting for their themes the contemporary German political issues of the 1960s.[13]

With their adaptation of *Antigone,* the group refused to privilege any one source of the play as the "correct" translation. Peer Raben, the director, passed out a pamphlet to the audience that read:

> During rehearsals of texts of individual scenes learned from memory by the actors various versions were employed spontaneously. The result has been organized by me, supplemented with Brecht's legendary version (of *Antigonemodell 1948*) so that this production is based upon a number of different translations and adaptations.[14]

Even though the Action Theater challenged hierarchy (the primacy of the author or of the artistic personnel within the troupe), the Munich cultural press continually individualized the source of its performances. Fassbinder first emerged publicly in the theater's two-line advertisement in October 1967 for its production of Georg Büchner's *Leonce and Lena,* though the play was produced collectively by four directors. The short public review recommended the play based on its reputation as a classic and the fame of its author without noting that the troupe had so radically altered the play that only the title remained.[15]

The first major public recognition of Fassbinder as a director and artist came with the production of Ferdinand Bruckner's play *The Criminals.* Although a newspaper review of Fassbinder's solo directorial debut in December 1967 was positive and lengthy, Fassbinder was seen as an adapter and not an interpreter of the 1920s leftist work about the criminal class and the courts.[16]

When Fassbinder did finally achieve public recognition as an *Autor* and director of the play *Katzelmacher,* the press's reception was conditioned by his association with the film world.[17] In the review, Fassbinder's work played a secondary role to the filmmaker Jean-Marie Straub's staging of the adaptation of a short Bruckner work. The play was reviewed under the headline "Beyond the Culture Industry. A Premiere and a Straub-Production in the Action Theater." *Premiere* referred to Fassbinder's production. This headline suggested that Straub, with his name recognition, primarily as a filmmaker, outranked the theater director (Fassbinder—the author of the "premiere" work).[18]

Although the article mentioned Fassbinder, the style of the Action Theater troupe introduced the piece:

> The Action Theater romps elsewhere; it is a virtual enemy of culture and the public; it is politically left, and it destroys the holy sanctuaries and modes of cultural representation of culture. . . . They have obtained nearly everything that one cannot get without money; they have a good ensemble; . . . they have directors who are capable of creating their own "homemade" style, which serves the intentions of the company excellently. But above all they have authors [*Autoren*] in the ensemble who can write just those texts which the Action Theater can and wants to present.[19]

An important concept in the Fassbinder legend takes hold here. The reviewer perceived the artist's (Fassbinder's) success as part of the Action Theater collective's political and aesthetic stance; the artist writes and directs within the strictures of what "the Action Theater can and wants to bring about."

The idea of the individual artist being subsumed in the collective's identity is repeated in the experience and reception of the collective's most notorious work, *Axel Caesar Haarmann,* in June 1968. (The title is a political reference to the Roman dictator and to Springer's first and middle names— Axel Caesar.) The play was a highly charged example of *Demonstrationstheater,* or theater based on the forms of the 1960s protest movement. Even though Fassbinder had gained some renown for his previous directorial work and a

Süddeutsche Zeitung report of his arrest at the demonstrations in Paris in May 1968, he receded into the background as the collective responded to the attempted assassination of Rudi Dutschke, a leftist student organizer.

The troupe's first national review in *Theater heute* made no reference to Fassbinder, who appeared at the end of the play. He announced that the authorities were shutting down the performance and began to hose down the audience while demanding that the hall be cleared.[20] Instead of attributing the performance to any one individual's genius (Brecht, Peer Raben, or Fassbinder)—the traditional German theatrical analysis—the critic viewed the performance as an outgrowth of the troupe's collective or countercultural personality (see chapter 4). This review serves as one of the few recognitions of the troupe as a collective author—a political and cultural victory for its iconoclastic attack on the primacy of the individual author in German bourgeois theater. More significant is the emergence of a new public discourse in which the troupe's private existence is conflated with its aesthetic mode.

As I discuss more fully in chapter 4, the reference to the Living Theater's Artaudian style of theater allowed the *Süddeutsche Zeitung* reviewer to make sense of the Action Theater troupe's alternative theatrical as well as living styles; he removed the distinctions between theater and life. This conflation is evident in the second paragraph of the article:

> The attractiveness of the Action Theater results from engaging young actors and theater-possessed amateurs [*Laien*] in spite of a number of dilemmas, in spite of an unfavorable site, quarreling, and a lot of dust that drifts under the nose without the audience's awareness, yet it is intentional (in any case, symbolic).[21]

Here, even the theater's poverty and filth were an extension of the "aesthetic" experience. The "ensemble's house politic" resulted in "the heating up of the theater as a political arena of action."

More importantly, the review dissolved much of the difference between the public and private spheres. *Axel Caesar Haarmann* was, according to the review, the equal of any of the "spontaneous" or nonacted antiestablishment or anti-Vietnam War demonstrations going on in the street. Indeed, the troupe overstepped the comfort of aesthetic distance and the theater was closed down by the Munich authorities in June 1968. The closing had its intended political result: the antiauthoritarian collective lost its structure and disbanded.

antiteater (1968–74)

The troupe was reorganized under Fassbinder's direction in July 1968. Renamed the antiteater, it evolved into a more classically organized theater as Fassbinder came to the forefront as the central creative personality. The "Fassbinder troupe" surfaced in July performing Peter Weiss's *Mockinpott* at the Academy of Visual Arts. The program explained the transition as a polemical style harking back to the dada manifestos of the 1920s: "antiteater = ensemble of the Action Theater, antiteater = socialist theater, antiteater = information."[22] Fassbinder argued publicly that his growing role (along with that of Peer Raben) was not a political change, but rather a matter of expediency — an organization's need for a head.

A subtle change occurred in the critical reception of the productions, however; the role of the collective's political/aesthetic philosophy receded and Fassbinder became the motivation behind the group's creative drive. There was hardly any attempt to distinguish Fassbinder as an individual from what had been traditionally reported as the *group's* aesthetic and politics. The reviews offered no biography, interviews, or comparisons with his previous works to distinguish him from the collective. Fassbinder simply was the antiteater. In the words of one Munich reviewer of *Iphigenie*, it was "Fassbinder who had learned Goethe's *Iphigenie* in school" and it was his style that was capable of revealing "the hypocrisy of authority."[23]

The antiteater allowed Fassbinder to stabilize his career-long pattern of combining his idiosyncratic adaptations of the classics (Jarry's *Orgie Ubu*, Goethe's *Iphigenia on Tauris*, Sophocles' *Ajax*, Gay's *Beggar's Opera*) with his own plays (*American Soldier, Preparadise Sorry Now, Anarchy in Bavaria, Blood on the Cat's Collar*). Admittedly, his penchant for producing the classics fits into a German tradition of "updating" them for contemporary audiences, but the degree to which they were altered was still rarely addressed. The press traded on the established acceptability of the canonical authors in their choice of reviews and their evaluations.

Still, why did the established cultural critics *Frankfurter Rundschau, Frankfurter Allgemeine Zeitung,* and *Süddeutsche Zeitung* fail to distinguish Fassbinder's individual expressive method from the original author's intent? They had done so in their reviews of the relationship between the collective's staging and the canonized original author's intent. Their silence about Fassbinder and his aesthetic position suddenly disappeared when he finally received national exposure. This change attests to the institutional difference in reception of the traditional high-cultural realm of theater and the popular world of film and television.

The German Fassbinder as Film-Television Maker: A Growing Institutional Division

One cannot overemphasize the change in the critical reception of Fassbinder's art when he made the jump from theater (traditional, but limited, access) to film (mass reception) and television (even broader reception). Admittedly, his work was relegated to the margins of popular reception as he challenged the forms and institutional structures in both theater and film. Just the costs of producing and selling a small, nonmainstream film called for a larger audience and a wider sphere of exhibition (no longer tied to a theater but now to a name). Even the institutions of the German art cinema (festivals, art film houses, federal prizes, the journals) increased a film's, as opposed to a play's, accessibility to a national audience. But more importantly, the move to film was not limited to the more rarefied or less-seen exhibition method of the art cinema circuits, but included television exhibition, which led to Fassbinder's early film success. These distinctions between forms (theater and film) and method of diffusion (performance, art cinema exhibition, and broadcast) must be seen as the complicated but central key to the peculiarly sensational reception of Fassbinder's oeuvre in West Germany.

One needs to examine also the institutional influences of the art cinema on the reception of Fassbinder's first films. Although Fassbinder had made two previous short films, he released an eighty-eight minute film, *Love Is Colder Than Death* (*Liebe ist kälter als der Tod,* 1969), for the first time at the all-important Berlinale film festival in June 1969.[24] Although the film did not win any immediate critical acclaim, the conventions tied to a film premiere at the Berlinale resulted in interviews that singled out an individual authorial source. Traditionally, the interviewer seeks parallels between artists and their work.

Additionally, as a major state-funded showcase, the Berlinale accorded Fassbinder a number of important articles in national newspapers — the *Berlin Tagesspiegel, Film* (the German film fan magazine), and, most notably, *Frankfurter Allgemeine Zeitung.*[25] Comparable to an interview in the *New York Times,* this newspaper's notice signaled the change in Fassbinder's potential to reach a middle-class audience. After this breakthrough, a number of interviews specifically about the film ensued, with Fassbinder's long work in theater being at best a sidelight.[26] The attention culminated in a long interview in *Filmkritik,* West Germany's most prestigious film journal at the time, and the publication of the film script in *Film.*[27]

The second event that catapulted Fassbinder into the limelight was a one-day, thirteen-hour retrospective ("Showdown") devoted to his work: two films (*Katzelmacher* and *Love Is Colder Than Death*), two theater pieces, and one cabaret review in Bremen in November 1969.[28] Here Fassbinder was revealed to have the oeuvre that marks aesthetic individualism—a classic determinant of auteur/*Autor* status. The immediate catalyst for this event was the October premiere of his second publicly released film, *Katzelmacher,* at the Mannheim film festival, an event that always meets with wide publicity.[29]

The German critical reception of the Fassbinder "Showdown" at the Bremen State Theater was still limited to *Der Spiegel* and *Theater heute,* but their attention signaled Fassbinder's move into a general national, albeit "cultured," reception. The importance of the reviews lies in their national scope and in the degree to which they personalized Fassbinder's work, which heretofore had been judged by broader aesthetics and political norms.[30]

The German press's fascination with the Fassbinder legend began in *Der Spiegel* in December 1969 with a full-page article entitled "Fun Demands Consciousness—*Spiegel*-Reporter Fritz Rumbler on the antiteater chief Rainer Werner Fassbinder."[31] What is most significant in this article is how quickly Fassbinder had become the sole artist; the collective had receded into the background. The *Spiegel* article established three central themes— his youth (he was twenty-three), the quickness of his working style, and the amazing productivity of his short career: "In barely two years he has made four films, written five theater plays, adapted ten pieces, and produced in seventeen plays. In addition, he acted, presided over a theater commune, and smoked around sixty cigarettes per day." The merit of his work lay in its originality. Fassbinder is quoted as saying, "Everything is beautiful for us that rises as an alternative to the accepted."

Although the antiteater collective (the "us" Fassbinder refers to) is described as "Germany's most enthralling private theater troupe," Fassbinder is the only member to be painted as an individual: "like a phoenix from Munich's underground ... the boy wonder of the season." In fact, the article failed to mention any of the collective's other members by name, preferring to delve into three aspects of Fassbinder's biography: his unique aesthetic disposition (as a not formally educated child of the German middle class); Action Theater's connections with German terrorism; and *his* formation of the antiteater, where "he wrote his plays himself with the help of the collective." The collective as an experiment in nonbourgeois conception of the creative process now represented only "trouble" (*Kummer*) and at best a sexual outlet for Fassbinder's "promiscuity." As a result, the reporter argued, "it seems that the astounding personality of this early matured twenty-year-old holds this group together in crisis."[32]

Ironically, the death of the collective antihierarchical aesthetic was acknowledged in November 1970. "The End of a Commune," a West German television-made semidocumentary account of "the difficulties of communal work in our society" chronicled the antiteater events. A *Der Spiegel* review stated:

> Of Fassbinder's communards, almost all pay lip service to the ideal of common work and living group. In reality many are not ready to give up their private comfortable life out of comfort or fear of such an existence. And Fassbinder knows that too. He finds this disgusting contradiction simply depressing.[33]

The docudrama (broadcast nationwide during prime time) revealed that the antiteater was publicly recognized as an important and unique experiment in an alternative vision of authorship. Not surprisingly, the program chose to present a very negative view of this nontraditional concept of creativity and pointed to Fassbinder as its "true" source. Significantly, the collective responded (without Fassbinder) in a letter arguing that the film had "destroyed their quiet attempt at collective work form and had embraced a middle-class genius cult."[34]

The Art Cinema Fassbinder (1970–76)

The Fassbinder of the art cinema is the one with whom we are most familiar. His films circulated in the film festivals, art houses, and student film clubs of West Germany. It is through the festivals that Fassbinder was first noticed in America by *Variety*.[35] His privately financed films, usually shot in thirty-five millimeter, fulfilled all the institutional characteristics of the classic postwar national art cinema films (as opposed to his television work, either taped or filmed in sixteen-millimeter). Between 1969 and 1977 Fassbinder produced ten to twelve films that were financed privately within West Germany, including some of the most autobiographical and well known of his works: *Beware of the Holy Whore* (1970), *Ali/Fear Eats the Soul* (1973), and *Fox and His Friends* (1975).

As art cinema films, the majority were premiered at either the Berlinale (the Berlin film festival) or Mannheimer Filmwoche (Mannheim Week) — the two most powerful German festivals of the 1970s. During this period he also premiered a number of films at other European festivals — in Vienna (1969), Venice (1970), and Cannes (1972 and 1974) — and placed his films in big-city art cinemas: Cinemonde (Munich) and Kurbel (Berlin). The lion's share of his art films were distributed and often cofinanced by Filmverlag der Autoren, one of the major distributors of the "name" film *Autoren* of the New German Cinema.

By 1972 Fassbinder was a recognized institution within the important, albeit narrow, bourgeois art cinema. Ulrich Gregor of Berlin's cinematheque Arsenal contracted with Fassbinder to screen a series devoted only to the private art house films.[36] Although these films were being discussed and promoted by West Germany's film journals (*Filmkritik, Film,* and *Film und Fernsehen*), it was the mass-circulation publications that created the popular legend informing the educated and noneducated filmgoer of Fassbinder's authorial marks within the personal films. But more importantly, these publications established a series of contradictory discussions about Fassbinder's position as both *Autor* and autobiographical figure as he evolved into the star of his films.

Before I analyze these discourses, the term *star* needs to be defined. In *Stars,* Richard Dyer writes: "Stars are, like characters in stories, representations of people. Thus they relate to ideas about what people are (or are supposed to be like). However, unlike characters in stories, stars are also real people."[37]

In general, Fassbinder's filmic work lacked stars. He used his antiteater acting troupe — actors from the fringes of Munich avant-garde leftist theater circles — whose creative roles were suppressed in favor of individualizing Fassbinder as the artistic source. Only after his international successes of the mid-seventies did his actors (Hanna Schygulla, for example) evolve as recognizable stars. Even as they gained recognition, they were still primarily associated with the Fassbinder name (Schygulla was often described as "Fassbinder's Hanna Schygulla"). In 1972 Wolf Donner wrote an article entitled "The Boss and His Team":

> The strategy — to manufacture a name and a figure as the brand name — was a necessity in our society where interest is fixed more on a single personality than on groups and collectives. Fassbinder also had the experience that it is sometimes necessary to assert oneself in an authoritarian manner in a group.[38]

Given the general recognition of Fassbinder as the organizing agent of his films—a status peculiar to the art cinema director—he extended that role to an autobiographical level. He created a hazy line between the function of an *Autor* as the organizing agent and as the star who is constantly subjected to a real world versus fictional world comparison known as stardom. What is particular to the star's character/real person dichotomy that is not usually relevant for an *Autor* is the uncertain separation of the public self and the constructed or fictional self.

Elizabeth Burns (quoted by Dyer) argues that the "life as theater" phenomenon is one of the central concepts of stardom in that the actor "intervenes ... between the authenticity of his own life, of his own self and its past as known to himself (and as known or assumed at least in part to the audience) and the authenticated life of the character he is playing."[39] One can apply much of the star phenomenon to the public reception of Fassbinder as the lines between his films and his personal life became increasingly ambiguous during this period.

Although there is no one Fassbinder legend or image, there is a range of images associated with him that is limited by what the press, his institutional supporters, and Fassbinder himself said about the director. As a result, this polysemy called the Fassbinder legend did change over time. Some stars are able to create a stable image (John Wayne is an example), but in the case of Fassbinder, the tension between the privilege of his status as an *Autor* and the scrutiny of his life as a star created contradictions that slowly fragmented with increased national exposure through the popular medium of television, culminating around the broadcast of *Berlin Alexanderplatz* in 1980.

Fassbinder as Star *Autor*

In an attempt to isolate Fassbinder as an individual from his membership in the collective, the West German press described him as a psychologically differentiated individual with a specific biography. He was described as both ordinary and extraordinary, the classical contradiction associated with stardom: a spectator needs both to identify with and to be in awe of the star.[40]

Fassbinder's "ordinary" character boiled down to his physical appearance, his conservative middle-class origins, and his propensity for hard work. Unlike most authors and other artists, Fassbinder fell victim to the star image even as the press consistently remarked about his "ugly" appearance, which belied his status: "He looks like he has a permanent and classical case of the mumps: a stocky figure, sleepy eyes, shabby hair, stubbly hair, a little surly, a bit grumpy, a full moon face and stomach. That is — on first appearance — the rising genius out of Munich."[41] *Die Zeit* wrote an oddly racist description in 1970: "He does not have a refined artistic appearance; he looks sooner like a Mexican hacienda owner with a massive body, pocked face, and a walrus mustache."[42]

Not only did his appearance belie the star qualities he had attained, his background contradicted his radical politics. He came from the heart of conservative Bavarian respectability. According to *Twen,* he grew up "in a bourgeois milieu — father-doctor, mother-translator."[43] Many articles pointed to the fact that he did not even have the classic German *Bildung* (cultivation) that defined a German *Autor.* Representative of this reaction is the statement that "he left high school without a diploma for actor's school in order to gain some kind of 'preparation' to become an actor."[44]

Fassbinder's ability to work hard was also taken as a sign of his ordinariness. Countering the conventional concept of the artist's privileged position of not having to work for a living, Fassbinder was seen as having "earned" his position through near-"common" labor. For example, he was compared to an assembly line worker: Fassbinder "produces film and theater plays like the baker on the corner produces morning rolls [*Brötchen*]."[45] *Die Stuttgarter Zeitung* explained in a similar vein that Fassbinder was "the hardest working young filmmaker" and that his works were representative of mass culture in that they were "films to throw away" (a phrase repeated in the press).[46] Even the conservative *Die Welt* declared: "Once you meet him, you'll decide that he is an entirely ordinary guy."[47] With such descriptions, the press set in place the Fassbinder who was identifiable to the broad public.

Significantly, this ordinary side of Fassbinder also allowed the more hostile dailies to question why he was quickly anointed West Germany's leading young filmmaker. The *Die Welt* article began by turning the art cinema's evaluation of Fassbinder against itself:

> He made just one film and with it exploded onto the cultural scene like a rock star — leather jacket and boots. At the time, he was not taken seriously.... He and his film, which was described as being "like when a farmer plows a furrow into the land." (Henri Langlois, head of the Paris Cinematheque), were laughed at. It made no difference to him.[48]

On another level, one could argue that these comparisons of Fassbinder with the common man or his filmic work with rough physical labor were necessary elements for Fassbinder's acceptance by a wider German audience. On this level, he was solidly German and therefore deserving of state monies and recognition as a *German* artist. By 1976 Fassbinder began playing into this theme with statements such as, "As a German I can only make German films"; he said he wanted to be "a German Hollywood director."[49] But, more accurately, these statements balanced Fassbinder's more individualistic or "artist" side. As much as he was seen as having an affinity with the common German, the extraordinary Fassbinder—and relatedly the homosexual Fassbinder—were, nevertheless, the more popular objects of West German interest.

Like any star, Fassbinder was most often presented in terms of superlatives. Given that his background and his appearance were at best common, it was his psychology that took on the extraordinary quality. His propensity for hard work became superhuman, bordering on frenzied, in the press. A comparison of the following descriptions from two culturally different sources is instructive in this regard. *Hör zu* wrote: "This young man is not to be measured by any normal or middle-class rulestick. He creates like a horse. Writes a play in three or four days. Sleeps hardly at all. Smokes without interruption."[50] *Der Spiegel* described Fassbinder thus: "In two short years he has made four films, written five theater plays, directed ten plays, and produced seventeen plays, and add to that he has acted, run a theater commune, and smoked sixty cigarettes a day."[51] A similar tendency to present him as excessive can be found five years later in a *Frankfurter Rundschau* article:

> Rainer Werner Fassbinder is the most multifaceted and productive among our young artists: actor, playwright, film-television-theater director. In less than a few years he has made over twenty films (some for TV), not counting the radio plays and theater productions.[52]

One cannot deny that Fassbinder was a productive filmmaker. But the press's need to present him as extraordinary led them to characterize him as superhuman or nonhuman based not only on his productivity but also on his lifestyle.

As his film career and the resulting public recognition developed, his productivity became more directly related to his psychological makeup. Typical was a much reproduced interview in the *Stuttgarter Zeitung* in April 1974 (later published in a book and a number of newspapers). When asked about his pauseless work schedule, Fassbinder answered:

It has to do with psychological reasons that come from some-
where in the past. What they are, I also do not know. Still it is
true, for example, that I must assimilate all that I experience in
order to have the feeling of having experienced it.[53]

The correlation with emotional past and present experiences established
the individual psychological basis for the continuum between his films and
his life. Here his films were interpreted as a form of emotional release.

By 1976 there was a direct correlation in his films between these psychological sources and his autobiography. Most of the West German press
noted the number of directly autobiographical works in this mid-1970s period. By then Fassbinder had filmed *Beware of the Holy Whore* (1970), *Ali/Fear
Eats the Soul* (1973), and *Fox and His Friends* (1975). The ever antagonistic
Die Welt reviewed the autobiographical *Fox and His Friends,* with the director in the title role as a homosexual, in March 1976:

His works consist of quotations, found objects, and stories that he
has heard. And what is autobiographical in his work is sooner located in what he does not express. The laconic remark over his
intention to write a novel must be placed in context with his productions, his difficulties in his private life, and the frequently un-
veiled aggressivity over failures of his theater productions. The truth
comes sooner with the understatement: "I also have psychosomatic suffering which is really disturbing."[54]

The possessed or disturbed Fassbinder surfaced as the most frequent public
way of discussing his creativity. He said he worked so hard that there was
no time between projects. Even the liberal cultural weekly *Die Zeit* described him as an "exhibitionist" and the audience member as "a voyeur
without free will." The article concluded that "Fassbinder is not consider-
ate, he bothers us with psychosomatic agonies, homosexual fantasies, sadomasochistic excesses, and a lack of social responsibility."[55] In the eyes of the
press, Fassbinder's extraordinary psychological makeup singled him out as
an exceptional individual. He was not simply an actor acting out someone
else's role. Rather, Fassbinder the *Autor* exceeded a star's position; he was
not only actor and film character, but also the *sole* creative source of both.

The Television Fassbinder (1970–76)

Although Fassbinder continued to produce a number of independent films
under the production company titles antiteater, antiteater-X-film, and later

Tango Films, the majority of his films were done for West German television.[56] Why is this institutional distinction important? The made-for-TV movies were marketed for and shown to a broad prime time German audience who had limited knowledge of the conventions of the art cinema, but as taxpayers had a vested interest in public television productions. The question then becomes, How could a member of an anarchist leftist theater troupe whose explosive productions were closely associated with the disruptive student movement become the darling of state television? Obviously, the answer is not simple.

On one level, by 1970 Fassbinder fit television's needs. He was a recognized *Autor* coming out of West Germany's all-important (albeit leftist) theater community. He and his troupe had produced many of the canonized works of the German theater. Many of his films were first produced as plays as part of the Action Theater and antiteater. Given the tight nature of the collective's work method, Fassbinder could rapidly produce inexpensive films. He had demonstrated this in the past. Therefore, he fit comfortably into the constraints of the low-budget production method of the made-for-TV movie.

On the other hand, Fassbinder's recognition as an *Autor* was built around a lack of orthodoxy, whether it was his excessive dramatic style, his notorious personal life, or the outrageousness of his productions. The more important question then becomes, How did Fassbinder's television sponsors contain the explosive potential of both the *Autor*'s unorthodox style and his life? The answer lies in analyzing the division between the works that Fassbinder made as an independent art cinema filmmaker and those he did for television.

For television, Fassbinder's excessive style was channeled into what has been described as "melodramatizing" or popularizing two television genres: the classic adaptation and the socially critical made-for-TV play. Working from literary sources in the beginning of the decade, Fassbinder adapted canonical literary works. His political and iconoclastic "living theater" style (see chapter 4) was scaled down and promoted as a method of broadening the appeal of these high-art works. Fassbinder added a veneer of melodrama to his adaptations, creating what could be seen as the Hollywoodization of German high culture.

For the broad West German television viewership, Fassbinder's early works were promoted primarily under the name of and by the reputation of the original author. Although the initial films he produced were "original" to Fassbinder (*Warum läuft Herr R. amok?,* 1970, and *Rio das Mortes,* 1970), he soon settled into producing a series of adaptations (Carlo Goldoni's *Das Kaffeehaus,* 1970, Marieluise Fleisser's *Pioniere in Ingolstadt,* 1970, and Franz Xaver Kroetz's *Wildwechsel,* 1972).

What is most significant is the scant publicity these televised prime time works engendered. While the national popular press was alive with discussion of Fassbinder's less seen nontelevision films such as the prizewinning *Katzelmacher* (1969) and his continued work with antiteater, these adaptations were simply announced in the television listings as, for example, "Rainer Werner Fassbinder's adaptation of Carlo Goldoni's *Das Kaffeehaus.*"[57] In other words, the authorship of these adaptations, altered as they were from the original, was not included in the public appraisal of Fassbinder's "creative genius."

The articles did, however, provide evidence of the mounting theme of diversity and productivity as signs of Fassbinder's uniqueness. The headline of an April 1970 article on Fassbinder in West Germany's most read magazine, *Hör zu,* openly displays this equation: "The Revolutionary with a Heart: He produces for three. He makes film, television, theater. He calls himself a 'revolutionary.' He does not love just one — Rainer Werner Fassbinder is a Unique Person [*Unikum*]."[58]

Simultaneously, a whole other Fassbinder existed in the independent German film world: the confessional Fassbinder. His works for the more select art house circuit were markedly different; they were original and idiosyncratic. This stylistic code has been aptly described by film academic Eric Rentschler, who speaks of Fassbinder's "appropriation of the melodrama and his codes (expressive lighting, theatrical tableaux, garish decor with narrow interiors, mirror reflections, heavily enunciated music at crucial junctures)."[59] But what Rentschler and others do not describe was how this authorial code was conditioned by and functioned differently within the two media. In his privately funded films, Fassbinder used his melodramatic style to question the larger issue of the reliability of the auteur/*Autor* as an expressive individual.

Fassbinder's amazing career in two very different institutions — the mass medium of West German television and the high-culture world of the art cinema circuit — was built around a delicate balancing act between Fassbinder the producer of popularized classics and socially conscious family melodramas and Fassbinder the confessional *Autor.* In one of his few statements on his television work during this period, the director underlined the self-consciousness of the division between his work in television and in theater and film: "Solely in television is it different [from film and theater productions]. There one interacts with a varied public. And I find at the moment that it is better to tell people something."[60]

Eight Hours Are Not a Day: Fassbinder and the Social Critical Television Genre

In 1972–73 Fassbinder came to the attention of a broad West German television audience with the Westdeutscher Rundfunk production of his workers' series *Eight Hours Are Not a Day* (*Acht Stunden sind kein Tag*). Collins and Porter's study of the genre of workers' films chronicles the political furor created by anticapitalist films, and particularly Fassbinder's popular contribution.[61] What they did not analyze is the degree to which Fassbinder's original contribution was a departure from his cycle of literary adaptations for television. Because of its unprecedented scope (five episodes totaling seven hours and forty minutes; only *Berlin Alexanderplatz* exceeded it in length), the series became a center of public attention. More importantly, it was an unprecedented marriage of the popular German middle-class genre (the family series) and a larger leftist experiment in workers' rights associated with the educational ideals of the Third Channel.

Although Fassbinder was chosen to direct this series based on his reputation as a leftist, the decision was also based on his ability to popularize bourgeois genres—the family series—a choice that the producing television station emphasized. Peter Märthesheimer, Fassbinder's television producer, wrote a long intellectual explanation of the series' objective entitled "The Occupation of a Bourgeois Genre." Appearing in *Fernseh und Bildung,* the article attempted to legitimize the series for German intelligentsia based not on Fassbinder's fame as an *Autor* but on the importance of using the conventions of middle-class fiction for working-class inspiration. Märthesheimer wrote:

> They [the protagonists] only become so striking because the forms of expression which formerly belonged to the bourgeois and petit bourgeois milieu, are in *Eight Hours* introduced for the first time into the proletarian milieu, and with these forms stories are told in a completely different way. This transplantation has two advantages—one of aesthetic effect: how the characters behaved was very striking, "distanciated" against the given background; the other of ideology: the apparently unlimited scope for the action and

> behavior which bourgeois culture allows its heroes in the novel,
> [in] the theater and even in the family series, addicted to eclecti-
> cism and the cult of the private, offers an effective lever to make
> problematic the established, regimented and constrained working-
> class milieu.[62]

What is significant here is how Märthesheimer uses "bourgeois culture"
genres to legitimatize the form and content of the Fassbinder series. Previously, Fassbinder's work for public television had been promoted as adaptations of established literary works of the educated middle class. But here, in
a curious turnaround, when Fassbinder produced an original and political
television film his creative role and political reputation receded into the
background. The central issue became the right of working-class culture to
be exhibited via the same forms used for bourgeois culture. In a sense, the
discourse of Fassbinder's popularizing established literature remained the
same. Now, however, it was the form and content of those traditions that
were being translated. Fassbinder's skill, then, lay in being a consummate
craftsman translating a middle-class genre to a working-class milieu.

Discussion about the appropriation of a bourgeois form by a working-
class genre continued in the popular press. In an article in *Konkret* entitled
"Is the Proletarian Wave Coming?" Fassbinder argued:

> One can use any genre to put across a message, whether you want
> to introduce a new sensitivity or political content. Family series
> are what Germans like watching. That way you create a potential
> audience for the first half hour. You're over the hill then if people
> haven't turned off. Then such and such a family comes regularly
> into their homes and they can do what the characters can do.[63]

As Collins and Porter point out, the producers clearly planned to use
"a familiar compromised genre as a vehicle for raising political consciousness of the German working class TV audience, through the audience's identification with the characters and the actions of an 'occupied' family series."[64]
In fact, one of the most common strains in the critical discussion of the
worker film was what an abrupt switch the style and content of the series
was for Fassbinder, who had heretofore worked only on classical adaptations for German television and on his own privately produced films.[65]
Moreover, in one article Fassbinder was challenged for his lack of appro-
priateness for a working-class narrative because of his "autobiographical
background" as a child of the middle class (and therefore alien to the lower
class). In response, he agreed:

Ah, yes, I don't really know what it is really like. I just have my idea of it. And I have worker friends and when I have written up my ideas I give them the text so that they can read it and discuss it with me. Then I alter the text until they finally say—yeah, it's like that near enough.[66]

Fassbinder's response differs from that of a German *Autor* in the degree to which the content and form of the series do not conform to his "cultivation" (*Bildung*) nor to his other works. At best, Fassbinder's reputation as a popular filmmaker with leftist sympathies corresponded to the series' sense. The conservative backlash highlighted that side of Fassbinder.[67] Yet another example of how Fassbinder's role as an established *Autor* receded into the background can be found in the academic/professional journal *Kirche und Rundfunk*: in a long article entitled "Eight Hours Is a Long Day" Fassbinder's participation is mentioned in one line.[68] Again, the article echoes the theme of Fassbinder as the popularizer of established forms, or in this case the popularizer of another class's experience.

Although *Eight Hours Are Not a Day* was widely seen (41 to 45 percent of the German audience) and popular (60 percent of that audience rated it "good" to "very good"), the series was still politically controversial. For the cultural representatives of the middle class, the political moment in the production of *Eight Hours* came not with the choice of Fassbinder, a known radical, but rather in the WDR production of an *Arbeiterfilm* devoted to working-class entertainment and activism. Aesthetically, it was attacked in *Die Zeit* as Fassbinder's "stylistic mishmash."[69]

But the main thunder came from the established institutions of both the right and the left, which attacked the series for a political naïveté about how the workplace functions. On another level, the problem was presented as the inability of the producers to distinguish between fiction and reality. The major criticism lodged against Fassbinder was that he had "a notion of political activity that does not go beyond the realms of private experience into the traditional areas of political struggle and debate."[70]

The debate over *Eight Hours* had more to do with the application of middle-class conventions of goal-oriented protagonists to a working-class milieu—a potentially explosive concept for the middle-class individuals who ran the various governing boards of Westdeutscher Rundfunk (see chapter 2). According to Collins and Porter, the governing board (*Rundfunkrat*) did not cancel the series, but imposed strict guidelines on Fassbinder: he could produce future episodes only if he took into account the criticism against the first five. Seeing the new restrictions as "too daunting," Fassbinder withdrew from the series. Since WDR saw the film as "authored" by Fassbinder, they discontinued it, arguing that they would have a credibility problem without him.[71]

By 1973, because of the notoriety associated with directing the working-class series and the corresponding public interest in his class origins, Fassbinder was a well-known figure in the German mass media world. He went on to produce three shorter *Fernsehspiele* within a social critical genre: *Like a Bird on the Wire* (*Wie ein Vogel auf dem Draht*, 1974), *Fear of Fear* (*Angst vor der Angst*, 1975), and *I Only Want You to Love Me* (*Ich will doch nur, dass Ihr mich liebt*, 1975–76). Yet the correlation between Fassbinder's life and his work for television continued to grow with the production of these "original" works. In an official television publication, Märthesheimer interviewed Fassbinder in 1976 and asked him whether the themes of matricide and denied love in *I Only Want You to Love Me* were autobiographical. He responded: "Yes, that is true in a certain sense. It is the case that all my films have also something very personal to do with my life."[72] There was a growing relationship between Fassbinder's television work and his life, but the overt political nature of his television films was continually denied in favor of the theme of emotional exploitation.

Separating out the actual politics of Fassbinder's personal life from the quasi-political theme of sexual exploitation became necessary for state television's spokespeople. By the mid-seventies they had become increasingly nervous about their support of anything that smacked of politics, given the change in political climate brought on by the rise of terrorism and the resulting *Tendenzwende*. As a result, from 1976 to 1980 West German television produced only two Fassbinder works after six years of at least two a year. Both adaptations (Oskar Maria von Graf's *Bolwieser*, 1976–77, and *Women of New York*, 1977, adapted from Clare Boothe Luce's *The Women*) were produced without much publicity or critical notice.

By 1975 the distance that television had been able to maintain between the *Autor* and Fassbinder the individual began to break down as Fassbinder and the success of his independent confessional feature films became a constant issue in all West German dailies. In addition, he had gained a reputation as a representative of German culture in that he had won every major West German prize and state subsidy.[73] West German television (particularly Westdeutscher Rundfunk) still wanted to produce Fassbinder's work. By the late 1970s, as a recognized feature film *Autor*, Fassbinder could dictate his choice of materials; he was no longer constrained by the need to produce the works of other authors.

Still, Westdeutscher Rundfunk canceled two major television projects with Fassbinder during this period. In 1977 they canceled his adaptation of Gustav Freytag's *Credit and Debit* (*Soll und Haben*), a canonical nineteenth-century German novel about a Jewish merchant. Two years earlier his aborted theatrical production on the postwar Frankfurt building speculation, *The Garbage, the City, and the Dead* (*Der Müll, die Stadt und der Tod*), had been branded "anti-Semitic" by the mass West German press, although it was supported by the cultural press.[74] The television station thought this history would make it too difficult for the planned 1977 television adaptation of another text about Jews by Fassbinder.

In 1978 the station pulled out of producing *The Third Generation* (*Die dritte Generation*) because of its theme of terrorism and Fassbinder's connection to the Baader Meinhof terrorist group. Fassbinder published a rebuttal to WDR's withdrawal in the widely read liberal daily *Frankfurter Rundschau*:

> Reality, everyone seemed to agree, was the province of television, which is unfortunately a public institution and as such committed to a balanced approach to reality — or is it a balancing act, an undiscriminating pluralistic approach, in which anything and everything has legal rights, especially the legal system?[75]

For all Fassbinder's growing tabloid fame by 1978, German public television was able to ride out the crises by either not producing or pulling out of Fassbinder's more personal and political works or deflecting Fassbinder's biography away from the productions. Television maintained his high-culture status as the producer of the work of other *Autoren*, yet he was also a figure of popular culture whose sensational life was melodramaticized in the popular press. Fassbinder was able to be ordinary as a representative German *Autor* and extraordinary as a star/personality.

When Fassbinder's *Berlin Alexanderplatz* premiered on West German television in 1980, the West German populace knew the television Fassbinder for melodramatic adaptations of other authors' works. They also had access to news accounts of his life stemming from his autobiographical films. But these worlds had remained relatively separate because Fassbinder's television works were not *his* films or *Autorenfilme*. The art cinema and television spheres had been separated by the institutional split in the production of independent film in West Germany in the 1970s. When Fassbinder produced West German television's biggest production to date, an adaptation of Alfred Döblin's *Berlin Alexanderplatz*, and declared "I am Biberkopf" (the protagonist), the two separate worlds collided. The result was the biggest

West German media controversy since the airing of the American series *Holocaust*. The airing of *Berlin Alexanderplatz* represented the meeting of high culture and popular culture: Fassbinder's life as melodrama.

The Fassbinder legend began to force the West German public to question what Foucault describes as "the legal and institutional systems that circumscribe, determine and articulate" authorship. By embroiling the content of his films so closely with his own life, Fassbinder exploited, questioned, and fell victim to the mechanics of the bourgeois construction of aesthetic individualism. Indeed, to be a legend a director must be in the impossible position of being ultimately knowable as a popular star yet ultimately unknowable or removed as an author anointed by the middle class. Perhaps it is the taboo nature of his exploration of the context of aesthetic authority that led Fassbinder to christen his work "incest film."

4 / Shock Pop: Fassbinder and the Aesthetics of the German Counterculture

Thomas Ammann just called to tell me that Fassbinder just killed himself. Well, he really was strange. When he came to the office he was reeeally strange. And I say somebody's strange, you know that they're strange. He was thirty-seven and forty movies.
Andy Warhol[1]

Warhol's dispassionate and typically voyeuristic chronicling of a star's death makes the unusually self-conscious acknowledgment that he and Rainer Werner Fassbinder were both "strange." Despite their differences, the comparison between the two artists/directors figures strongly in Fassbinder's international reception. Fassbinder's legend has often been compared to Warhol's "decadent, camp sensibility of the New York demi-monde."[2]

Both gay, Fassbinder and Warhol are famed for their countercultural lifestyles as leaders of entourages and artistic troupes — groups that served as ambiguous sources for their sensationalized promiscuous sexuality and as an exploitable pool of labor for their factory-style productivity. Further, solid questions remain about the degree to which the two artists did indeed produce their *own* work and whether their art did not originate instead in their ability to manipulate the star-making machinery of the culture industry.[3]

Biographical comparisons to Warhol aside, beneath this level of analysis lies a deeper, unexamined source of Fassbinder's films: American pop culture of the mid-1960s. "Popism" (Warhol's term) was an American movement that glorified a new cultural pluralism based on artistic and cultural forms capitalizing on the immediacy and pleasure of commercial culture. In 1965, Allen Kaprow summed up the sources of this new American movement for West Germans:

> First, the mass media publications of the newspapers and magazines; here one finds the comics, the want ads, the headlines, the photo exposés and the common graphic designs. Second, the radiating stars or the images of youth; these have the appearance of advertising photos and billboards similar to television and film techniques of photomontages and slow motion filming in order to create a single "frame" or a strip of film. Third, the world of the fast food stand, the supermarket, the discount center which offers the battlelines of necessities, prepackaged goods, household tools.[4]

The American pop culture movement of the 1960s remade consumerism into a youth culture—pop art, rock and roll, and countercultural activities— entailing an ambiguous mixture of vaguely antiestablishment activities and pleasure in consumerism. The 1960s pop movement is comprised of pop art and popular culture united by the remaking of the signs and products of commercial capitalism. Obviously, pop art and popular culture are not the same. Pop art could serve as a sharp critique of mindless consumption and capitalism. One needs only to consider James Rosenquist's *F-111* (1965) and Peter Saul's *Society* (1964) to see how pop iconography enhanced the paintings' indictment of America's cultural economy. As a whole, American pop culture and art celebrated the more ephemeral pleasures of the postwar consumer boom.

German pop never entered into this incestuously close relationship between American pop culture and capitalism. Germans adopted America's consumerist culture as a rebellion against European high culture's hegemony in the first half of the twentieth century. Indeed, the German pop movement represented a major break from the old left's subservience to European modernism as a form of resistance. Whereas pop's popularity in America preceded the anti-Vietnam War movement, West German interest in pop grew simultaneously with the country's rising youth-based antiwar movement. Richard McCormick has characterized the German student movement in the 1960s as specifically antiauthoritarian in that it was based "on the ideal of personal refusal: each committed individual would refuse to cooperate with a system seen as authoritarian and immoral."[5]

American pop as a reaction against the dictates of modernism served as an iconoclastic model for the art and protest forms of the rising German New Left. Although Warhol's and Robert Rauschenberg's pop art enlisted popular culture in its deflation of high-art abstraction, it was easily assimilated into the art gallery scene. It took a German political movement to keep pop from being totally swallowed up by the German marketplace. Andreas Huyssen argues for the specifically political nature of the German adaptation of American pop when he writes: "In short, pop became the synonym for the new life style of the younger generation, a life style which rebelled against authority and sought liberation from the norms of existing society."[6]

The pop movement of German youth was conscious of the potential problem in using the political and economic products of America as a countercultural agency. They remade these American pop art and commercial images to point out the contradictory relationship of the ruling German bourgeoisie to America in the 1960s: simultaneous support for the American political economy and utter disdain for American commercial culture. This poaching of American pop culture by the German antiwar generation can be defined as a "popular" culture movement—the disenfranchised use of American consumer culture against German established or high culture for political empowerment. Even though this movement filtered its appreciation of pop through Europe's own anarchistic traditions (Antonin Artaud's theater, for example), this use of commercial culture as a popular political form represented a remarkable break with the Frankfurt school's critique of popular culture—a form of mass deception by the culture industry.

Interpreted within this historical and national context, Fassbinder and his film work stand as an example of the generational and class battle within German leftist culture. Even though the cultural and popular press attempted to remove Fassbinder from a social or collective context by nominating him as an *Autor*, his work was firmly rooted in a historical aesthetic in which a German subculture used American popular culture's pleasurable immediacy to combat the rigidity of high culture. Wim Wenders also participated in this "pop"-ularization of German culture through his antiauthoritarian films; films such as *Alice in the Cities* (*Alice in der Städten,* 1973) and *The American Friend* (*Der amerikanischer Freund,* 1977) served as somewhat critical homages to the cultural democracy of rock and roll and popular film. But Fassbinder took up the forms of American pop culture, pushing them beyond even the antiauthoritarian use. Fassbinder achieved what Warhol could sanction: he politicized them, made them "strange."

Brecht and Fassbinder: The Problems of Brechtian Cinema

It is difficult not to speak of Bertolt Brecht in discussing German leftist culture and the use of form as a critical agency. Fassbinder's films share Brecht's interest in politics and form. In fact, many of them have strong affinities with Brecht's working-class subject matter and his alienating performance style. Fassbinder's films follow Brecht's dictum that the ideology not only of content but also of form must be made manifest.

One has only to remember the painfully self-conscious scene of Emmi and Ali in Hitler's favorite restaurant in *Ali/Fear Eats the Soul* to recognize the influence of Brecht's class consciousness and formal alienation. Here, the newlyweds—a white cleaning woman and a black North African guest worker—sit down to their wedding dinner in a completely empty restaurant. The camera isolates them within the door frame in a long shot; they appear out of place and embarrassed by the waiter's disdain of their race and class. Self-consciously quick cuts between waiter and couple create a series of Brechtian tableaux as these individuals come to represent social types.

But what about Fassbinder's choice of remaking an American 1950s melodrama—Sirk's *All That Heaven Allows*? Just the choice of a Hollywood film reflects a certain attraction to the simple forms of popular culture. Although a Brechtian reading of Fassbinder's work is based on ample textual evidence, it fails to take into account the historical context of the reception of Brecht in the 1960s. In fact, Fassbinder rarely played into the Brecht industry of the 1960s and 1970s. When he was asked about Brecht's influence, he replied, "No. Kluge's alienation is intellectual like Brecht's, while mine is stylistic."[7] Indeed, how do we reconcile such Brechtian textual analysis of Fassbinder's films with the filmmaker's own proclamation that "American cinema is the only one that I can take really seriously, because it's the only one that has really reached an audience"?[8]

A closer look at German youth counterculture and theatrical forms in the late 1960s reveals that Brecht and his work stood as part of the "established left"—a culture represented by the complacent bourgeoisie of the Sozialdemokratische Partei Deutschlands (the SPD of Willy Brandt and Helmut Schmidt) and the more authoritarian left represented by the Kommunistische Partei Deutschlands (KPD and East Germany). The young left saw the old left as either ameliorators or Stalinists who had failed to mount an effective resistance to the American military-industrial machine that occupied not only South Vietnam but also West Germany itself in the 1960s.

This youthful distrust of established leftist politics culminated in 1966, when the socialists (SPD) under Willy Brandt took over the West German government for the first time since the 1920s through a partnership with the liberal Freie Demokratische Partei (FDP) and the conservative Christlich-demokratische Union (CDU). For the rising student movement, this euphorically hailed "Grand Coalition" served as bitter evidence that a "New Left" had to be constructed. The German Students for a Democratic Society (SDS), growing out of the SPD, broke with the party in 1959 over the party's refusal to adhere to Marxism. The SDS began as early as 1964 to organize teach-ins about South African apartheid, the Vietnam War, and Iranian repression, as well as street demonstrations against German involvement in these imperialist actions.[9] While the German student left had a number of markedly doctrinaire groups — Maoists, Trotskyites, KPD followers — there was a growing suspicion of hierarchical and traditional authority.

With the reinstitutionalization of the left as represented by the SPD within German politics, Brecht had become acceptable. By the mid-1960s plans were under way to create a major government-funded Brecht archive in his hometown of Augsburg. In 1967 and 1968 — the central years of countercultural uprisings in West Germany — Brecht's plays were among the works most commonly produced by major state theaters. In 1967, *The City of Mahagonny* played in Wiesbaden, Frankfurt, and Stuttgart.[10] In May and June 1968, as Paris and Berlin erupted in unprecedented student riots, the prestigious Munich Kammerspiel produced Brecht's *Three Penny Opera*.[11] Even the city-sponsored youth forum in Baden planned a production of a Brecht *Lehrstück* for teenage edification. The state television networks produced five of his works between 1966 and 1969. The television revival of Brecht's plays culminated in 1967 with the national broadcast of *St. Joan of the Stockyards* and *Trumpets in the Night*. In the 1960s, according to Knut Hickethier, the television networks treated Brecht's works as classics — a term that underlines their acceptability within a prescribed bourgeois cultural tradition.[12]

This list of Brecht productions does not, however, speak to the relative political content of the chosen Brecht play. Nor does the Brecht revival reveal how the Brecht plays were further politicized through the production process by references to the Vietnam War and the German class struggle. Television's appellation and use of a "classic" can be seen as an astute move to depoliticize the applicability of Brecht's plays to the 1960s. The popularity of Brecht productions in the late sixties reveals that his plays and his name no longer carried a destabilizing threat, as they did during the politically unstable 1950s and early 1960s. No longer was it practically verboten to produce the East German's work within West Germany. This change led a *Theater heute* writer to entitle an analysis of Brecht productions in 1968 "How Dead Is Brecht?"[13] That same year, novelist and political activist Peter Handke, in an article on protest theater, declared Brecht's work to be "harmless."[14] In fact, so established was Brecht as a sanctioned playwright that Fassbinder's avant-garde/political Action Theater in Munich never produced even one of Brecht's plays in its countercultural repertory.[15]

The German New Left in the 1960s: Pop as a Political Antiaesthetic

Although Brecht's works stood as a major model of leftist cultural resistance, the young German counterculture directed its wrath principally against any established culture. The movement was distinctly anti-intellectual, devaluing modernist notions of distance. Even Brecht himself would have supported such a break from his works in that he argued: "What was popular yesterday is not today for the people today are not what they were yesterday."[16]

American pop culture served as a prime vehicle with which to undercut the dead forms of the German bourgeois arts. First and foremost, pop art was associated with a part of consumer America — a "nonculture" without a tradition of high culture — in the eyes of the German cultural establishment. Schooled in the 1950s on the abstract expressionism of Jackson Pollock and even Paul Klee, the German arts establishment as a whole did not take this new art seriously.[17] Pop art was the child of commercialism, but one based on a broad visceral youth-based appeal with a subcultural origin in the American underground art movement of Andy Warhol and Allen Ginsberg, as well as in comic books and the rock and roll of the Velvet Underground and the Grateful Dead.

According to a think piece on pop culture in the *Süddeutsche Zeitung* in November 1967, a naive preindustrial cultural democracy pervaded the American movement:

> Participation is unquestionably the key word. In the self-written songs of Bob Dylan, in Joan Baez's guitar ballads in which appears a young, herbal, and humane America, and in the rhyming teenage rebelliousness of Janis Ian ("Society's Child"), the division between art and reality and spectator and performer is abolished.... Songs are musically rhymed observations about the current situation. Whatever happens is commented on. Ideologies are taboo. The joy of

playing mingles with the displeasure over the world's responsibility for the Bomb. Participation does not mean engagement in the sense of left and right ideologies — which have credibility among these youths. Participation is a natural expression of a feeling of life — it is untroubled, but concerned, as well as untesty and cheerful. It demands dignified human relations.[18]

Here as elsewhere in German culture, American pop culture was associated with feelings, immediacy, and tactile pleasures. For many traditional German leftists the pop-inspired American counterculture was more concerned with dropping out of established "uptight" adult culture in America and refusing to engage in the discourses of modern capitalist existence and class domination.

Indeed, the hippie utopian vision often translated for Germans into avoiding economic and political responsibility for American culture in favor of a communal sensory voyage into drug-oriented pleasures. German historian Jost Hermand contends that early American pop art — an antecedent to hippie culture — ran parallel to the growing legend of the Kennedy era (1960–63), which gave America a huge surge of self-confidence. As evidence, he quotes pop artist Robert Indiana on pop's ideology in 1963: "It is the American Dream. Optimistic, generous and naive.... It is the American myth. For this is the best of all possible worlds."[19]

Andreas Huyssen suggests that the German interpretation of American pop culture corresponds to Roland Barthes's theory of *jouissance*: pop culture represented pleasure gained by escaping the control of the culture through the sheer delight of the perceptual play of forms. Barthes's pleasure derives from "distancing the signified" by foregrounding the signifiers.[20] Although the pleasure is antipolitical, pop art's *jouissance* took on a powerful ideological role when it was integrated into the political context of both German traditional culture and the emerging counterculture. The German youth appropriation of American pop culture was based on an urge to engage the issues of capitalism and domination after the postwar occupation. Like every popular culture movement, the German movement is riddled with contradiction. It played into the colonizing power of the American media and commercial culture, intending to reveal "the complicity between aesthetic taste, and economic and symbolic power" in postwar Germany.[21]

Writing in exile, Brecht had actively encouraged "pleasure," but he argued for a pleasure based not on transgression or artistic convention or evasion of social control, but on ideological enlightenment. In his essay "Theater for Pleasure or Theater of Instruction," he writes:

Learning has a very different function for different social strata. There are strata who cannot imagine any improvement in conditions; they find the conditions good enough for them. . . . But there is also a strata "waiting their turn" who are discontented with conditions, have a vast interest in the practical side of learning, want at all costs to find out where they stand, and know that they are lost without learning; these are the best and keenest learners. . . . Thus the pleasure of learning depends on all sorts of things; but none the less there is such a thing as pleasurable learning, cheerful and militant learning.[22]

For Brecht, one could never escape ideology. Pleasure is found in distancing oneself from the trap of bourgeois ideological control through Marxist "learning." Even when he writes about a boy's physical pleasure in wolfing down food in the play *Life of Galileo,* Brecht argues that a "self-indulgence" must be allowed in order to teach a social lesson.[23]

Increasingly through the late 1960s, the use of pop iconography was directed at the bourgeois-dominated traditions of high culture in West Germany, where canonical art and literature were treated with reverence. The British subcultural movements of the 1960s coalesced around a similar rebellion against the hegemony of the bourgeois culture in an assault on style through a bricolage of popular iconography as represented by the rockers, beats, and teddy boys.[24] In fact, Andrew Ross argues that the British experienced a similar subversive pleasure with the arrival of American popular culture and pop art in the mid-1960s: "For Britons, the importation of American popular culture, even as it was officially despised, contained, and controlled, brought with it the refreshing prospect of a boycott of traditional European judgments of elitist tastes."[25]

Whereas the British drew on their own popular traditions in working-class and Cockney culture, the German pop movement lacked an indigenous popular culture. The concept of *German* culture or even "popular" culture had been tainted through association with nazism. At best, this culture has become kitsch—a sad imitation of high art. The occupying or "liberating" American forces provided the commercial and cultural commerce that became the basis of German pop irreverence.

Nevertheless, German pop's reception strongly differs from that of its American counterpart as a result of the strength of the German bourgeoisie's cultural capital and its resistance to an American-based art movement. Like dada in the 1920s, German pop was a direct reaction to a high-culture milieu; American pop was born within the friendly environment of consumerism. Consider the headline of a guest editorial in the prestigious *Theater heute* by a countercultural theater troupe (quoted in chapter 3): "Destroy the Bourgeois Theater." Such polemics exemplified the centrality of class issues in the arts for the youth rebellion. The degree to which pop culture was political in America was based on its resistance to a broad, ill-defined, puritanic "establishment." In his comparative study of German and American pop reception, Hermand calls this late German pop period (1967–69) "shock pop." It was brought on by the loss of the West German political optimism that had initially spawned the popularity of pop art:

> The Vietnam war, the Black Panthers, the SDS Movement, the Paris May 68 disturbances, the German SDSers, the involvement in the problems of the Third World, and the widespread campus unrest: all these contributed to the feeling that nothing more was to be gained by human sensitivity and closeness to nature. The political rockers therefore replaced the slogan "be nice to one another" with only a dirty sneer.[26]

One of the first attacks on *deutsche Kultur* by this more militant pop movement was directed at the purity of the German language — a traditional focus of German nationalism. The American words *nonprofit, pop art, happenings,* and *underground* became standard vocabulary for a German youth who wanted to undercut the dominance of German as the language of all culture. For example, free alternative rock and roll concerts sprang up across West Germany in 1967, often billed as "nonprofit" in English.[27] West German art galleries began to exhibit "pop art" paintings as early as 1963; the Akademie der Künste in Berlin culminated in a show devoted to Andy Warhol at the Neue Nationalgalerie in Berlin in March and April 1968.[28]

But for many German cultural critics American pop art and culture were seen as shock pop — destabilizing or intrusive. The New York avant-garde film movement (the New American Cinema), with its fascination with the everyday and the materiality of commercialism, became the darling of the alternative film clubs, particularly in Munich — the home of Fassbinder's Action Theater. The New American Cinema's debut there in 1964 was described as having initiated the German interest in American pop art films' use of the everyday, commercialism, and breaking rules. When a Warhol film premiered in Munich in May 1968, the local reviewer declared that it had an "unashamedly anarchistic form."[29] P. Adams Sitney returned to Munich a month later, during the intense political activism of June 1968, and presented a program of Ron Rice, Claes Oldenburg, and

Warhol films. Again, the press highlighted the destabilizing influence of the "underground" films. One reviewer argued that their merit lay in their ability to force the spectator "to reorient himself to what appears common by having the rug pulled out from underneath himself."[30]

Pop Art's Theatrical Spectacle: The Happening, The Living Theater, and the Action Theater

By 1965, Cologne was recognized internationally for another form of American pop spectacle: the happening. The happening preceded the New York pop art scene; many of its practitioners were artists and musicians — Claes Oldenburg, Robert Rauschenberg, John Cage. Happenings represent an important historical transition from the perceptually based abstract expressionism to the more conventionalized world of pop and commercial iconography. Often called "painter theater," these theatrical experiments began in art galleries and studios in the 1950s as a cross between painting and performance — a modest subgenre of spectacle.

The conventional Aristotelian separation between stage and audience was eliminated in the happening and replaced with a more vertiginous construction of space in which participants (not actors) performed among spectators. Accepted theatrical concepts were broken down: there was no plot (yet performances were rehearsed) and no clear ending. Often people off the street would be integrated and audiences had to be told to leave. Happenings were deliberately impermanent: the focus was the physical moment. As a result, their content defied clear explanation. They were designed to tease and abuse the audience through surprises and provocations: shocking statements, loud noises (banging on an oil drum, several radios playing simultaneously), and physical intimidation of the audience (sprinkling them with water, sneezing on them, driving them out with a lawnmower).[31] Peter Wollen has termed these performances the "theatricalization of minimalism" that resided in pop art.[32]

When the Germans appropriated American pop art and the happening, they repeated the simplicity of forms, the emphasis on physical pleasure, and the ability to shock by breaking down aesthetic distance. German pop owes more to the American cultural movement's physicality and antirationalism than to its intellectual appeal. In fact, the German model for its emotionally charged theater did not come from the cool and intellectual distanciation of Brecht's Epic Theater but rather from the New York-based Living Theater, which kept the happening aesthetic alive in Europe into the

1970s. The Living Theater began its nomadic tour of Europe with its Artaud-inspired happenings, performing *Antigone* in Krefeld and Munich in 1967.[33]

The group was renowned for a highly visceral and violent theatrical form that physically and psychologically jolted the audience's complacency through a pseudoimprovisational staging of its plays. As one critic argues, the American troupe desired "to reduce the structure of drama itself until the form and the theme should be synonymous until, that is, the drama should cease to inform and start to re-enact."[34] This participatory ethos in theater arts was based on emotional reaction and the consequent physical response, resulting often in a political action in the context of the German antiwar movement. It rejected the intellectual complexities and ambiguities of modernism, including Brechtian political modernism, but it was still perceived as a political theater in its form and its refusal to adhere to traditional classical norms of theater.

For one German critic the happening aesthetic was closer to psychodrama, which allowed the participants to develop creatively and emotionally through breaking rules.[35] It was directly linked to the teach-in and sit-in methods of the youthful vitality of the German protest movement. In fact, during a guest performance in Munich in February 1967, the Living Theater performers began a confrontational sitdown strike in the public lobby when a member was arrested on suspicion of auto theft. The founders of the troupe, Julian Beck and Judith Malina, responded that the action was an extension of their theater: "We try to tear deep into the physical feelings of the spectators. One can also establish compassion physically."[36]

Taking their cue from these American abstract "events," the German counterculture used the form to attack the bourgeois tradition of aesthetic distance and contemplation. With student demonstrations erupting in the streets, the countercultural theater collectives integrated the forms of the protest movement into the presentational form by breaking down the separation of the audience from the performance and invading the auditorium with the actions of a protest demonstration. The ultimate aim of this agit-prop theater was to decompose the intellectual resistance of the audience to involvement in antiwar activities. Like pop culture, this theater integrated the forms and actions of the everyday into representation. For the German counterculture, the line between performance and political action was to disappear. Nevertheless, German shock pop returned a seriousness — an aesthetic of political immediacy and action — to pop.

It is not surprising, then, that Fassbinder's avant-garde theater troupe appropriated and combined a number of strains in American pop art culture and patterned itself after the American troupe, initially calling itself, in English, Action Theater.[37] Indeed, the theater collective served as a recognized leading example in Germany of the Living Theater's agitprop method in the late 1960s. The German company was a collective like the Living Theater, existing on the margins of Munich's cultural scene much like the off-off-off-Broadway American troupe. The Munich troupe adapted and sytematically perverted canonical German and classical plays and their performance traditions. It performed its version of the Living Theater's *Antigone* just half a year after the American troupe visited Munich. The Action Theater publicized its production as "more like a central African festival than a meaningful, collective expression of emotion."[38] A local critic wrote of the production that "they stammer, stamp, become rigid, and die; the moaning bodies wind through the spectator's area and horrible cries permeate the walls of the hall."[39]

Although the troupe's production of John Gay's *Beggar's Opera* followed the Brecht/Weill tradition of a satiric operetta, Fassbinder ended the play within the Living Theater sensibility by introducing the last scene with a quick succession of silly doggerel and prayerlike dialogue and then closing the play with all the actors creeping onto the stage and barking. When Fassbinder took over the troupe in 1969, he continued to rewrite the Living Theater's work for the new antiteater group; he adapted the Living Theater's *Preparadise Now* into *Preparadise Sorry Now* (1970). As early as June 1968, a critic argued in *Theater heute*:

> It of course strikes one as grotesque that the Action Theater refers to Brecht and that [idea] has threatened the continuation of his ideas.... The Action Theater ... comes out of the world of the pop and hippie culture (an example being the staging of *Leonce and Lena*) and visually out of the world of comic strips and film.[40]

In general, the troupe cut into the power of the plays' traditional messages by using pop art's method of quoting from commercial or popular culture — most often from rock music and Hollywood film. In Fassbinder's production of Bruckner's *The Criminals* (1967), he integrated the music of the Rolling Stones, and he was criticized by the established press in Munich for not being historically correct.[41] In 1968 the troupe staged Goethe's *Iphigenie* with electronic rock music as a "third chorus." One writer described the performance as a kind of collage: "Lines from Mao or Paul McCartney were assembled exactly like scenic quotations out of comic strips or the Living Theater."[42] Such irreverence for historical truth exemplifies the more dada-inspired political iconoclasm in German pop art as opposed to its American counterpart.

Consider how the Action Theater's notorious piece *Axel Caesar Haarmann* reveals the troupe's debt to the spontaneity and immediacy of their American model. A highly charged example of demonstration theater coming during the feverish protest days of June 1968, the play was organized around the forms of the student movement: mass demonstrations with banners and posters, the chanting of antiauthoritarian slogans, and intervals for sit-ins and teach-ins. Fassbinder appeared at the end of the play and hosed down the audience à la riot police. The aim of the performance was to ignite iconoclastic pleasure, anger, and ultimately action, not Brechtian distance and realization. *Axel Caesar Haarmann* exemplified the power of the naive immediacy of American pop culture within the more restrained European political intellectualism.

Perhaps the most infamous example of the Action Theater's agitprop was *Chung* in June 1968. It was to be performed on the street as well as in the theater with the express purpose of responding to the state's new emergency law. On the day of the play's premiere, the Action Theater's premises were ruled a fire hazard by the authorities and the theater was closed.[43] Since Fassbinder predicated so much of his life on breaking social taboos (including the left intelligentsia's), the most politically explosive moments of his works derived from pop art's emphasis on immediacy and the everyday, resulting in the lack of orienting boundaries between political action and theater.

Ultimately, Fassbinder and Action Theater as well as the pop art happenings owed much of their action orientation to Antonin Artaud — the "other" theorist of modernist theater. Fassbinder's films reveal Artaud's influence on his work far more than Brecht's. The film *Satansbraten* (1975–76) begins with a quotation from Artaud's *The Theater and Its Double*.[44] *Despair* (1977) is dedicated to "Artaud, Vincent Van Gogh, Unica Zurn." And in 1981, the year before his death, he wrote and directed a film, *Theater in a Trance,* that combined dance pieces with Artaud's writings.

Artaud's theory remains just as potentially revolutionary as Brecht's in that it too questioned the role of representation in social change. But the Frenchman's object was the psychological subjectivity of the individual, a subject that Brecht rarely considered. More than Brecht, Artaud rejected society. He viewed European society as paralyzed by bourgeois conformism that revered established canonical works as fixed literary texts "that could no longer respond to the needs of the times."[45]

As an anarchist and antirationalist, he became the nemesis of the European bourgeoisie with his refusal to participate in traditional bourgeois culture as well as the communism of the avant-garde left of the 1920s. Unlike Brecht, Artaud never left a clear semiotics of his theater during his early formalist period. Even though he called for a fixed language of gesture based on Balinese dance, gendered breathing differences, and ideograms, he refused to explain this language in any detail, claiming that Western civilization ossified culture through theory and formal rules.

Nevertheless, Artaud's major work, *The Theater and Its Double* does offer an outline (at times contradictory) of an aesthetic theory and its potential praxis as a political action theater. As opposed to Brecht's intellectual alienation effect, Artaud's theory called for catharsis as the central experience of the theater of cruelty—a catharsis that transcended the dominant social constraints of spoken and written language and communicated on all sensorial and intellectual planes.

To create this prerational ritual and to achieve purgative catharsis, the spectator/participant observes or performs certain violent actions that allow spectators and performers to purge themselves of violence in their daily lives. As to any guidance for the actual direction of an Artaudian performance, there is little evidence left from Artaud's theater work.[46] Jerzy Grotowski's Polish Poor Theater and Judith Malina and Julian Beck's Living Theater have come to represent the most "orthodox" Artaudian theater performances.

But the problem still remains: Artaud's theory defied the notion that representation can adequately replicate the power of the original experience.[47] Artaud's theater could never be "performed"; the theater of cruelty transcended representation. Theater is not a representation of life. It *is* life. But it must transcend social control. Artaud stated: "I have therefore said cruelty as I might have said 'life.' "[48]

The "Artaud paradox" embodies the contradictions involved in the counterculture's appropriation of cultural norms. Given Artaud's rejection of all rational discourse, most particularly Marxism, his theory fed into the youth counterculture's rejection of classical Marxism in its rational and scientific guise. His essay "No More Masterpieces" was reprinted in *Theater heute* in May 1968, and *The Theater and Its Double* was translated into German that year.[49] His antirationalist statements in the Surrealist Manifesto inspired the May Paris student revolt: the students quoted Artaud's inflammatory language in their leaflets.

As Martin Esslin points out, Artaud "exemplifies the profound identity of all political attitudes based on the primacy of emotion over reason and the inevitable resort to violently aggressive action."[50] The spontaneity and ephemeral nature of political actions and street protest theater of the 1960s were derived from this Artaudian disdain for social control and cultural rigidification. But at best Artaud's theater could take place only once.

Herein lie two philosophical parallels between Artaud's theater and Fassbinder's films. The first is the lack of a clear delineation between representation and the artist's immediate political existence. For many, Artaud's theory of theater found its purest form in his own transgressive public life. Fassbinder traded on the German tabloid press's sensationalized accounts of his anarchistic lifestyle in his films. His films are distinguished by unparalleled dependence on personal confession. As will be explored in more depth in the next chapter, in the European art cinema the director often represents "the author," and therefore a spectator interprets a film as a "personal statement"—a reading strategy not encouraged by Hollywood films. Fassbinder throughout his career produced films that logically extended this "personalism," films in which his authorial presence became biographical or even confessional.[51]

In fact, he pushed the confessional tradition of the art cinema to question the orthodoxy of any ideological position—even his own. And what distinguished Fassbinder's confessional style from that of the other art cinema confessionalists (e.g., Fellini, Pasolini, and Truffaut) was his pop culture iconography. As early as *Katzelmacher* (1969), Fassbinder films began to play out a tenuous relationship between Fassbinder the person whose highly publicized life transgressed bourgeois social norms and Fassbinder the artist sanctioned by the very class that his personal life affronted.

We need to reconsider in this context how the popular press responded to Fassbinder's mixing of the art cinema and popular culture as a critique of "art" and "the artist." Consider how the bourgeois press compared Fassbinder's work to the mass production of consumer goods. He was often compared to an assembly line worker. He was described as one of the hardest-working filmmakers. And his works were described as representative of the disposable nature of mass culture, as the much quoted phrase "films to throw away" indicated. In other words, when Fassbinder's work crossed the line from aesthetic distance to the pleasures based on sensationalism and immediacy, as well as emotions and visceral perception, his work was perceived by the dominant press as ephemeral and less important—like popular culture.

A second parallel between Artaud and Fassbinder is that both looked to violence and physicality as forms of social transcendence. Fassbinder's films were marked by violence throughout his career. He moved from a cardboard cutout, comic book use of it in early films such as *Why Does Mr. R. Run Amok?* (1970) and *The American Soldier* (1970) to an unrelenting sadomasochism in late films such as *Fox and His Friends* (1975), *In a Year of Thirteen Moons* (1978), and *Berlin Alexanderplatz* (1980). In his search for an escape from societal, sexual, and economic control, Fassbinder uses the visceral nature of violence as an ambiguous source of the films' power. Kaja Silverman, Eric Rentschler, and Thomas Elsaesser have commented on the assault on the body in *Thirteen Moons* and *Berlin Alexanderplatz*.[52] Silverman and Elsaesser argue that in masochistic abandonment Fassbinder finds a utopian moment within the patriarchal power relations where the characters accept their "lack" and take pleasure in it: beautiful suffering. Silverman argues that "despair and suffering function at times to 'secrete' an intense and simultaneous joy."[53]

This "utopian masochism," as Silverman calls it, not only carries on Artaud's aesthetic of violent pleasure but also extends the German student movement's demand for a greater awareness of subjectivity. Fassbinder responded by investigating the relationship of the personal and physical reality. The emotion and violence that were once acted on the streets as political theater by the students were now in the 1970s acted out as an assault on the character's as well as the spectator's psyche and/or body in Fassbinder's films.

Implications of Pop's Antiaesthetic for Understanding Fassbinder's Films

Ultimately, it is Fassbinder's use of melodrama that unites the violent visceral Artaudian tradition and pop art's playfulness. Indeed, most academic analysis of Fassbinder as a Brechtian stems from his pop appreciation of the American director of 1950s melodrama, Douglas Sirk. Fassbinder produced a number of melodramas that mimic if not quote Sirk's style; the best-known example is his remake of Sirk's *All That Heaven Allows* (1955) as *Ali/Fear Eats the Soul* (1973).

Fassbinder's 1971 essay "Imitation of Life: Rainer Werner Fassbinder on the Films of Douglas Sirk" offers the most concrete evidence of his relationship to the Hollywood director. Although the article is impressionistic, he defends Sirk based on the use of melodramatic excess as a formal political critique. He argues: "Sirk has said: you can't make films about things, you can only make films with things which make life worth living. Sirk has also said: a director's philosophy is lighting and camera angles."[54]

For Fassbinder, such formal consciousness in Sirk's melodramas led to social awareness in that, for example, the sets were heavily marked by the characters' social situation. In fact, he appears to state that Sirk's stylistic irony invokes Brechtian distanciation: "Douglas Sirk's films are descriptive. Very few close-ups. Even in shot-countershot the other person does not appear fully in frame. The spectator's intense feeling is not a result of identification, but of montage and music. This is why we come out of these movies dissatisfied."[55] This concept of "dissatisfaction" stemming from the formal method could easily be interpreted as alienation or the alienation effect (*Verfremdungs-Effekt*) of the Epic Theater. But the Fassbinder essay does not develop the ideological or class-based awareness that was Brecht's reason for such a method.

Fassbinder's essay more comfortably fits into a more contemporary form of American stylistic excess: pop camp. Although critics have discussed the influence of camp on Fassbinder's style, this aspect has not evoked the degree of scrutiny accorded to the more Marxist and structural Brecht theater influence.[56] (Only with the rise of gay studies have pop and camp begun to receive the analysis they deserve as a form of political resistance other than the classically conceived Marxist methods.) Indeed, if one reads Fassbinder's article carefully, it serves as an elaborate defense of a camp aesthetic. Andrew Ross defines the "camp effect" as "when the products ... of a much earlier mode of production which has lost its power to dominate cultural meanings become available in the present for redefinition according to contemporary codes of taste."[57]

American melodrama of the 1950s functioned as an oddly contradictory example of a disenfranchised mode of production for Fassbinder's camp sensibility. By the mid-1960s American melodrama's cultural power had begun to wane under the influence of the European art cinema's realism in Europe as well as in Hollywood. But the celebration of a Hollywood form through camp revival also served as a defiant act against the traditional German left, which spoke of American culture as cultural imperialism. Ultimately, for Fassbinder, who represented a countercultural figure on three levels (young, German, and gay), camp offered the opportunity to estrange the German establishment from the repressive class concept of tastefulness.

Within the cultural poaching endemic to the sixties pop movement, America of the 1950s took a privileged iconographic position. Pop art celebrated the period of Pax Americana and cultural consumerism, and Sirk's melodrama served as a prime example of this popular pleasure in its fascination with the everyday, the bricolage of consumption, and the intense "trivial" emotion. This period was in fact the period of the American occupation of Germany, and Fassbinder's postwar trilogy of *The Marriage of Maria Braun, Lola,* and *Veronika Voss* reveals an absorption with the bricolage of American popular culture in the 1950s. But Fassbinder's appropriation of Sirk went beyond uncritical pop appreciation; his analysis was fraught with an oddly self-conscious camp glorification of melodrama. His heightened language reveals an ironic use of an American form. Fassbinder writes: "And Sirk had made the tenderest films I know, they are the films of someone who loved people and doesn't despise them as we do.... America is really something else."[58]

Maternal melodramas such as Sirk's have always functioned as a privileged object of camp pleasure within the pre-Stonewall gay community. Gays not only identified with the marginality of the melodramatic form as a "castrated culture," they displaced their sexual identities onto the melodrama's heroine as a victim of patriarchal discourses on sexuality.[59] Consider the camp seriousness of Fassbinder's defense of the Jane Wyman character in *All That Heaven Allows*:

> And there Jane sits on Christmas Eve, her children are going to leave her anyway and they have brought her a television set for Christmas. It's too much. It tells you something about the world and what it does to you. Later on, Jane goes back to Rock [Hudson] because she has headaches, which is what happens to us all if we don't fuck once in awhile.[60]

This presentation of "the marginal with a commitment greater than the marginal merits"[61] exemplifies Fassbinder's camp intellectualism — the celebration of alienation, distance, and incongruity represented by the dominance of American culture in its taste and sexual mores. Instead of *V-Effekt* one is confronted with camp's ironic distance, which allows Fassbinder to find value in and to identify with these "low" or "trashy" commercial melodramas to undercut the dominance of German bourgeois cultural authority.[62]

Fassbinder's continual use of strong female protagonists extends the logic. Beyond an ironic Brechtian critique of American capitalism, Fassbinder's camp aesthetic is as much a celebration of American commercialism as a critique of it. As a child of the camp and pop counterculture of the 1960s, Fassbinder disdained the high seriousness of Brecht's political theory.

Additionally, these pop-art-inspired commercial references add a broader appeal to the emotional anarchy of Artaud's theater that underlines Fassbinder's excesses. Consider the dependence on the visceral appeal of pop iconography and violence in Kenneth Anger's *Scorpio Rising* (1962–64), Jack Smith's *Flaming Creatures* (1963), and Bruce Connor's *A Movie* (1958) and *Report* (1964–65). Arguably, such emphasis on violent physical appeal represents the old alignments of the avant-garde — apolitical formalisms. But one cannot discount the political power of the immediate freedom of the anarchistic subjectivity of the avant-garde form combined with the crass conventionality of American commercial iconography. Such a textual tension is represented in all of Fassbinder's films and keeps them from being marginalized and politically neutralized within a high-art avant-garde tradition of abstract film.

Here my analysis may appear to be a problematic postmodern reading of the political potential of Fassbinder's works: they seemingly refuse a doctrinaire adherence to any established left political philosophy and aesthetic strategy. Like many pop artists, Fassbinder glorified the commodity market by his choice of subject. Indeed, he echoed the ambiguity of this pop culture aesthetic in his self-proclaimed title: the "German Hollywood director." But postmodern readings often fail to take into account the historical and political context of film form as political resistance. The German counterculture sought to return a kind of Barthesian pleasure that had been repressed by intellectual and political ideologies. This pleasure results from the attempt to evade the policing action of the bourgeoisie as represented in all of the texts' ideology, whether it be on the right or left.

To some degree, Fassbinder's formal method derives from an element within the German New Left that refuses to privilege ideology over emotion and intellectualism over action. Similarly, Barthes argues that the pleasure of the text surrounds the attempt "to abolish the false opposition of practical life and contemplative life. The pleasure of the text is just that: a claim lodged against the separation of the text" and an insistence on the extension of erotic pleasure investment to objects of all sorts, including language, film, television, and political action — the breakdown of culture.[63]

As a result, one should consider the more modernist elements in *Chinese Roulette* (1976) or even *The Bitter Tears of Petra von Kant* (1972). These films evade a direct reference to contemporary sociohistorical reality as chamber works. As I will explain in greater depth in chapter 5, they both participate in a classical art cinema strategy: a playfulness that substitutes ambiguity for clear character motives and goals. The theme of the victim as victimizer (whether it is a crippled girl or a masochistic secretary) weakens its connection to a clear class, gender, or economic source.

But these readings—like postmodern culture in general—efface the history of these films' reception. We need to refashion postmodern theory so that we can discuss the break with modernism as a political act within a clear history. Indeed, within the countercultural activity of the German left in the 1960s, the dominant culture was represented by both bourgeois capitalism and an ineffectual established left. Fassbinder's appropriation of the bright colors and sensual forms—the general physical immediacy—of American pop art offered a clear political act in the face of a highly rigidified concept of culture and the resultant class system.

More often, the American references in Fassbinder's films as well as in the New German Cinema as a whole have been understood as a critique of American cultural imperialism. The ever present country music of the American Armed Forces Radio Network in the background of *Veronika Voss* (1981) seems a clear metaphor for social control when it is combined with the film's drug theme. Yet the sheer physicality of the high-key light of *Veronika Voss,* the Technicolor-like melodrama of *Ali/Fear Eats the Soul* (1973), the long takes that dwell on the everyday in *Katzelmacher* (1969), or even the general emphasis on emotional exploitation over class analysis allowed Fassbinder to explore a form that could not simply be swallowed up in a realist aesthetic nor, in its excessiveness, one devoted to intellectual distance and ideological "truth." Fassbinder's self-conscious use of mise-en-scène owes less to Brecht or even to a Brechtian-inspired Douglas Sirk. Although they are political in content, Fassbinder's melodramas evade the "negative hermeneutics" of Brechtian ideological criticism—the dismantling of all ideologies and utopian innocence.[64]

Finally, Fassbinder's film's films are pleasurable. The visceral pleasure takes several forms: the immediacy and tactile quality of the pop iconography, the physical assault of the violence, and the melodramatic emotion. The intensity of his style cannot allow the viewer to accept the simple sadness of the films' content or what Richard Dyer calls their "left-wing melancholy."[65] The erotic physicality of the Fassbinder form reveals a dream of another state that transcends the traps of ideological control that his films reveal — a state of immediate and erotic pleasure. Brecht would have found this pleasure profoundly bourgeois. Nevertheless, this utopian moment within the rigidity of the German cultural class system is what moves human beings to act — a thoroughly irrational act. This contradiction between left-wing melancholy and the utopian naïveté of pop forms is what makes Fassbinder's films so powerful. And perhaps such a tension is what differentiates Fassbinder from Warhol and makes the German director "reeeally strange" from a postmodern perspective.

5 / The Textual Fassbinder:
Two Institutional Genres

American cinema is the only one I can take really seriously, because it's the only one that has really reached an audience. . . . American cinema has generally had the happiest relationship with its audience, and that is because it doesn't try to be "art." Its narrative style is not complicated or artificial. Well, of course it is artificial, but it is not art. Rainer Werner Fassbinder[1]

Thus far, the issue of the Fassbinder film and the influences of American melodrama and European art cinema have been set aside in favor of chronicling Fassbinder's place within two major historical discourses — the *Autor*, and American pop culture. The tension between these two often antagonistic sensibilities broadly structured his historical reception in West Germany in the 1970s as the "German Hollywood director." Yet we need to look now at how these historical influences structure the Fassbinder text. Two specific institutional genres evolved out of these discussions of Fassbinder's authorship and popular culture: the melodramatic adaptation for West German television and the confessional film for the art cinema.

Of course, texts are always part of history. It is only the process of traditional criticism that has separated the two. Edward Said points out that "texts are worldly, to some degree they are events, and even when they appear to deny it, they are nevertheless a part of the social world, human life,

105

and of course the historical moments in which they are located and interpreted."[2] The Fassbinder film is as historical an event as the *Autor* discourse
within postwar German society.

Genre offers a strategy for uncovering the exchange between a film
industry/director and the historical audience. Genres result from a highly
conventionalized system of signs and codes and are recognizable by the
filmgoing and television-watching public. Film genres are associated with
the assembly-line production process of classical Hollywood filmmaking,
where genre allowed for variations on proven narrative conventions: the
musical, the western, and, most importantly for Fassbinder, the melodrama.
And now corporate American television has produced its staple genres of
the sitcom, the soap opera, and the detective drama.

But genre analysis is far from being a lifeless and ahistorical investigation of form. It negotiates the relationship between individual narrative
and society. Fredric Jameson argues that these conventions have a privileged position within the historical analysis of a text's ideological influence
with "the mediatory function of the notion of a genre, which allows the
coordination of immanent formal analysis of the individual text with the
twin diachronic perspective of the history of forms and the evolution of
social life." We need to look for generic connections and systematic deviations as "clues" that would return the Fassbinder text to the specific historical situation of the film. Ultimately, for Jameson this method "allows us to
read its structure as ideology, as a socially symbolic act, as a protopolitical
response to a historical dilemma."[3] By analyzing Fassbinder's genres, we can
see how he responded to the "historical dilemma" of the sanctioned role of
the *Autor* within West German culture in the 1970s. He created two genres
that are unified by his use of the melodramatic mode but sufficiently different in their form and content to serve the institutional traditions of television and the art cinema.

The art film is usually set in opposition to the genre film.[4] Through its
association with high culture, the art film is "valued for its unique qualities."[5] Looking at the connotation of art in Western culture related to the
art cinema, Pierre Bourdieu argues that the central intention of the modern artist is to be "autonomous" or "entirely the master of his product."
Within this aesthetic individualism, the artist "tends to reject not only the
'programmes' imposed a priori by scholars and scribes, but also — following the old hierarchy of doing and saying — the interpretation superimposed a posteriori on his work."[6] Although the art film flaunts this lack of

convention, we still must ask: How then does it speak? Given that Fassbinder was a child of the art cinema, an auteur, *Autor,* and public representative of German arts, how can we reconcile this status with the idea of a "Fassbinder genre"?

Art cinema directors are subject to genre restrictions much more than is generally accepted. They are subject to the commercial pressure of the independent film industry and state television, which depend on audience attendance/viewership and profit. Genre remains one of the means by which art film directors communicate. Many recent European filmmakers are associated with particular genres: Bergman with the *Kammerspiel,* Chabrol with the gangster film, early Godard with the detective film, and Wenders with the "road film," after which he has so self-consciously entitled his production company. In fact, one of the underlying form and content tenets of the art cinema is its breaks with and adherence to the classical Hollywood norms.[7] To look at Fassbinder's films simply as examples of European art films removes the historical cultural and personal specificity of their origins.

Fassbinder, too, operated within a system of historical constraints. As David Bordwell suggests, Fassbinder's success may be a result of his chameleonic "narrational personae" from film to film. For Bordwell "there is a 'realist' Fassbinder, a 'literary' Fassbinder, a 'pastiche' Fassbinder, a 'frenzied' Fassbinder and so on."[8] But when these changing films are seen within their historical institutional context, a discernible pattern or set of genres emerges. Indeed, as the "German Hollywood director," Fassbinder worked more closely with the popular idiom of the Hollywood melodrama than any other art cinema director did. Given Fassbinder's unprecedented productivity (over forty films in seventeen years), he was able to create a recognizable set of subgenres using melodrama as the model.

Fassbinder produced two of his own genres: the literary adaptation for television (*Fernsehspiel*) and the confessional film for the art house circuit. We need to understand the broad characteristics of these genres, and then we can apply them to specific films. *Bolwieser* relates to canonical Hollywood or "classical" narration and exemplifies Fassbinder's melodramatic adaptation for television, while *Chinese Roulette,* with its debt to the art cinema, represents Fassbinder's confessional melodrama. These two texts are exemplary for several reasons: both are available in America and are possibly the most familiar examples of these genres here;[9] both were produced in 1976; and both would have been fresh in the memories of West Germans as the most recent film of each genre before *Berlin Alexanderplatz* (1980).

Finally, neither film represents the best example of its genre — *Martha* and *In a Year of Thirteen Moons* are better examples — but these choices will show the changing of film codes within the genres. Fassbinder inscribed his melodramatic signature on the entire body of his films. This signature reconfigures Fassbinder's use of genre by introducing seemingly non- or antigeneric elements — authorial subjectivity — into his films. However, I prefer to explain how Fassbinder's "textual force" actually extends the conventional notions of genre to create a complicated, often ironically playful representation. Indeed, it is the clash between genre and authority subjectivity that allows the historical text to manifest itself in Fassbinder's films.

The Melodramatic Literary Adaptation: *Bolwieser*

Between 1970 and 1980 Fassbinder produced eighteen *Fernsehspiele* especially for television: eight literary adaptations; seven original works; two from psychological case studies; and one cabaret production.[10] As I argued in chapter 2, the *Fernsehspiel* is a specifically West German genre known for the filming of canonical literary works. To the Germans' credit, their concept of the "canon" (or the realm of the classics) has always been ideologically broader and more international in scope than American public television's. In the postwar years, the canon considered for television took on a self-consciously "non-German" flavor in the attempt to "democratize" German tastes. The majority of the original authors of the Fassbinder adaptations were well known in Germany, and their other works had been produced on television.[11] Fassbinder's literary adaptations did expand beyond television. In fact, his three attempts at feature film adaptations — Fontane's *Effi Briest* (1974), Nabokov's *Despair* (1977), and Genet's *Querelle* (1982) — became international successes. But on the whole, Fassbinder reserved adaptation for television.

He adapted primarily twentieth-century works, with one venture into the nineteenth century: *Nora Helmer,* from Ibsen's *A Doll's House.* All the works he chose had politically progressive or social critical content. He adapted American liberal middlebrow fiction (Daniel Galouye, Claire Boothe Luce, and Cornell Woolrich), German twentieth-century critical theater (Marieluise Fleisser and Franz Xaver Kroetz), and Weimar novels (Oskar Maria von Graf and Alfred Döblin). Only Döblin's *Berlin Alexanderplatz* employed a modernist self-consciousness that could not translate into Hollywood "invisible" narrational forms without substantial change. Additionally, one can see a general similarity in these television adaptations; almost all the protagonists emerge from the middle class (with the marked exception of those of *Berlin Alexanderplatz*), as opposed to the overwhelming number of proletarian and marginal protagonists of Fassbinder's art cinema films.

Each one of the film adaptations integrates a play of three narrational forms: the original literary author, classical Hollywood narrative, and Fassbinder's style. The necessity to use the author's name and adhere to the logic of the original story related to Foucault's theory of authorial function: "Literary discourse was acceptable only if it carried an author's name; every text of poetry or fiction was obliged to state its author and the date and place and circumstance of its writing. The meaning and value attributed to the text depended on this information."[12] Fassbinder respected the original work's integrity much more within the state institution of television than in the leftist countercultural theater. The original literary work frames the story in his television adaptations.

By "story" I mean the chronological, cause-and-effect chain of events occurring within a given duration and spatial field.[13] The way Fassbinder adapted the literary source remained true to the original on the level of the story, whereas classical Hollywood narration functions on the level of plot: how the events of the story are directly presented to us. The classical Hollywood narration often makes difficult literary texts more accessible by establishing a linear causality.

Following Hollywood's lead, every Fassbinder adaptation has a well-defined protagonist, as indicated by the use of characters' names as the films' titles (*Martha, Nora Helmer, Bolwieser*). Each protagonist is endowed with well-defined traits: Martha is a lonely middle-class spinster; Hanni of *Wildwechsel* (Jailbait) is the sexually premature teenage daughter of a strict, lower-middle-class Catholic family. And each protagonist is goal-oriented in the classical Hollywood sense: Berta of *Pioneers of Ingolstadt* wants to have a love affair, and *World on a Wire*'s Dr. Fred Steller hopes to create artificial intelligence.

Additionally, the construction of time and space in these adaptations conforms to the Hollywood system of continuity in which cause and effect dominate the narrative's progression. Given the constraints of television production, the adaptations are often filmed as interior dramas confined to a few well-constructed and easily identifiable stagelike spaces (bedrooms, living rooms, and common public places such as bars).

Despite the fact that these adaptations are largely governed by the content of the original text and Hollywood plotting conventions, Fassbinder did affect both the story and the plot. None of the television films fit these narrational paradigms at all moments. Fassbinder's greatest influence was felt at the level of style, or through what I term his "melodramatic mode."

Here I employ the term *mode* as distinct from *genre*. Derived from *modus* (manner), *mode* has explicit musical connotations.[14] Applied to melodrama, it allows me to designate a larger set of recurring features similar to those associated with textual "realism." Although Fassbinder used some narrational conventions of Hollywood melodramas, he borrowed more from their style in his television adaptations. These films are distinguished by a heightened emotional tone or a melodramatic stylization that can indicate the larger invisible hand of melodramatic fate.

In *The Melodramatic Imagination* Peter Brooks argues persuasively for melodrama's role as a mode.[15] In this view, melodrama overlaps and competes with realism and tragedy, maintaining complex relations with them. Melodrama refers not only to a type of aesthetic practice, but also to a way of looking at the world.[16] Historically, an author or director working in the melodramatic mode had recourse to such broad and excessive devices as character types (villain, victim, hero), repeated events, and amplified music, gesture, and visual displays. Such repeated plot devices and visual and aural stylistics have made melodramatic works popular with the nonliterate.

Melodrama (I will argue more fully later) evolved into a genre within certain well-regulated institutions (Hollywood and the nineteenth-century American and British stage). It is the Hollywood version (the 1950s Universal melodramas) that Fassbinder quotes in his original confessional works. But with his television work Fassbinder had to adhere to the original story and was confined by the conventions of television plotting.

This use of melodrama as a mode also fits into Fassbinder's appropriation of American popular culture as part of the pop self-consciousness of the 1960s. Here Fassbinder's melodramatic style functions as an affront to the "sophistication" of the canonical original as he popularizes the work through broad strokes: character typing, highly punctuated music, excessive mise-en-scènes. His use of melodrama enlivened the literary source through the visceral pleasures of vivid style, emotional intensity, and violence associated with pop culture. His television adaptations are so self-consciously melodramatic at times that they could be read as camp in that his melodramatics reveal the potential stereotypes of canonical literature. However, their public status as adaptations of canonical literature ensured that his adaptations would be read seriously.

A Fassbinder television devotee could pick out a Fassbinder story by the common theme of sexual and social exploitation of the powerless—particularly women—but the degree to which exploitation is emphasized depends on how Fassbinder chooses to amplify on the original character's social definition. In other words, the director stylizes his characters, establishing types or more classically conceived melodramatic figures. For example, in the Carlo Goldoni play *Coffeehouse*, the protagonist represents a "tiresome parasitic gossip and informer."[17] Fassbinder transforms him into a melancholy character, as much as a victim of society as a villain. There is a tendency in all Fassbinder's television works to dispense with distinguishing surnames and complex traits. His characters are reduced to generic Franzes, Hannis, Kurts, and Karls. In *Pioneers of Ingolstadt* the characters are named simply Soldier Karl and Servant Bertha. Given the repeated use of the same names for disparate literary characters, one becomes conscious of the broad strokes of a Fassbinder adaptation where the original story's incidents and logic are given a melodramatic breadth that makes the classical melodrama types—hero, victim, villain—more clearly discernible. Additionally, Fassbinder loosened the often complex narrative structure of the originals to create what one critic saw as "a simple step by step narrative" that typifies television drama.[18]

During this period of television production (1970–76), popular critics described Fassbinder's adaptation as mannerist, suggesting an exaggerated or affected adherence to a particular style or manner.[19] The term reveals the critics' resistance to Fassbinder's narrational intrusion into the original author's material. Fassbinder, however, admitted that he chose to adapt texts that he "could have written"—a possible reason for the repetition of themes in his adaptations and his other work.[20]

In classical narration, characters move toward goals to structure the causal logic. A cause-effect development is left dangling in each scene to be picked up in the next, usually through a dialogue hook. In Fassbinder's adaptations the characters are goal-oriented, but the links between cause and effect and especially the dialogue hook (e.g., "meet you at . . .") are more ambiguous if not nonexistent. For example, in *Martha* (1973), as the protagonist makes no plans from scene to scene, rarely is there a dialogue hook. Rather, she is caught up in a sea of external forces endemic to melodrama: either a villain (her husband) or fate. All she can do is react. As a result, scenes end with uncertainty about what the next event will bring. This episodic construction is emphasized through the use of fade-in and fade-out.

Fassbinder's major intervention into the narrational process, however, comes not through obtrusive camera work but through the mise-en-scène. The director's signature melodramatic style is often evident, but it does not function beyond contributing to the psychological subjectivity that marks melodrama within classical narration. As in the Hollywood melodrama, all expressive cinematic resources (gestures, lighting, setting, costume) work to convey inner states. Fassbinder's luscious signature sets pour forth saturated colors and excessive decor constrained only by television's limited production budgets. Martha's repression at the hands of her husband is represented through the overgrowth of plants. Similarly, in *Nora Helmer,* as Nora withdraws from society she shrinks behind the overstuffed Wilhelmian decor. Even costume reveals social and sexual characteristics: the many women characters of *Women in New York* (1977) are defined as old, young, fashionable, ugly, or beautiful by stereotypical outward appearances, thus creating the generalized types of the melodramatic mode.

The camera rarely intrudes into the slightly excessive mise-en-scène of Fassbinder's television works. Usually used to reframe the action, the camera movement can sometimes become unleashed from the characters. But this is reserved for emphasizing subjective states characteristic of the melodramatic form. In *Martha,* for example, when the title character encounters her husband-to-be in Rome, the camera circles the two. Their mutual attraction motivates the movement most immediately. Yet one senses an external shaping agent. This presence reaches its apogee with Fassbinder's *Fear of Fear* (1975) and its unusual intrusion of camera work. Here the camera's once "objective" or classical role slowly becomes more and more subjective (showing what the victim sees) until we lose all sense of what constitutes objective truth.

Finally, music — the heart of the melodramatic mode — functions as a strong (perhaps the strongest) subjective device in all Fassbinder's televisual films. Peer Raben remained Fassbinder's career-long composer. As a result, the television scores do not differ in temperament from those of Fassbinder's feature films, but they do tend to be simplified: a few repeated musical themes are associated with each major character. Keys and chords punctuate characters' discoveries, and the recurrence of reactions and actions intones the cyclical nature of the melodramatic world. *Martha,* the most generically conceived of the Fassbinder melodramatic television adaptations, uses music to mark each stage of the protagonist's realization of her husband's sadistic intentions. But even *Jailbait,* praised as more "naturalistic," uses intense music to climax the final fateful moment when Hanni reveals her miscarriage to her jailed lover.

This overview of Fassbinder's melodramatic adaptations for television reveals a consistency on three narrational levels: the original author's story, the classical narration, and Fassbinder's melodramatic signature. Generally these levels correspond respectively to story, plot, and style. Obviously, Fassbinder's changes in setting and ending offer a problem for such an equation. These departures did not go unobserved at the time. The West German bourgeois press harangued Fassbinder for any misappropriation of the original story's logic. For example, in a 1971 *Film und Fernsehen* article, Benjamin Henrichs argues that the Fleisser play *Pioneers in Ingolstadt* had a "modest social logic" but Fassbinder's broadening of the character's social types ruined the social subtext.[21] Franz Xaver Kroetz pronounced Fassbinder's changes in his *Jailbait* "pornographic" and won a lawsuit to have them deleted from the film.[22] The power of copyright had established the legal relationship between author and adapter, especially in the public arena of state television, limiting creative exploration. Fassbinder was legally bound to respect the intent of the original author.

This broad description of a Fassbinder genre can be used to analyze *Bolwieser*, released in the United States as *The Stationmaster's Wife*. Renowned as a "faithful Fassbinder adaptation," the television film reveals these patterns of narration and the degree to which Fassbinder's influence is stylistic, not narrational. This section describes the edited theatrical version (of the two-part television film) because of its availability in America. I discuss only elements that are applicable to both versions because *Bolwieser* is a classical example of an "amphibian film": made for both theatrical release and television broadcast. The film is a typical example of the use of the narrational concept of self-consciousness, which will explain the complex difference in authorial intervention in the two Fassbinder genres.

The story of *Bolwieser* centers on Xaverl Bolwieser, a weak petit bourgeois bureaucrat in a small Bavarian town in the 1920s. He marries Hanni, a woman with whom he is infatuated and to whom he ultimately becomes subservient. Bored and disgusted by her simple-minded husband, Hanni torments him by giving and withholding sexual favors. She fulfills her own desires through a series of affairs. First she has a rather public liaison with the butcher. She even convinces the unsuspecting Xaverl that he should lend her large inheritance to her lover as a wise business venture. Town gossip catches up with Xaverl and he confronts his wife. She denies the affair, promising no more public contact with the butcher. The three even take the gossipers to court and win the case. Aware of the veiled lies they are living, Xaverl perjures himself on the stand to protect Hanni.

Suffocating once again from life as Xaverl's wife, Hanni begins her second affair, this time with her hairdresser. The affair repeats the first in style and openness, but this time the ex-lover becomes jealous and tells Xaverl. He confronts her. She denies it. And as usual she convinces the cuckolded Xaverl of her virtue. Angry at the butcher's betrayal, Hanni calls in the loan. The butcher gets his revenge by turning in Xaverl to the police for perjury. Xaverl is convicted and sent to prison. There, weak and oppressed, he willingly agrees to Hanni's request for a divorce. He is sentenced to a nightmarish existence of denial, unable to pace, sleep, or even masturbate.

The film replicates the story of the Graf novel *The Marriage of Mr. Bolwieser* surprisingly faithfully.[23] First published in 1931, the novel was heralded as autobiographical, given Graf's origins in a small Bavarian village. But its fame was built more on Graf's satirical analysis of the psychological makeup of the German petite bourgeoisie in the 1920s — the central supporters of the Third Reich. Nicknamed "the Bavarian Gorky," Graf gained even greater recognition in German cultural circles for this novel. It was the last work that the socialist (possibly anarchist) Graf wrote before fleeing Nazi Germany. Although *The Marriage of Mr. Bolwieser* was burned by the Nazis, Graf's fame increased. In America he was also known for his odd form of Fassbinder-style persona: a German anarchist in lederhosen in New York City. As a result, *The Marriage of Mr. Bolwieser* and Oskar Maria von Graf were well established within literary circles when Fassbinder chose to adapt the novel in 1976.

The plot of the television film owes much to classical narration. The so-called critical realism of Graf's narration — by an omniscient third person — fits comfortably into the *Fernsehspiel* genre's reliance on "invisible" narration. Fassbinder's narrational influence is felt when he collapses the two plot structures into one. In the Graf novel Bolwieser has two simple goals: to run his train station by the clock and to have a happy marriage. Graf uses these two lines to interweave psychological analysis with commentary about the politically repressive nature of prefascist small-time German bureaucrats.

Characteristically, Fassbinder reduces the two lines of plot (the romance and the social goal) to his recurring theme that the personal is political. Although it is evident in the television film, this change is more noticeable in the condensed theatrical film available in America. His focus in both versions is Bolwieser's need to maintain his love life as he obsesses over his wife. Such narrowing gives the story a more condensed melodramatic flavor as the characterization of the protagonist takes on a crazed edge. For all the intensity, however, this excessively narrow world still does not affect classical narrational clarity.

Fassbinder's Bolwieser is a classical protagonist. And like most Hollywood characters, he is goal-oriented (he wants to maintain his marriage). Unlike a John Wayne character, however, Bolwieser is a reactive, not an active, agent. The active agent in the film is the antagonist, Hanni. Given that most popular culture characters have inherited their traits from nineteenth-century short fiction and melodrama, the characterization of a simple cuckolded husband fits the lack of complexity that Hollywood films thrived on. Additionally, as a Fassbinder theater troupe actor, Kurt Raab brings none of the fullness that a popular star persona might, whereas Elizabeth Trissenaar, a well-known German stage actress, brings her reputation for playing femmes fatales to her fuller and more active performance as Hanni. The dichotomy between a weak protagonist and a strong antagonist is announced at the very beginning. Behind the opening credits, a photographic still of the nuptial bedroom kiss erupts into action. Passionate undressing begins, only to be interrupted by Hanni's refusal to get pregnant.

Verbal and visual redundancy underscore (almost maniacally) Xaverl's simple traits. Hanni continually refers to him as "fatty" and "my cock," while he is seen working at his adding machine, tearing at Hanni, eating, and passing out drunk in a cyclical fervor. Hanni is depicted in more idiosyncratic scenes of visual display: parading on the streets, dancing, peering in the mirror; she is often shot in soft focus and halo lighting.

The film communicates Xaverl's central conflict and goal from the start: Since Xaverl and Hanni conflict, how will they maintain their marriage? The film then becomes an ongoing series of causally linked episodes in a never-ending game of Hanni's indiscretions and Xaverl's forgiveness. The film loses much of the forward projection characteristic of a classical film because of the cyclical nature of the relationship, but the plot does progress: Xaverl's will slowly breaks down. In the end, there is a decisive tying up of all plot lines. Xaverl is put in jail and Hanni divorces him.

The film's use of space and time is subsumed under the need to tell the story. If Fassbinder uses the ambiguity of spatial relations in his private features such as *Third Generation* (the labyrinthine corporate skyscraper as a metaphor for alienated existence under capitalism), he displays none of that playfulness in *Bolwieser*. The film is shot in five well-defined interiors; less

than one-sixth of it is shot outdoors. The melodramatic mode motivates
such interiority. Spatial relations are "realistic": historically "correct" set-
tings, decor, and related mise-en-scène. Each scene functions within continuity rules of space as shot size is dictated by constructing establishment,
breakdown, and reestablishment of scenic space.

There are, however, some idiolectal norms within *Bolwieser.* Fassbinder
substitutes sophisticated camera work that follows the character's movement
for classic editing. As a result, the camera movement heightens character
interactions. This method evokes the same spatial patterns that editing would
create. For instance, in one scene Xaverl arrives home. The minute he enters, he coos for wife. The camera tracks with him to where he finds Hanni
supposedly still crying in the same spot from the morning's fight. In other
words, the camera retraces the movement of the previous scene — a redundant action, but one that gives the interactions of the marriage a repetitive
feel.

Although the repetition of these scenes borders on an endless flow of
marital altercations, each scene breaks down classically: exposition of the
new marital problem, the body of the film where characters act toward
their goals usually ending in a fight, and the resolution of some of the goals
with "I promise ..." And then goals open up, indicated by the dialogue
hook ("I'm going to my hairdresser's ..."). In the end, boundaries of all
scenes are clearly demarcated by either cuts or dissolves. The specific use of
the fade-to-black at the end of certain scenes gives the melodrama's narration a chapter quality. The film's narrational presence subtly organizes the
flow into concise segments for our understanding.

Nevertheless, the narrational moments partially betray *Bolwieser's* narrational invisibility. There is a rhythmic use of fade-to-black and intricate
camera work that swirls around the actions and ends up viewing the action
from an obscured view behind curtains, cut glass, and plants. Sometimes
the camera startles us, zooming in quickly on a reaction. Moreover, the
music that rises and falls with the emotion sometimes is so loud or so dis-
cordant with the mood that we notice it. Herein lies a narrational presence
that slips out from behind the "invisibility" or "objectivity" of classical
narration and asks us to be conscious that some being or force guides the
film's diegetic world.

Not every film, of course, has a narrator. Film theory has demonstrated
that a classical Hollywood film offers itself as the source of its own narration. For example, in a generic Hollywood film such as *Four Girls in Town,*
a 1955 B picture, viewers are unlikely to look to the director/screenwriter

(Jack Sher) or even the studio (Universal) to make sense of the classical narration. The Hollywood film effaces its own production, creating an internally consistent logic that critics often cite as its greatest power to persuade.[24]

But what of these classically narrated films that supposedly break through their internal consistency and "rupture"? For example, Jane Feuer notes that such moments open up "a textual space which may be read against the seemingly hegemonic surface."[25] As I outlined in chapter 1, these "excessive" moments are what Fassbinder critics look to with the director's use of melodramatic style to create "open texts." In other words, their disruptive quality "opens up" the hermetically closed narrational consistency of the Hollywood text. But do they? Is the canonical narration of Hollywood films so seamless that such "breaks" stand out?

All films reveal a degree of awareness of their own making. From the Hollywood practice of grouping characters for our best view to Max Steiner's heavily laden, searing scores to the artificial montage sequences (e.g., Susan Alexander's performances across America in *Citizen Kane* [1941]), all these moments reveal what might be called a degree of self-consciousness. Instead of the political use of *defamiliarization,* as in Godard's *Tout va Bien* (1972), the term *self-consciousness* describes a strategy that breaks from realist convention of fourth-wall drama. It means "the extent to which the narration display[s] a recognition that it is addressing an audience."[26] Consciousness of the production as a production does not destroy the fiction, but serves as a momentary reminder of what the viewer already knows: the constructed nature of film and television.

But recognition of the Fassbinder film as a film does not automatically lead to a break in the internal logic of its narration and ideology, as Brechtian analysis of Fassbinder's work would have it. Rather, these self-conscious moments in Fassbinder's and Hollywood films (direct address, heavily laden music, an emotion-filled Sirkean landscape) are codified by the established conventions of genres. With Fassbinder's use of one of the most self-conscious of Hollywood genres, his melodramas often motivate their breaks in classical narrational logic around melodrama's defining characteristic: intense subjective narration when the film either enters the psychological state of a character or indicates the external influence of the guiding hand of melodramatic fate.

Usually accepted as a genre that subsumes almost everything under emotional impact, melodrama extends its affective influence to the plot as well as the film's style. As a genre, melodrama is omniscient in its delineation of a character's emotions, which creates greater irony and other "dissociated emotions."[27] Although *Bolwieser* is not a melodrama, Fassbinder depends on melodramatic omniscience to increase the sense of Xaverl's own culpability. As a result, we are not confined to Bolwieser's perspective; that would play on our sympathy too much as we experience simultaneously with him the revelation of Hanni's unfaithful acts.

Rather, the omniscient narration allows us to know more than the protagonist Xaverl knows. Xaverl is often there to witness what we experience as omniscience (the glances, the touches, the pregnant pauses), but he is either too stupid to understand or too weak to acknowledge it. But Fassbinder undercuts the emotional potential of melodramatic omniscience, producing none of the classic sympathetic identification with the protagonist. Even in the film's "big scene," — the courtroom perjury — Xaverl's wide range of knowledge is nearly acknowledged. But he perjures himself, refusing to take on the responsibility that expressed knowledge of his wife's indiscretions would entail.

Unlike the horror film, melodrama does not suppress information. We learn everything about the protagonist — even his deepest feelings. The melodramatic narration in *Bolwieser* continually spins out new blows to the protagonist's well-being. Our interest is maintained by questioning what will happen next, as the plot tells all. Usually melodramatic suspense is constructed around carefully timed "coincidences" or surprises, those fateful moments that critics argue are so transparently "false." *Bolwieser* avoids this melodramatic characteristic; a surprising coincidence is not an important factor. Instead, our interest is guided by the *expectation* of coincidence, such as Bolwieser catching the lovers in action.

Fassbinder teases us as he unleashes the camera from an illicit embrace between the lovers to track across the room to an open door. Classical narration would call for Xaverl to arrive, but when he does not appear, the teasing shot calls attention to the fact that in Fassbinder's world melodramatic fate plays no role. It also underscores a central Fassbinder theme: victims victimize themselves. They are not controlled by a social or anonymous force such as fate, to which melodrama traditionally points. But as much as Fassbinder manipulates the narrational logic of a classical melodrama, the film does not break from the classical film's internal coherence.

Yet what marks *Bolwieser*'s significance is the fact that the film prevents the classical identification with the protagonist. Fassbinder may have played down the more overtly "political" or "social" plot line of the Graf novel (Bolwieser as petit bourgeois functionary of prefascist Weimar), but he has substituted a critical perspective: no longer can one accept the melodramatic types of hero, villain, and victim. The victim as his or her own victimizer contradicts both the active agency of the classical protagonist and the passive victim status of the melodramatic Mary Pickfords, Mildred Pierces, or even the Sirkean Cary Scotts. Yet it also undercuts the potential critique of the social sources of victimization. There are no simple or direct social causes in Fassbinder's melodrama or even his melodramatic adaptations: only what Elsaesser calls "vicious circles."[28]

This Fassbinder genre contributes to the codes of melodrama not because of plot, but rather because of style. The film is filled with melodramatic mannerisms. Such an argument supports the assertion that melodrama is a mode, not a set of established narrational conventions of a genre. It covers the classical film with a redundant blanket of mise-en-scène and music. Kurt Raab's near Delsartian performance as the weak, hen-pecked husband makes abundantly clear the character's motivation. And finally, the excessive score constantly changes tone as it creates musical themes for each character and the repeated situations of Xaverl's dilemma. But it serves the same purpose as in any Hollywood score. The style telegraphs the simple lines of classical narration. Ultimately, the melodramatic mode takes the parsimony of the classical text and elaborates it into an even more transparent (legible) story.[29] When this melodramatic stylization combines with classical narrational techniques and the adaptation of the canonized literary story, it results in the production of Fassbinder's television genre: the melodramatic adaptations.

The Confessional Melodrama: *Chinese Roulette*

Fassbinder's "genre" of the confessional melodrama, which evolved directly from art cinema, encompasses seventeen original feature films made between 1969 and 1978.[30] I have emphasized the influence of Hollywood on Fassbinder's use of melodrama, but his process of confessing his "extraordinary" life owes its largest debt to the art cinema's generic codes. The art cinema organizes its films on three levels: objective realism ("real" problems, "real" locations, natural lighting); subjective realism (revelation of the human condition); and authorial expressivity (the director as author organizing this fragile world). Those who are acquainted with Fassbinder's oeuvre know that his films characteristically deal with a highly subjective accounting of the human condition under psychological, sexual, and social repression. Fassbinder presented this highly emotional analysis of character psychology by continually weaving his authorial marks or personal interventions into this hermetic arena (his camera work, his heavy use of framing, his obscured vision, and even his melodramatic character types). This is the Fassbinder who fits comfortably into the postwar art film world of Bertolucci, Bergman, and Rohmer. But Fassbinder steps beyond these directors' roles as an authorial presence within the film text. "Fassbinder" functions as more than the organizing presence. Characteristically, he takes the auteur role and extends it to the most unexamined area of German concept of *Autor:* the director as an exceptional and therefore worthy individual.

This phase of my argument depends on an understanding of how these films employed the narrational mode of the art cinema. New German Cinema was a reaction to the postwar dominance of Hollywood aesthetic and economic methods within Germany. German art cinema directors worked within a modernist notion of objective realism where the vagaries of contemporary everyday life took precedence over Hollywood realism's adherence to a coherent set of events. Often compared to an Italian neorealist director in his early years, Fassbinder filmed in locations where he lived (especially Munich and Bavaria).

As a result, the streets of Munich become the backdrop for Fassbinder's much praised "verisimilitude" or street life realism of *Katzelmacher* (1969). The film replicates the deadly boredom of unemployed youth. In general, Fassbinder features take place in actual German bars, streets, and homes. In addition, he employs natural exterior lighting and reserves stylized lighting for his interiors. Further, Fassbinder attains "realism" by his choice of nonactors for major roles. These roles are for members of his extended family and acting troupe. Often his mother and his lovers (El Hedi Ben Salem as Ali or Armin Meier) play important parts. By extension, Fassbinder's theater troupe functions as a noncommercial source of actors; the renowned closeness of Fassbinder and the actors creates an ambiguous game of realism and fiction in his films.

Fassbinder's ongoing interest in contemporary social issues creates another level of realism that must be seen against the romantic or politically amorphorous issues that Hollywood films have traditionally represented. Fassbinder's films tackle the problems of sexual and social repression within West Germany. *Fox and His Friends* is a study of homosexuality and capitalism; *Ali/Fear Eats the Soul* deals with contemporary German racism; and *Mother Küster's Trip to Heaven* examines personal repression by the mass media and the authoritarianism of the Communist Party. Fassbinder's use of sexual explicitness and extreme violence, or "topical realism," was traditionally prohibited in the classical Hollywood film.

With the thematic realism of the art cinema comes the concurrent "realistic" strategies that loosen the tight or "artificial" causality of the dominant cinema. In Fassbinder's as well as in many art director's worlds, causal ties often break down or do not exist at all. His alienated protagonist acts inconsistently: Fox spends his lottery winnings aimlessly; Ali leaves Emmi without explanation. Additionally, coincidence plays an especially strong role in Fassbinder's art films: Emmi meets Ali as a result of a chance rainstorm.

Chance and coincidence — as in melodrama — become central to the art cinema plot (consider the role of chance in Thomas's life in the classic Antonioni art film *Blowup* [1966]). In fact, almost all of these Fassbinder's films lack the well-defined goals of classical narration. *The Third Generation* exemplifies this: a terrorist's goal falls apart and therefore fails during the terrorist act. The plot of *Fox and His Friends* is predicated on an obvious example of chance — winning a lottery.

Fassbinder uses chance as a plot device throughout his oeuvre, but he translates chance into the melodramatic heavy hand of fate and therefore a theme of victimization. Mother Küster is victimized because of her husband's murder/suicide. The Revolutionary Poet of *Satansbraten* is driven partly mad by his stifling middle-class existence. And a good portion of *In a Year of Thirteen Moons* is spent in the attempt to discover what in her childhood caused Erwin/Elvira to become a "victim." Again, such emphasis on a controlling outside agency is underscored by an episodic structure. This directly relates to the plots of adaptations such as *Bolwieser* and *Effi Briest,* both of which end sequences with fades-to-black, seemingly revealing the end of a chapter or the influence of outside force.

In Fassbinder's original films, the role of chance or being victimized motivates a plot structure of either a random review of the protagonist's life (as in the biographical *In a Year of Thirteen Moons*) or a series of chance encounters (*The American Soldier*). Even the title of *Thirteen Moons* bespeaks chance, referring to the strange occurrences that come about when planets align. On this level, one can argue that Fassbinder's emphasis on plots with indirect causal references to social and sexual victimization are more "true" to contemporary political "reality" than the linear plots and the active, self-determining characters found in classical narration. As a result, we have a "realist" level to a Fassbinder film.

Without a dependence on the goals and action of canonical narration, Fassbinder emphasizes character reaction or psychology in his studies of oppression. If classical Hollywood narration is based on action, Fassbinder's art cinema work is marked by floundering reaction. As in classical narration,

Fassbinder's characters and their effects on each other remain pivotal. But classical characters lose a sense of purpose and goal orientation in Fassbinder's films; they are caught in a web of vague external forces that do not allow them to act. This kind of characterization fits into the art cinema's link with subjective realism. In Hollywood films, psychologically defined characters carry the action. In the art cinema, where goals and the cause and effect chain of events are absent, the plot moves closer to an intense psychological study of character as individuals slide from one event to another.

In *Fox and His Friends,* for example, Fassbinder ironically presents his protagonist's lack of clear-cut traits within the plot. Fox works as a carnival performer—Fox the Talking Head. He is a goalless individual who reacts to the more active, goal-oriented characters such as his wealthy gay antagonists who fleece him of his lottery winnings. Like Fox, Fassbinder's characters continuously question their lives, whether it is Mother Küster, Walter Krantz in *Satan's Brew,* or the terrorists in *The Third Generation.* Some characters—a cleaning woman in *Ali/Fear Eats the Soul,* for example—are introduced and never reappear. A more striking example is the young hoodlums who appear out of nowhere to rob and kill Fox at the end of *Fox and His Friends.*

Whether it be a search, a trip, an idyll, or the making of film, the survey form of narration is a common thread running throughout the art cinema (from *Blowup* to *8½* to *Wild Strawberries* to *Contempt*). Such a narrational technique structures the art cinema's characteristic exploration of the modern condition. Fassbinder uses a random plot structure to emphasize character repression. Without the purpose and free will of the classic character, the Fassbinder hero sinks into a melancholic form of subjugation. The goallessness of a Fassbinder figure is more explicitly and consistently determined as either interpersonal or social repression than in other art cinema films. Although it is similar to melodrama's use of a larger force guiding the predetermined actions, the nature of that force becomes much more ambiguous within the existential crises of Fassbinder's characters in his art films. Fassbinder's films adhere to David Bordwell's general statement about the art film: "Thus the art film's thematic of *la condition humaine,* its attempt to pronounce judgments on 'modern life' as a whole, proceeds from its formal needs: had the characters a goal, life would no longer seem so meaningless."[31]

Fassbinder's films slow down classical narration and allow characters to dissect their feelings about lack of power and control. In *In a Year of Thirteen Moons* the role of emotions comes to the fore as the protagonist hysterically narrates her life during a slaughterhouse scene. She goes through therapy and listens to a nun's long recital of her childhood in an orphanage. Similarly, in *Katzelmacher* one finds "dead time" in the interactions of the characters. And in other less explicitly arty films such as *Mother Küster, Ali/ Fear Eats the Soul,* and *Germany in Autumn,* one still sees characters who continuously discuss their feelings. Fassbinder's characters tend to express themselves more directly through fights (*Ali*), public pronouncements (*Mother Küster*), or telephone conversations (*Germany in Autumn*) instead of the surreal dreams associated with other art cinema directors.

The intense subjectivity of Fassbinder's art films motivates a less clear concept of space and time. Like Fassbinder's elaborate use of camera work and mise-en-scène in his melodramatic television adaptations, his stylistic devices can be motivated through an appeal to the subjective experience of his character. Like the jump cut that embodies energetic youthful lifestyles in Godard's *Breathless* (1959), Fassbinder's camera movement often emphasizes the emotional interconnectedness of his characters. His spatial device of obscuring our vision by shooting through windows can indicate just how impenetrable the characters' feelings are.

Fassbinder creates common characters (a cleaning woman, a prostitute, a circus worker, a housewife) who experience the same pain and emotion that their middle-class art cinema cousins do. They tend to shudder on the verge of emotional breakdown as they realize the pain of ordinary existence and existential misery. But with few exceptions, Fassbinder's characters do not have the education and volition associated with the anointed middle-class protagonists that typically populate classical art cinema films (*L'Avventura, The Conformist, Wild Strawberries, The American Friend*).

The role of capitalism is hinted at throughout Fassbinder's films: Mother Küster's husband murders his supervisor out of anger at ex-worker exploitation; capitalist management is in cahoots with the police in *The Third Generation*; and Emmi and Ali must face ongoing racist incidents in a "postfascist" Germany. But as in most art films, Fassbinder's political analysis is limited. These incidents become significant only when they impinge on Fassbinder's psychologically individualized characters. His "political message" at this level falls at best into what Richard Dyer has aptly called his "leftwing melancholy."[32]

Separate from this subjective realism, however, is Fassbinder's authorial expressivity. The director assumes a formal narrational role within the film. Given the ambiguous subjectivity of these character portrayals, the spectator has always had recourse to Fassbinder (as well as to any director) as the overriding intelligence to understand the meaning of the film. Just the phrase "a Fassbinder film" connotes a degree of artistic authority and freedom that Hollywood directors rarely experience. Although he has often been chastised for his public manipulations of his position as director, almost all art films view the author as "a textual force who communicates (what is the film *saying*?) and 'who' expresses (what is the artist's personal vision?). Lacking indefinable stars and a familiar genre, the art cinema uses the concept of authorship to unify the text."[33]

Since the art film is sold as a product of an artist, the art cinema invites the viewer to see the director as a narrational principle. This procedure demands a culturally competent viewer who frequents art theaters and who knows the films of Fassbinder. This sophistication enables the viewer to pick out the Fassbinder signature: such formal devices as the heavily laden mise-en-scène, the multilayered sound track, and the pristine camera work as well as the themes of sexual and social exploitation. Each of Fassbinder's films figures as the newest chapter in his oeuvre on sexual and social repression in West Germany.

Within the film, these authorial marks come to the fore through Fassbinder's repeated violations of classical narration. These breaks with classical form are quite subtle in that Fassbinder more than most art cinema directors depended on the classical conventions of melodrama. In his more explicitly art cinema films (*The Third Generation, In a Year of Thirteen Moons, Katzelmacher*), there are a number of deviations from the classical film: overexposed sections of film (*Katzelmacher*), slow motion (*Thirteen Moons*), and stressed and elliptical editing (*The Third Generation*). One has a difficult time subsuming these devices to character subjectivity because they often counter the character's emotions. Rather, these interventions can be read as authorial commentary.

In his more melodramatic works (*Ali/Fear Eats the Soul, Mother Küster's Trip to Heaven*), conventional character typing and stylistic devices are clearly related to the character's emotional states. There is, however, an even greater ambiguity as to whether we are dealing with the generic melodramatic codes of subjectivity or art film authorial intervention. The art films encourage a greater emphasis on reading the breaks in the classical melodramatic canon as authorial. The enigmatic ending of *Ali/Fear Eats the Soul*—Emma stands over the sickbed exchanging strangely ambiguous glances with the doctor—calls for at least two readings. One can understand this self-conscious moment as forming a sad acknowledgment between the wife and doctor that Ali's health problems are endemic to the position of a guest worker, but there is another valid reading given the "unnatural" expression of the doctor. Fassbinder offers ironic commentary about the Emmi/Ali situation. This is part of the game that is typical of art films, particularly Fassbinder's. With his films the viewer is often forced to choose between the subjective codes of melodrama and those of authorial commentary.

Finally, Bordwell adds ambiguity — a complex final level — to the interpretative process of art cinema narration. He argues that objective and subjective realism and authorial expressivity are incompatible as textual strategies.[34] On one level, Fassbinder attempts to create a "real life" verisimilitude through which he examines contemporary West German issues (homosexuality, women's rights, postwar German authoritarianism). His filmmaking is a conglomerate of "nonacted" moments: the spontaneity of his acting troupe, his performance in *Germany in Autumn,* the "natural" performance of El Hedi Ben Salem in the title role of *Ali/Fear Eats the Soul.* According to Bordwell's argument, such realism seems incompatible with authorial commentary when, for example, Fassbinder intercedes with his flowing camera work. It directs us from character action to refracted images, to images within images. Here Fassbinder's creative role appears.

Typically, an art film hovers on three levels of narration as we construct our interpretation around a balance of character subjectivity, life's untidiness, and authorial vision. There we remain, caught in an ambiguous play between levels exemplified in the open ending of the film. Fassbinder's characters do not have clear-cut goals. Within an episodic structure, the typically powerless protagonist wanders from one encounter to another, at the mercy of more directed individuals or even vaguely indicated societal institutions. An open-ended conclusion allows Fassbinder to proclaim his lack of hope for social change, but it also emphasizes a lack of internal control. The director surfaces as a humble individual who cannot completely organize the complex realities of twentieth-century existence. The story no longer counts. It is the process of telling that matters.

Fassbinder, however, offers yet another level of narrative resolution: his autobiography. The director's personal history enters the film at a number of levels. First, a knowledgeable viewer would recognize that his films contain seemingly endless references to his personal life. His acting troupe and friends, his mother, and his lovers act and even star in his films. And Fassbinder often uses the films to reenact his personal relations in a less-than-veiled way. For example, *Beware of the Holy Whore,* Fassbinder's *8½,* was publicly proclaimed as a film about the interpersonal problems within the commune during the making of *Gods of the Plague*; it is littered with clues to which character represents which troupe member. He cast his male lovers in eight roles and his mother in eleven, including, in *In a Year of Thirteen Moons,* a film about a transsexual suicide, a nun at the protagonist's former orphanage. In a long monologue she tells of his motherless childhood as the source of his abnormal sexuality, creating an indirect parallel between the character's and Fassbinder's lack of maternal love. This autobiographical self-consciousness is painfully explicit in *Germany in Autumn*: Fassbinder, his mother, and his lover Armin Meier play themselves, and Fassbinder openly reveals his dictatorial and emotional personality as he bullies them.

Fassbinder also extends the art cinema practice of dedicating one's works to other directors. Fassbinder's pseudonym, Franz Walsch, appears in connection with eleven of his films as either a character or as the editor of the film. The name is yet another insider's game. It is a conflation of the names of Franz Biberkopf, the protagonist of the Döblin novel *Berlin Alexanderplatz,* and the American director Raoul Walsh. More directly, Fassbinder dedicated films to Chabrol, Rohmer, Straub, Peter Zadek, and Artaud. In fact, he made unusually personal dedications. *The Bitter Tears of Petra von Kant* (1972) is "dedicated to the one who here becomes Marlene," a reference to Irm Hermann, a close woman "associate" from his communal acting days. In one of his most autobiographical films, *Fox and His Friends* (1975), the director plays the homosexual of the title, named Franz Fox. In a particularly self-conscious move, Fassbinder dedicates this dissection of the gay world to his gay lovers: "For Armin and all the others."

By the time Fassbinder dedicates *The Third Generation* (1978–79) "to a true lover—and hence probably to nobody," his textual melancholy about the possibility of love is read against his transgressive biography as a homosexual and a leftist who is reputed to be promiscuous and violent. This unusual level of autobiography serves as part of a realist aesthetic: Fassbinder's films are about "real" and personally "experienced" events and people. This subjective realism was built, to a degree, on the Action Theater's Living Theater tradition, in which theater acting is as "real" as offstage life.

On another level, authorial intervention, associated with the art cinema, gives these autobiographical works an intensity one might associate with the nervous whisper of an individual seeking public acknowledgment of his sins. Fassbinder's confession becomes a commodity (as he sells the audience the prurient pleasures of his personal life) while he uses the films as a form of therapy—a classic art film trope. Foucault argues that some societies have openly dealt with sex through erotic art, but under the influence of Christianity, modern Western society has become a "confessing society." This recent process of monitoring, recording, and categorizing sex has made it "an object of great suspicion ... the fragment of darkness that we each carry with us."[35] Although the sensationalism of an autobiographical reading is often discouraged by academic readings, which value more abstract and thematic understandings, it conditioned the social reception of Fassbinder's films. Indeed, part of Fassbinder's attraction is related to how his confessional mode connects to this "fragment of darkness" in Western culture.

Fassbinder's revelation of his transgressions proved difficult for German society, and even for the cultural press. Even after he had gained international success and renown, Fassbinder continued to confess, most particularly with his planned film, *Cocaine* (about his drug addiction), and with his adaptation of Genet's confessional work *Querelle* (1982), an expressionist homosexual fantasy. Admittedly, I have chosen to discuss the most explicitly autobiographical of Fassbinder's films. If my argument about his confessional melodrama is viable, it should apply to his less overtly personal works as well. For that reason, I will now apply this model to *Chinese Roulette* (1976), which has been received as one of Fassbinder's most perfectly realized art films.

The film's narrative involves a married couple who leave each other for a weekend. Supposedly, Ariane Christ goes to Milan and Gerhard Christ leaves for Oslo. Instead they both arrive at their castle in the country accompanied by their respective lovers, Irene and Kolbe. Their crippled daughter, Angela, seems to have arranged this uncomfortable meeting; she too arrives, with her mute governess, Traunitz. The castle is kept by a housekeeper, Kast, and her writer son, Gabriel. After a period of uncertainty the couples continue their trysts, remaining together at the castle.

On the second night Angela convinces the castle's inhabitants to participate in a game of "Chinese roulette." The game revolves around telling veiled truths. The eight people divide into two groups of four. One group secretly chooses a member of the other group, and that team asks questions to discover the identity of the chosen individual: If this person was a wild animal, what would he be? If this person went to live on a desert island, what would she take with her—a person, a book, or a thing? The questions and answers become more pointed and cruel as the game progresses: What would this person have been during the Third Reich?

The questions reveal more about the individual who answers than they do about the game's chosen individual. Nevertheless, as the questions and answers become more macabre, the game climaxes with Angela's revelation that she has singled her mother out as the game's victim. The mother reacts by pulling out a gun to shoot Angela, but instead shoots her governess. In the epilogue the woman survives, and Angela confronts Gabriel about plagiarism. In the final frame of the film we see a processional pass by the castle. Another shot rings out and the image freezes. We do not know who shoots or who gets shot.

The film's title, *Chinese Roulette*—a game—echoes an essential art cinema narrational strategy: playfulness. The retelling of the story seems easy but belies the complexity of the plotting. To break down this film's complex plot relations, let us employ the scheme of "objective realism," expressive or subjective realism, and narrational commentary that I used in my survey of Fassbinder's art films. Then we will be able to get at the complex "game" of this film's narration.

Chinese Roulette offers limited objective realism with its on-location shooting (an apartment, Munich's airport, a village, and a castle). Unlike most of Fassbinder's art films, *Chinese Roulette* is confined to a rather self-consciously stylized *Kammerspiel* of interiors, high-key lights, and twirling camera movement. A greater sense of realism comes from the film's contemporary subject matter—the ambiguous games families play because they are unable to communicate. Such realism can be extended to the film's highly elliptical treatment of cause and effect. We are never totally sure whether Angela is responsible for the couples' meeting.

With a modernist sense of reality, the film refuses to convey the motivation for Angela's anger. Is it a result of her handicap, or does it emanate from her relationship with her mother? The film's opening is emblematic of its tenuous play of cause and effect. Whereas in classic narration the beginning is reserved for establishing motives and goals, Fassbinder's film opens with a mysterious scene in which Frau Christ and Angela listen to an opera while they are perched on window sills separated by a large expanse. Meaningful glances are exchanged while opera dominates the sound track. An enigmatic close-up of the mother's cigarettes arranged on top of a mirror is inserted into this scene, which seems to last a long time as the camera cuts between the motionless mother and daughter. But nothing happens. When the mother finally asks the daughter, "Nice?" we are unsure of the referent. What motivates their lack of action? More puzzling, how does this scene contribute to the story?

The lack of action and clear-cut motivation dominates the movie. A blind man comes to the castle to beg, but drives away in a Mercedes-Benz. While she is driving, Kast is cut short by another motorist and whispers angrily, "fascist," while the music emphasizes the statement's importance. In attempting to make sense of these elliptical actions, we have recourse to a concept of modern verisimilitude in which relations between characters and the effects of their actions are not always clear. The opening scene establishes an ongoing pattern of indirect communication. The actual game later in the film makes the pattern explicit.

The attempt at objective realism is quickly undercut by subjective narration. From the very first scene, the film becomes a play of meaningful glances. Often we are given point-of-view shots and eyeline matches while the connecting space between glancing characters is missing. Characters look at each other across large distances, pulled together spatially only by eyeline matches. For example, Angela watches her mother and her mother's lover the morning after the first night of the lovers' tryst. The interchange is done through a series of eyeline matches and no conversation. Angela looks at her mother and lover offscreen. The next shot is a medium long shot of the mother looking back. Space between the two is symbolically elongated. And when Angela grunts "ya, ya," the mystery of these subjective interactions overwhelms us.

The initial meeting of the couples on their illicit weekend also involves a play of looks. Gerhard Christ and his lover go to bed. At the door we see them passionately kissing. As the door opens, the camera moves in and refocuses, revealing Ariane Christ on the floor with her lover. The camera slowly begins tracking and panning around the room. It pauses to frame the figures as their images are split up by the glass cabinets that serve as the focus of the room. The camera circles; the characters rearrange themselves, and the camera portrays a new set of relationships through glances (usually eyeline matches) and figure placement.

Fassbinder communicates hardly any information about his characters directly. He allows only fragments of knowledge: the parents took lovers after the child's illness. They hate the child. Herr Christ financed his lover's business. Herr Christ and Kast were involved in some seemingly political activity ("Ali Ben Basset was murdered in Paris"). Gabriel digs into luggage and finds a dildo, which he replaces in a panic. Often the most sociopolitical information or action becomes inconsequential to the plot.

Like classical narration, the film relies on psychological causation, but it emphasizes the art cinema's lack of clear-cut motives, traits, or goals for us to puzzle over. The characters are defined not by what they say but through physical appearance and gestures. The housekeeper, Frau Kast, wears loud synthetic clothing and her hair is garishly orange and coiffed in a matronly manner. Gerhard Christ's lover is distinguished by her beauty, high-fashion clothing, and excessive make-up. Most ironically, Angela looks like an angel child, with long blond banana curls and sweet feminine dresses. The characters are distinguished not by actions but by oddly accentuated mannerisms that belie their appearances. Angela's metallic clumping echoes ominously through the castle but is contradicted by the aura of innocence projected by her dolls. Frau Kast looks at her dowdy visage in the mirror, licking her lips and rubbing her breasts seductively. Herr Christ's beautiful lover smokes continuously. And Kolbe, perhaps the least distinguished and most passive character, reveals another side when he jumps on Frau Christ in bed and bites her like a vampire. The fact that these actions contradict appearances points to the fact that the characters are far more complicated than they can express.

If they do express themselves, it is elliptically through stories (Herr Christ's trip to Syria), readings (Gabriel's reading of his manuscript), or indirect questions (the game). In one of the few direct moments of character display, Gerhard Christ asks Kolbe if he loves his wife. He answers, "I got used to her . . . Perhaps that is love." *Chinese Roulette*'s characters are inarticulate art cinema figures. Their lack of direction is displayed in their circling of each other. As viewers we notice how these details give the character away. But given the constant undercutting of each clue, Fassbinder refuses us the pleasure of subjective understanding.

This emphasis on characterization is essential because the plot is minimal. In fact, the plot is constructed around a modernist device called a boundary situation — that moment of knowledge that is the goal of the art film character's search. Boundary situations are described by Bordwell as "pointed situations in which a presented persona, a narrator, an implied reader in a flash of insight becomes aware of meaningful as against meaningless existence."[36] In *Chinese Roulette* this meaningful moment comes with the game. The importance of the game is underscored by how directionless the plot is; characters go their separate ways in the house only to be brought together by the game.

But the questions still remain: What does the game of Chinese roulette reveal? How does it do so in a film that is noncommunicative? The boundary situation, like the *Kammerspiel* in a Bergman film, allows the characters to explain their feelings and mental states. Given how in many art films the plot is compressed to highlight the boundary situation, it functions to reveal prior events, as in Bergman's *Persona* and Kurosawa's *Rashomon*. Until the game, *Chinese Roulette* is an existential mystery: Why is this child hated so much? What is she capable of? The game plays with the boundary situation conventions of the art film. It makes a "game" out of interest in the subjective reality.

At Angela's suggestion, the questions begin, harmlessly at first. Until this scene, the film has suppressed character interaction, preferring an ambiguous web of glances and eyeline matches. Here the characters interact, but the questions and answers reveal as little as the knowing looks and ambiguous references of the rest of the film. Gabriel's, Traunitz's, and Angela's answers grow more and more ominous. Answering the question "How would the person die?" Gabriel says, "Garroting"; Traunitz responds, "The person is already dead"; and Angela coolly comments, "A slow natural death, very slow and very conscious."

Even when we find out that they have been describing Angela's mother, our knowledge is still limited by this particular rendition of inquiry into character. Chinese roulette necessitates half-truths: enough information to keep the game going, but veiled and ambiguous. On this level *Chinese Roulette* stands as a metaphor of the narrational practices of the art cinema: the game of objective and intense subjective realism.

Yet on the third level of art cinema, the authorial commentary remains to a degree separate from the actual game. How does Fassbinder come to the forefront in the film and, ultimately, the game? By stepping beyond the limited self-consciousness of classical narration, *Chinese Roulette* continually bares its "constructed" nature as it pushes its stylization to such an "excessive" level that the presence of the author/director obtrudes.

Here the camera exceeds the subjective stylization of *Bolwieser*. Reserved for the scenes involving interactions among the couples, the moving camera initially dances around them in a classical manner in that it follows character movement. But its movements in general are based more on creating visual games with figure placement. Either the camera settles on an image of two or three players, revealing the multiple layers of their subjectivity and relationships, or it tracks circularly around the room, catching a figure's reflection in the glass cases and thereby creating a multifaceted image of the individual. These images can be read as the projection of the characters' emotional or subjective perception of the situation. Similarly, the music often emphasizes the suspense and discovery involved in the process of revelation. Horns blare on the sound track and the camera zooms in on the mother in classic melodramatic fashion as she realizes that she is the object of the game. But such a subjective understanding is undercut by the patterned nature of the stylistic treatment, giving a sense that an outside force is guiding this event.

Beyond the highly stylized nature of the game's staging, Fassbinder's presence is felt through the illogical nature of the film. He declares his presence in the opening scene, when the opera we hear suddenly stops as a door opens. No story logic can explain this. His authorial commentary surfaces as Gabriel reads aloud his existential manuscript. The camera pans across a beautiful landscape, revealing a crucifix dissolving into a steer's skull. We could read these images as a character's visualization of the reading, but as the camera floats through the room, Fassbinder offers no cues for the connection. Rather, here as well as in the pristine camera work, the opening sound track, and the odd, nonsensical references (the blind man with the Mercedes, the dildo, the political references), Fassbinder's organizing presence is continually felt. Even the presence of Anna Karina, Godard's actress and lover, makes us conscious of Fassbinder as part of the institution of the art cinema. And *Chinese Roulette* is only one chapter of his oeuvre. Ultimately, we accept these nonobjective or subjective interactions as Fassbinder's signature. In lieu of stars and genres, the art film organizes itself around the director as a textual force, giving meaning to the play of different kinds of realism.

Chinese Roulette has been critically described as a "high art melodrama,"[37] illustrating why melodrama is sometimes described as a protomodernist sensibility. In *Chinese Roulette* Fassbinder makes apparent the odd similarities between the narrational conventions of melodrama and art cinema. Both modes slow down the plot in favor of subjective display, the revelation of mental states. In both forms Fassbinder's film style becomes an embodiment of these subjective states. Melodramatic changes in the musical score, for example, mirror the emotional dilemmas that both Xaverl and Ariane Christ experience as they fall victim to outside forces.

The shared melodramatic traces are seen to differ in the two Fassbinder genres when one considers the lack of causal ties in Fassbinder's art cinema works as opposed to the more causally related actions of the protagonists of his adaptations. If there are moments of self-consciousness in his television films, they are much more the workings of fate, whereas in his art cinema works the plot lines are so tenuous that a more overt and modernist concept of textual construction is necessary. The author/director comes forward as the humble force organizing the inconsistencies of the text. The final image in *Chinese Roulette* is a long shot of the castle from outside; an indiscernible procession moves by and then a gunshot rings out. Here we are conscious that Fassbinder refuses external logic and leaves open his humble and incomplete product. The film has exposed the fallibility of both the modern artwork and the modern artist: they cannot make complete statements.

Chinese Roulette is actually one of Fassbinder's less overtly autobiographical films. There are no direct references to his life, to his notorious proclivities toward homosexuality, drugs, and leftist politics. The film operates in a social vacuum made possible by its intense character subjectivity. The theme of promiscuity and perverse sexual pleasure fits comfortably with the Fassbinder autobiographical persona. Nevertheless, the film is not autobiographical.

On the other hand, Fassbinder's textual presence is made even more apparent in this ambiguous work than in a majority of his other works. With this film there is no question of Fassbinder's guiding presence as we attempt to reconcile the ambiguity with the game of character subjectivity and authorial expressivity. One cannot make sense of *Chinese Roulette* without positing an expressive individual or *Autor* who guides this film.

Finally, his contradictory roles as both controlling agent and humble art cinema director become important for the public reception of Fassbinder. The art cinema director takes on a more visible and iron-handed role in the construction of a film than his commercial counterpart. But the modernist ambiguity endemic to the art film intentionally foregrounds the incapability of the artist/director to produce a work that communicates clearly. Within his more art cinema-influenced films, Fassbinder reveals a degree of aesthetic and intellectual vulnerability. Such a refusal or inability to speak in some ways contradicts the concept of the *Autor* as an anointed communicator.

As long as the textual strategies of his more pronounced art and confessional films remained separated within the institutional confines of the art cinema, Fassbinder was accepted as a member of the art cinema. But by introducing these previously separated genres to the public in *Berlin Alexanderplatz,* Fassbinder engendered a legitimation crisis, and the crucial but unexamined assumptions of German film authorship in the 1980s came into relief.

6 / *Berlin Alexanderplatz*: The Interplay of Fassbinder's Textual Voices

"I am Biberkopf."

On the eve of the broadcast of West Germany's most spectacular television series, *Berlin Alexanderplatz,* Rainer Werner Fassbinder declared that he was Biberkopf, its protagonist.[1] Not only did he claim this unusual identity, he also wrote a long and painfully self-revelatory essay for the cultural weekly *Die Zeit* in which he explained how the Döblin novel had been the central creative impetus for his film career; how the novel stood as a "life's script"; and finally, at his most confessional, how the novel had allowed him to come to terms with his growing realization of his homosexuality.[2]

The connection between their country's best-known modernist novel and their most notorious film director shocked the West German viewing public. The publicity value of Fassbinder's declaration is self-evident. But from a critical perspective, how does it change our understanding when a director states publicly that he is the protagonist of his film? Fassbinder's confession seems to mimic Flaubert's infamous pronouncement that "Madame Bovary, c'est moi!" but is it no more than a personal affirmation of the creative process that underlines all film, literature, and philosophy? Should we conclude with Friedrich Nietzsche that "every great philosophy has been the confession of its maker, as it were his involuntary and unconscious autobiography"?[3]

These questions are appropriate given the disregard of autobiography in film and television studies. Although the art cinema, with its reliance on the director as a textual formal presence, has elicited a number of confessional readings, the discipline as a whole has failed to address the issue of film autobiography.[4] Part of this hesitancy is predicated on the problematic nature of stars and now directors; film and television spectators can often ignore the distinction between the fictional and the real, replacing the real lives of actors and now auteur directors with their film roles. This form of reception pushes film understanding beyond a simple reflection theory to what might be called a correspondence theory. Masking the role that representation plays, the autobiographical film appears more real or more true to life than less personal films. This is a powerful twist in the realist ideology that plagues film and television reception. The Fassbinder legend resulted from a similar discourse, as we saw in chapter 4; the popular press conflated the melodrama of the director's public life with his films. Sensationalism thrives on private revelations. But should we accept Franz Biberkopf as a direct embodiment of Fassbinder in *Berlin Alexanderplatz*?

Significantly, of the recent academic criticism of Fassbinder's *Berlin Alexanderplatz,* it is the German analyses that draw the most direct correspondence between Fassbinder the biographical individual and the content of the series. This critical stance stems from a combined German interest in content analysis and the centrality of the *Autor* in film and television reception. The most prominent example is a book-length study of the series, Achim Haag's *"No One Can Silence Your Longing": Rainer Werner Fassbinder's Berlin Alexanderplatz.*[5] Subtitling his book "Reflection on Autobiography and the Dissolution of the Self," Haag takes Fassbinder's confession at its word. He sees the *Autor* as the interpretative key; he begins with a discussion of Fassbinder's confessional essay and then studies the "biographical parallels" between Fassbinder and Döblin. Using the work of Gilles Deleuze, he argues that the sadomasochism of the series reflects Fassbinder's unresolved conflict with his father (a common interpretation in the German cultural press) and that each character serves as a facet of Fassbinder's personality (e.g., Reinhold as Fassbinder's alter ego). He concludes that the complex use of narrative voices (especially the first person) reveals Fassbinder's lifelong tension between collective/society and the artist/individual, which slowly self-destructs along with Franz.[6]

The three major academic analyses in English agree that as a result of Fassbinder's statement autobiography is central to interpreting the series, but they limit their willingness to draw a direct correspondence between the director's life and the film's narrative.[7] They focus on the themes of homosexuality and physical violence as the central biographical elements. A key moment remains *Berlin Alexanderplatz*'s epilogue, "My Dream of the Dream of Franz Biberkopf," in which Fassbinder openly draws parallels between his psyche and the protagonist's.

Eric Rentschler cautions his readers not to let Fassbinder's *Die Zeit* essay overdetermine their interpretation and argues for a metaphoric understanding: the violence of the series reenacts the mistreatment of Fassbinder as "other" in postwar West Germany. When Fassbinder appears in the epilogue, like his protagonist he is violated—cut off by the frame. Rentschler argues:

> We find traces of ... undeniable violence in these images and in this narrative—and, to be sure, on the body of the director who wears his scars defiantly. Fassbinder recognized the terms of dismemberment: the same history he wished to represent was the one that (mis)shaped him. He knew what he knew; he, too, had to pay for it dearly.[8]

Thomas Elsaesser and Kaja Silverman make a credible case for Fassbinder's central ideology as social transcendence through suffering violence, or what Silverman calls "masochistic utopianism." Their analyses are based on a number of shared assumptions about autobiography. First, both accept Fassbinder's statement that the novel helped him come to terms with his homosexuality, and therefore the series becomes a meditation on his sexual subjectivity. Second, both see the autobiographical elements in the series not as a matter of parallel events in Fassbinder's personal life but as Fassbinder bringing his persona to the text through his "narcissistic investment" in Franz Biberkopf. Also, Fassbinder breaks stylistically with the oedipal logic of Hollywood classical film by calling attention to the male gaze. The series critiques not only the violent power of the dominant heterosexual society over Biberkopf/Fassbinder but also Hollywood's sadistic regime of the male gaze, of which Fassbinder as a homosexual and a filmmaker was a victim. Silverman argues that "the masculinity that Fassbinder works to demolish in *Berlin Alexanderplatz* is his 'own.'"[9]

To a degree, these critics have historicized Fassbinder's form by combining his personal history as a homosexual and *Berlin Alexanderplatz*'s aesthetic, which turns the traditional visual pleasure of the classical Hollywood film against itself. But the analyses ignore the historical specificity of *Berlin Alexanderplatz*'s form and reception outside of the fact that his work was a response to the dominant heterosexuality in German society and film form. Neither the academic nor the popular press in West Germany addressed the role of the gaze nor even the prevalence of looking/watching in the series. This does not deny that the series breaks with dominant psychic mechanisms, but the point still is that we need a more historically informed interpretation if we are to understand the series' ideological role.

Finally, these film analyses fail to recognize the historical fact that *Berlin Alexanderplatz* was made for television, not film. Their arguments are premised on a highly specific specular theory of theatrical film viewing, which differs radically from television viewing. In fact, recent psychoanalytic critics point out that the concept of a voyeuristic gaze fixed on a larger-than-life screen in a darkened theater is not applicable to the diminutive television set in an illuminated room full of distractions that compete for the viewer's attention.[10] Since viewers concentrate on and participate in television at different levels, one psychological model cannot possibly account for all experience.

The concept of self-consciousness and its relationship to Fassbinder's previous uses of it represent a more historical understanding of autobiography and *Berlin Alexanderplatz*. As I demonstrated in chapter 5, Fassbinder's films fall into discernible generic patterns, particularly around the issue of self-consciousness or the textual addressing of the constructed nature of the filmic text. Film theory, however, has traditionally employed Emile Benveniste's linguistic analysis of *enonciation* to describe the process of extradiegetic intervention in the film's fictional world. Application to film of structural linguistics, as of psychoanalysis, has a number of problems for a historical understanding.[11]

Film theory and criticism have appropriated Benveniste's linguistic categories in an attempt to describe the filmic enunciative process. These categories allow the subjective nature of filmic construction to be explored. Christian Metz and Mark Nash both employ Benveniste's categories (particularly the concept of "shifters" — the change in pronoun address) in their analyses of the semiotics of film address. The "classic realist text" or the invisible narration of classic Hollywood presents itself as *histoire* bestowing on itself the status of objective narration. Ethereal intrusion within the *histoire* of the film, such as point-of-view shots in Dreyer's *Vampyr* that cannot be attributed to character, indicates the existence of "I" as a narrating presence in the film.[12]

There are a number of problems with the use of Benveniste's *enunciation* concepts in film. There can be no strict equivalence between verbal language and film; they can only help construct the subjective interventions in the film. Unfortunately, these linguistic concepts underline the film's psychoanalytic subjectivity and the ideological subject. Such theories deal in absolutes (first- and second-person address) when the awareness of the film as a text is more a matter of degree, as the term *self-consciousness* suggests.

In order to demonstrate this complex interaction of extrinsic historic norms of Fassbinder's genres and the intrinsic formal pattern of the film, I divide my analysis of *Berlin Alexanderplatz* into two parts. Because of the series' length — fifteen hours and twenty-one minutes — I cannot offer a comprehensive analysis of the film's narrational procedures. Rather, I will demonstrate the film's use of Fassbinder's two generic worlds: the melodramatic television adaptation and the confessional art film. Fassbinder utilizes three methods to bring his narrational presence to the forefront against a relief of classical and Döblin narrations: the voice-over narration; the repeated flashback to Ida's murder; and, finally, the epilogue.

Analysis of the complex play of narrational sources or self-consciousness in *Berlin Alexanderplatz* provides an instance of how the film interweaves the different narrational modes and voices of Fassbinder's heretofore separate genres. The result is a mesmerizing ebb and flow of classical melodrama, Döblin's and Fassbinder's competing modernist interjections, and personal confession. The series calls attention not only to the constructed nature of the work, but also specifically to the issue of *Autor.*

Although homosexual desire ties Fassbinder's life to *Berlin Alexanderplatz,* the series points to his guiding influence much more directly through its complex weaving of his narrational voices. More than in any other of his television adaptations, Fassbinder makes the work his own. Through the fifteen hours, he slowly exchanges narrational personas not only with Franz Biberkopf but also with Döblin as his modernist history of the Weimar period recedes before the iconoclastic culture of the seventies and Fassbinder's confessional voice. In the end *Berlin Alexanderplatz* represents a cultural battle between the authority of canonical German modernism and the antiauthoritarianism of pop culture played out for the broad German audience through television.

Berlin Alexanderplatz and Classical Narration

On the level of story, Fassbinder faithfully adapted the original Döblin novel. One can summarize both the television series' and the novel's story as follows: Franz Biberkopf is just being let out of prison in Berlin as the film begins in 1927. He was once a transportation worker and a pimp. He has spent four years in prison for beating to death his lover, Ida. Although he has an uncontrollable temper, he pledges to become an honest and respectable citizen upon his release. Franz's oath is mitigated by the fact that Germany is in the midst of a depression and work is impossible to find.

After a series of marginal jobs selling tie clips, homosexual magazines, fascist newspapers, and shoelaces, Franz meets Reinhold, a criminal to whom Franz is immediately attracted. Reinhold and Franz form a strong bond as Reinhold trades Franz his girlfriends in exchange for his friendship. He also introduces Franz to Pums, the head of a local gang of thieves. Franz joins the gang and in his first heist loses his arm when he is pushed out of the escape vehicle. Still undaunted, Franz survives the accident and renews his pledge to be respectable. He falls in love with the young and naive prostitute Mieze, who against his wishes continues to work in order to support Franz. Seeing the couple's romantic bliss, Reinhold jealously attempts to seduce Mieze, and when she rejects his advances he murders her. The realization that his best friend has killed the love of his life destroys Franz's tenuous emotional facade. He has a nervous breakdown. During a nightmare-filled stay in a mental hospital, Franz is rehabilitated as a "useful member of society." In the end the "new" and "respectable" Franz returns to Berlin as a menial parking attendant.

Simple recounting of the major events belies the complexities of the famous 1927 Döblin novel. If self-consciousness is defined as the way that narration shows a recognition that it is addressing an audience, the novel speaks almost continually to its audience through its direct address, its elliptical construction, and its contradictory clash of narrative tones. The 635-page novel spins a story that is as much about Berlin and the proletarian activities of the Alexanderplatz (a central business square in Berlin) as about its protagonist (even though the complete title of the novel — *Berlin Alexanderplatz: The Story of Franz Biberkopf* — would indicate the opposite).[13] Franz Biberkopf may be the protagonist, but he is decentered. He must compete with a polyphony of voices. In fact, the plot focuses on his struggle against the external forces of the city and Germany society to keep his goal: to be upstanding.

The novel was hailed as Germany's equivalent of James Joyce's modernist study of Bloom and Dublin or Dos Passos's montage of New York life. The German author strings together a series of short, undeveloped images of Berlin's big-city culture. The associational structure revolves around serious and often quite tragic snippets from newspaper articles, official city documents, and advertisements on the walls of Berlin. For example, Döblin inserts a section called "Local News":

> Quotations on April 18 around 11 o'clock were: I.G. Dye Stuffs 260½ to 267, Siemens & Halske 297½ to 299, Dessauer Gas 202 to 203, Wald Cellulose 295. Bids for German Oil at 134½.

> To return once more to the streetcar disaster in Heerstrasse, all those seriously injured in the accident are improving.

> On April 11, Herr Braun, editor, was liberated from Moabit prison by an armed party. It was a regular Wild West scene. A search is being made for them.[14]

In contrast to this reportage is the influence of the futurists in the energy and exuberance that the novel's rat-a-tat pace of images evokes. The work also echoes the dadaists with its childlike, nonsensical humor spun into the whirling pastiche of interventions into the story's logic. (Consider the section title "Gallop-a-trot, Gallop-a-trot, little Horsey starts trotting again" or the repeated interjection of "cock-a-doodle-doo" in the "Fourth Book.")[15]

Through the nonlogic of his narrative, Döblin destroys the convention that the fictional world is an imaginary world unto itself within which one identifies with the protagonist. He replaces the illusion with a modernist concept of reality resulting from the vagaries of modern human life. This depiction is similar to the subjective realism of art cinema that I described in chapter 5. Döblin's play of contrary forms allows him to question the intelligibility of the world while simultaneously giving his characters and events an existence that transcends the limits of fiction.

The author's direct intrusion is infrequent and surprising, reminding the reader that Döblin is in control of what at times seems to be an out-of-control text. "Once again, we return to the text," he announces.[16] Or consider this: "Karl, Reinhold, and Mieze want that; backwards Mieze, Reinhold, and Karl; and also Reinhold, Karl, Mieze, all of them want that." Here Döblin displays his capricious control of his characters. And such narrational inconsistency deflects character development.

Ultimately, Döblin's self-consciousness is guided by irony. He mocks his characters, particularly Franz's attempt at self-reform. Döblin passes judgment on the simple story that governs this novel. Chapter titles such as "Spirited White Slavery" (which is about Franz and Reinhold's trading of girlfriends) often add black humor to unpleasant acts. As much as the narration borders on being out of control, we are conscious of the guiding presence of a narrator. And through his irony, we are aware of the correct political point of view: Döblin's socialist humanism.

The novel's political commentary emanates not only from Döblin's politics, but more significantly from a much larger German literary movement that Russell Berman has called "left modernism." This group of writers includes the authors whose works Fassbinder chose to adapt for television (Graf, Fleisser, and Döblin). Their modernism is not united around the excessive play of form that we associate with Brecht's theater or the modernism of the French novel, for example. Their challenge took place on the level of content.

German leftist modernism was based on a political concept of the individual's role in society. A number of writers self-consciously broke with the institution of private contemplation that had dominated nineteenth-century German literature. Writers such as Döblin and Graf (*The Marriage of Mr. Bolwieser*) challenged this romantic tradition; their protagonists are consumed by crises of individuality. These writers believed their ultimate aim was to substitute a collective sensibility for the romantic individualism of earlier works. Bolwieser, for example, is promised individual happiness in marriage, but Graf reveals that Bolwieser's weakness resides in his distance from the villagers or the collective. Likewise, Franz Biberkopf pledges to better himself, but he is crushed by the city because of the impossible nature of his personal mission.[17] Given his emphasis on modernist form, Döblin offers a contrast to the more conventional narratives of the other German leftist modernists such as Graf and Fleisser. But one can still see Döblin's debt to German left modernism: his novel's central tension is the relationship of the individual to the city.

Since the chaotic and ironic structure of *Berlin Alexanderplatz* is one of the striking features of the novel, Fassbinder's use of classical Hollywood narration in his adaptation impresses one as a remarkable break with Döblin's modernist intent. In Fassbinder's film Berlin recedes in importance and Franz Biberkopf emerges as the central causal agent. The significance of this change lies in the fact that Fassbinder's (as opposed to Döblin's) socially oriented *Berlin Alexanderplatz* returns to the individual as the last refuge against the onslaught of societal repression. But in the case of the more classical and melodramatic Fassbinder version, the individual's failure is his own as well as a result of society's exploitation. This theme is structurally represented in the ambiguous play of Hollywood classical, melodramatic, and art cinema narrational techniques.

The film clearly defines the protagonist Biberkopf in the first episode. In part he is just a simple child (his reaction to his release from prison, his innocent exuberance over his sexual release after raping Minna — Ida's sister), but he is also part animal. The film reveals this not only in the rape scene, but also in the flashback in this first episode to his brutal murder of Ida. Most of the time we are confined to Franz's point of view. A central question of the film is, Are his actions self-willed or the result of a larger "force"?

The traits of the protagonist are repeatedly underscored by Biberkopf's "signature" love bite — half sexually arousing for and half inflicting obvious pain on his girlfriend/victim. The actor, Günter Lamprecht, emphasizes this dichotomy: he has the facial gestures of a child and the body of a bear. In fact, these contradictory traits are similar to those of the fundamentally flawed characters in literary naturalism where pregiven causes propel the action because the protagonist has no self-will. Here Franz is granted greater potential for self-will.

Like a Hollywood protagonist, Fassbinder's Franz Biberkopf is clearly goal-oriented: he wants to be an upstanding member of German society. Throughout all Franz's trials and tribulations, this goal remains the film's central organizing principle. In a typical Fassbinder move, the director combines the larger social issue with a personal goal as Franz's repeated attempts at economic independence fail, resulting in his exploitating his girlfriends through violence, abandonment, or prostitution.

The connection between romantic and societal exploitation becomes the hallmark of the television series. Where the novel's structure revolves around Franz's drifting as a directionless picaresque, Fassbinder breaks down his fifteen-hour film into a repeated cycle of episodes. He obsessively repeats the classical Hollywood plot pattern: an undisturbed stage, the disturbance, the struggle, the elimination of the disturbance. But as the spheres of his sexual relations and his social mission collapse repeatedly, the repressive nature of Franz's existence becomes even more emotionally disturbing.

The episode entitled "A Hammer on the Head Can Hurt the Soul" exemplifies this classical pattern. Franz attempts to resolve his unemployment by selling shoelaces door to door. He begins to sell shoelaces with his girlfriend's "Uncle" Lüders. He scores a financial "success" through a sexual liaison with a widow customer who pays him, but this moment of triumph is undercut by Uncle Lüders's backmailing the widow for her sexual indiscretion with Franz. Lüders's betrayal causes Franz's emotional breakdown; he disappears, distraught. Franz's friends corner Lüders, forcing him to find Franz and make up for his act.

Although the disturbance is not totally eliminated (Franz does not return), we have a resolution in that Franz's lover Lina and his best friend Merk realize that Franz will not return. They immediately couple, revealing the limited nature of their moral system. In fact, Franz's disappearance accounts for the next episode, in which Franz is drunk. Again the pattern is repeated: Franz's drunkenness becomes a spiritual as well as a physical battle, which he wins and returns to the world of the "respectable." When one surveys the entire series, excluding the epilogue, one sees how these causal links within an episode become a repeated pattern throughout the entire fifteen hours. Although the series shares Hollywood's plot linearity, its length allows for an unrelenting ebb and flow of cyclically repeated moments of triumph, conflict, and failure. The variations in the cycles maintain the viewer's curiosity but underscore our questions about the degree to which Franz's actions are self-willed or determined by an outside force.

Additionally, the sheer length of the series is adapted for the epic form. Each of the fourteen episodes offers Fassbinder a chance to develop a subplot, a facet of Berlin, or a representative character. But the range of these changes is limited. Whereas Döblin's narration moves effortlessly through both the streets and the dens of proletarian Berlin, Fassbinder's *Berlin Alexanderplatz* retreats to the interiors of an underworld. The artificiality of the sets of the Bavaria Atelier's "Berlin" studio harks back to the claustrophobic Hollywood gangster films of the 1930s, and the vaseline-coated lens conveys a blurred image that connotes memory and the past. We are conscious that German history is being recreated for us—the history not of a city or an individual, but of a psychological persona who represents the people of the prefascist period.

Augmenting the character-centered nature of *Berlin Alexanderplatz* is the fact that three-fourths of the film is shot in stagelike interiors. Most of the action takes place in the atmospheric dens of Franz's apartment and his pub. These scenes swing from moments of romantic bliss to Franz's acts of violence against his lovers. It is a world in which Franz Biberkopf exerts authority. These domestic areas are clearly delineated and provide a relatively controlled haven in the film; the streets of Berlin, however, are not spatially clear, as cars and faceless people whirl by. The ever present threat of the street intrudes on Franz's interior world through the use of expressionistic neon lights and thunderstorms that cast their blinking, garish light into the domestic arena.

Fassbinder's expressionist sensibility is evident in his portrayal of the streets as a chaotic world of action where Franz comes into contact with society's injustices (the amputation of his arm, thievery, a gang member's beating). The film announces this dichotomy in its first shots: the title "The Punishment Begins" is superimposed over Franz's horrified face as the rising noises of the street overwhelm him when he is released from the more "comforting" interiors of prison. Fassbinder reverses Döblin's celebration of the city by using the closed studio space to create a womblike world that parallels the unstable psychological needs of his protagonist.

Additionally, nearly every episode functions to introduce a new individual or set of characters. Following the classical cinema's reliance on character-centered action and the art cinema's use of overt parallelism, Fassbinder presents a vast array of characters. This intensifies the film's survey form as each character represents an aspect of Berlin's subculture: Dreske, the communist; the Jewish sausage salesman; Invalide, the bourgeois rightist; Glatzkopf, the master of the street of prostitution. Together these men symbolize the intercession of Weimar social and political reality into Franz's existence. They signify a challenge to Franz's pledge to separate himself from social involvement in order to be a "good citizen."

These attempts at social realism, however, are dwarfed by the overwhelming presence of the domestic sphere—the realm of women and emotion. Much of the forward projection of the narrative relies on the endless exchange of women as Franz's sexual partners. They function within the narrative to define different sides of the protagonist's emotions as his goal is tested throughout the film. His fatal flaw is a combination of violence and vulnerability with women; the "exchange" of women stands as a symbolic portrayal of the child/animal dichotomy. The novel refers to sex as one of many elements in life; sex and violence are the central underlying tensions in Fassbinder film. The violence done to women in *Berlin Alexanderplatz* borders on being unbearable. Yet slowly we become aware that Fassbinder parallels the violence of masculine dominant culture or "the street" with the nuturing of the feminine domestic sphere. This split explains the conflicting characteristics of Franz, who exhibits both violent masculine traits and gentle feminine traits.

Franz encounters women in the domestic world he inhabits. They are not distinguished by their goals or even by their varying social positions, since they all tend to be either prostitutes or jobless. Rather, the film defines them according to classical norms of physical and emotional types; consequently, they are portrayed as strikingly passive. The "fat Polish Lina" of the novel is transformed in the film into the slim, doe-eyed Lina played by Elisabeth Trissenaar (an even more traditional female role than the more active Hanni she played in *Bolwieser*). She is defined by her Catholicism and her unquestioning belief in Franz. The widow is represented as frail and nervous. She is followed by Franze, who is overweight and sentimental. The next woman, Cissy, is defined by her theatrical style and exaggerated emotions. Emmy is playful. And the final woman, Mieze, perhaps the most developed female portrayal in the series, has the depth of a child. Nevertheless, as a childlike prostitute, she is the most ideal woman, a classic portrayal of desire as she plays out male fantasies of the passive and dependent sexual child/woman.

Melodrama: Subjectivity and Self-Consciousness

This emphasis on women and the domestic realm emanates from Fassbinder's use of the melodrama genre. His television adaptations are marked by a high degree of emotional subjectivity endemic to their melodramatic style. In melodrama everything is subsumed by the subjective display of emotion. Classical narration typically works on an "objective" level to display what characters say or do. Many classical Hollywood films, however, move temporarily to subjective moments (a point-of-view shot) but return quickly to the objective reporting of external character action. Up to this point, I have presented *Berlin Alexanderplatz*'s narration as objective, but an inordinate number of subjective narrational devices clash with the forward momentum of the narrative. As Thomas Elsaesser has pointed out, the narrative is "anything but economical."[18] How do we reconcile these melodramatic moments with the classical narration?

Throughout the series, Franz Biberkopf teeters on the verge of emotional breakdown. His instability and volatility cause him to beat, rape, and murder women. This becomes particularly overwhelming to the viewer because the women are simple melodramatic types who are subjected to sexual violence usually reserved for pornography. The most symbolic portrayal of a woman is the repeated flashback of Franz's brutal murder of Ida. Ida is pure victim. We see only her bloody visage as she screams before collapsing. On this level, Fassbinder's characterization of women differs little from the physical or emotional melodramatic types of Hollywood except that the codes of the art cinema allow for the open display of violence and sex. And like the women he brutalizes, Franz falls victim to the violence of the patriarchal culture and the street as he too slowly becomes a melodramatic type — a victim.

Yet we are still sympathetic to his plight. How is this accomplished? And how do we balance such violent emotionalism with a theory of classical narration? Fassbinder critics suggest that the emotional excess ruptures the film's objective status. They assume that there is a norm of plausibility that, when it is stretched, shatters the film as a self-contained and self-sustaining world, creating a self-consciousness of the text as "text." But as a whole, Hollywood melodramas have avoided this through a careful give and take between objective and subjective narration. Excessive moments are recouped. *Berlin Alexanderplatz* offers a test of this, given the extreme emotional states that motivate much of the film's action.

Although in chapter 5 I described Fassbinder's use of melodrama as primarily stylistic, it serves an important narrational role in *Berlin Alexanderplatz*. Melodramas usually depend more than other genres on omniscient narration, which allows the audience more knowledge than the protagonist. It enhances the emotional tension as the character discovers what we already know.

Berlin Alexanderplatz, however, confines itself to Franz Biberkopf's restricted knowledge (in contrast to our omniscience in *Bolwieser*). The series is more like the detective genre, which demands unusual identification with the protagonist. Yet instead of the objective third-person use of the camera in these classical Hollywood films, *Berlin Alexanderplatz* demands a deeper psychological understanding of its protagonist. From the opening scenes of the first episode, "The Punishment Begins," Franz's punishment becomes ours as we dip into his subjective point of view. At least three-fourths of the film directly follows Franz's action, which deepens our identification with his triumphs and failures. The film stays with Franz most closely at the beginning and the end, partially to establish and reestablish our identification with him. The pattern illustrates the degree to which character subjectivity guides the film's narration.

Fassbinder uses a number of devices to develop Franz's emotional perspective as the narrational strategy. On an objective level, Franz acts in an extremely volatile manner in the opening episode. He is defined by his horrified and pitiful reaction to being released from prison, but we get even greater insight into his emotional state through the internally subjective flashbacks to his murder of Ida. This act of extreme violence is repeated four times within the series. Nevertheless, melodrama is a genre that conventionalizes such extremes: it "assumes violent and overly-charged attitudes."[19]

Whereas Döblin maintains the ironic distance of a modernist as he reports scenes such as Ida's murder, Fassbinder dispenses with much of the distance. Fassbinder's Franz acts out all the graphic emotional details endemic to the genre. Although the voice-over and superimpositions offer some distance, the objective narration of what Franz does and says takes on emotional immediacy when it is laced with the subjective memory of Ida's bloody face appearing in close-ups as she breathes her last words.

Brutal acts are carefully juxtaposed with scenes of Franz's tenderness and childlike innocence. He rapes a woman, but he brings her aprons when he has no money. After attacking Mieze, he takes the battered woman to the country in a halcyon scene that leaves the claustrophobic confines of the Berlin interior for the first time. The Franz who can beat, rape, and murder can also sing national songs with heartwarming gusto and make beer glasses talk. He can worry about a caged bird's health and simply beam his warm-hearted smile and women melt. Such contradictory extremes of behavior create the emotional ebb and flow of the melodrama. The unpredictability arouses our curiosity; we never know how Franz will react as either victim or victimizer. Consequently, we are forced into a contradictory position: we attempt to understand the emotions of a personality, but the personality is essentially two-sided and lacking in complexity.

Indeed, the most common indication of Franz's emotions is the internal commentary or mental subjectivity. Such devices include dreams, fantasies, memories, and hallucinations. Fassbinder employs an unusual number of cinematic equivalents for mental images in *Berlin Alexanderplatz*. In fact, the sheer number of them tests the traditional balance between the subjective moments and the objective narrational frame that defines the classical melodramatic code.

Three of the most subjective scenes in the film — the Ida flashback, Franz's endless drunk, and the dream in the epilogue — are all solidly grounded in objective narrational cues. The flashback to Ida's murder occurs as a guilty memory when Franz is emotionally aroused. The flashback reappears as he rapes Minna and as he beats Mieze (an evocation of his initial act). The hallucinatory quality of the later scene (Franz lies drunk throughout) is apparently motivated by alcohol. The scene becomes a haze of shapeless biblical images, disembodied voices, and fragmented actions.

The subjectivity of this scene is furthered by an aural depth. A steady din of voices overwhelms the scene as the beer man's wife gossips about the lives of her neighbors. Simultaneously, a single voice sings a maniacally repeated series of high chords. The game of chess between Franz and his neighbor wavers between the symbolism of a quasi-biblical revelation (as in Bergman's *Seventh Seal*) and a sober, but also highly literate, game of chess (à la *My Dinner with Andre*). Even Fassbinder's voice-over narration throughout the film is ambiguous: it could be either an externalization of Franz Biberkopf's thoughts or Fassbinder's or Döblin's musings. This play of textual motivation becomes more explicit as Fassbinder's ethereal presence becomes increasingly dominant throughout the series.

The epilogue's dream sequence shares this playfulness as Fassbinder announces it in the episode's title: "My Dream of Franz Biberkopf's Dream." On one level, there is an obvious case of Fassbinder commentary ("My Dream" with the 1970s pop iconography in a 1920s milieu is the most obvious cue). But the dream is still textually motivated—the hallucinatory nightmare of nervous breakdown. It is framed by Franz's stay in the hospital.

Significantly, temporal relations in *Berlin Alexanderplatz* are motivated in an even more ambiguous way. They go beyond *Bolwieser*'s use of fade-in and fade-out as a temporal device. In fact, the series lacks devices to indicate duration. We often cannot tell how much time has lapsed between episodes. How much time passes between Franz's disappearance after Lüders's betrayal and his reappearance drunk in a rented room in the next episode? What is the time frame between Franz's being crushed under the car and his apparent recovery in Eva's apartment? We never know.

In classical narration, characters fill in these gaps, explaining in the dialogue how much time has passed. Or pages jump off a calendar to tell us the time lapse between events. There are just enough textual cues in *Berlin Alexanderplatz* to provide some logic to the film's causal construction, including a few dialogue hooks ("Let's go to Neue Welt"). But overall, unexplained temporal gaps remain. These gaps relate specifically to the changes in the narration of Franz's subjective states as he grows more unreliable and unstable as a protagonist and point of identification.

The narrative parallels the indeterminacy involved in Franz's emotional health. All we know is that this is 1927 in the Weimar Republic. The amorphous use of film time stands in direct opposition to how the film so self-consciously states historical time. Perched at the moment of the rise of fascism, the film draws attention to the "times" through a loosening of temporal cause and effect. Here the role of history determines structure as time stops in the film. *Berlin Alexanderplatz* offers a case study of the prefascist person-ality—the psychological history of the people of the Weimar period. Again, the classical importance of a goal-centered protagonist recedes across the fifteen hours in the face of another competing narrational presence: the larger force of history.

The temporal gaps in *Berlin Alexanderplatz* increase the sense that a larger, arbitrary force is now in control. Conventionally, in similar classical melodramas, the narration often skips over time. We wonder what has hap-pened in the interval, but the narration forces us to accept it and move on to a new plot. Fassbinder combines selective suppression of information with an unprecedented subjective depth of information about the protago-nist's character, thereby adding a heightened self-consciousness to his series. A noticeable hand guides the narrative. What exactly "it" is—fate, history, or the author—we learn only over the course of the fourteen-hour series and specifically in the epilogue.

The few times when we depart from Franz's knowledge are part of an important narrational strategy: they come when Franz is physically or psy-chologically crushed by betrayal—when Lüders blackmails the widow, when the car runs over Franz's arm. The scenes reveal the reactions of others (particularly women), not Franz's. His girlfriends' tormented lack of knowl-edge about his state calculatedly wrings emotions from us. The film con-trasts the extremely emotional and distraught reactions of the women to the more pragmatic reactions of the men: Lüders's uncaring reaction to Franz's disappearance, the Pums gang's lack of reaction to Franz's supposed death.

Although it is used sparingly, this omniscient narration grows more prevalent over the course of the film, paralleling Franz's growing failure to accomplish his goal and therefore to control the narrative as a classical pro-tagonist does. Each failure of Franz's pledge further loosens the viewer's tie to his point of view. The most marked change comes when Franz is run over by the car halfway through the series. His dismemberment signals a kind of emasculation within the narrative. He becomes an inactive protag-onist, bordering on either a modernist figure in existential crisis or a melo-dramatic victim unable to act. We see Franz's physical abilities discussed by the Pums gang as basically "nondangerous." In his absence, Mieze and Eva discuss *their* decision for Eva to have a baby by Franz. Here women take over the protagonist's defining power—his animal sexuality.

Through the growing number of his narrational absences, Franz is sym-bolically weakened or feminized as he becomes associated with the domes-tic world and feminine passivity. Reinhold takes over the plot. This process begins when Reinhold stops Mieze in the stairwell and is completed in one of the film's most emotion-filled scenes, when he assaults and murders her in the woods. This scene repeats the central power game for Franz and Reinhold: the control of women. And Franz's feminization reaches its apogee in the dream, where Franz is seen in drag.

The movement of power is underscored in two cinematic ways. First, the scene breaks away from the closed and safer interior spaces of the city and moves to the forest, which dwarfs and overwhelms these small human figures. Second, Reinhold's assault calls to mind not only the setting of Franz and Mieze's most idealistic moment, but also the motions and the space of Franz's earlier fall in the woods. This scene is the death of Franz's narrational ability to direct the story. He loses control of the action that defines the classic goal-oriented protagonist as Reinhold visually takes over Franz's space. The intensity of the viewer's former emotional identification with Franz's goal is matched by the viewer's despair at this switch in narrational strategy. Franz's absence is painfully conspicuous in a film that was marked by his omnipresence. Once a relatively active agent and brutalizer of women, Franz is now only a passive protagonist: a victim of his own victimizing.

Finally, it is necessary to address the relationship between fate and self-consciousness in *Berlin Alexanderplatz's* melodramatic narration. So far I have posited two narrational forces: the film as its own narrator, as in classical Hollywood films, and the intercession of history in this stylized restaging of a historical period. But melodrama presents yet another narrational force: fate, which has been defined as "the principle or determining cause or will by which things in general are believed to come to be as they are or events to happen as they do."[20] This narrational cause has varied in connotation with the changing influence of religion, economics, and ideology on melodrama's short history. All these potential sources are cited in the Fassbinder series, which chronicles, with biblical overtones, an impoverished underclass caught between the rising forces of communism and fascism.

This amorphous presence of fate is also made manifest through narrative strategies. First, the Fassbinder series revolves around coincidence. Characters such as Merk and Eva appear out of nowhere, like avenging angels sent to rescue Franz from the depths of his emotional crises. Consider the parallel euphoric presentations of these two characters as they arrive on the scene. Merk runs into Franz by chance on the street below Minna's after the rape. The change in tone is noticeable. Horns blare when Merk steps out of the dark in a shot-reverse-shot sequence. Merk calls: "Franz." Franz answers quizzically, "Merk?" Their initial formality is replaced with a close-up of the two men hugging—an affirmation of a love that transcends Franz's previous violence. Similarly, Eva later appears out of nowhere to rescue Franz during his drunken bout. As she steps out of the dark, she says, "It's me, Eva." Similar music soars. A correspondingly stylized introduction to Reinhold also occurs. He too steps out of the shadows. He does not hail Franz, but stutters satanically as eerie pipe music rises—a noticeable contrast to Eva's parallel appearance. This stylization of "good" versus "bad" makes the patterning of coincidences conspicuous.

In fact, chance encounters—the Hasidic Jew of the Zannovich tale and Franz's spiritual renewal, the rightist and the selling of the *Völkischer Beobachter* newspaper, the widow and Lüders's deception, and the beating of Bruno with Franz's subsequent involvement in the Pums heist—steer Franz's actions as much as his own self-determined goals. Although there is no set pattern to these coincidences, their repetition over nearly fifteen hours increases the feeling that the external influence of melodramatic fate is at work.

This chain of chance meetings is augmented by the staging. As the camera disengages from Franz and cranes above the growing chaos of the street in the opening shots, we become conscious of the style of the series. Traditionally ascribed to Fassbinder's filmic signature, the style of *Berlin Alexanderplatz* exceeds the classical narrational method of unobtrusive storytelling. The most noticeable and repeated stylistic devices are what many describe as Fassbinder's devices: camera movement that obscures our clear view of the action, continual reframing based on visual patterns and not character movement, and, finally, the most striking device—the use of music.

Against the background of melodramatic narration, these moments of stylization can be "naturalized" as either an externalization of the protagonist's inner states or the intrusion of fate. These devices become apparent when Franz loses emotional balance: the courtyard spins, the sound track becomes an indiscernible clatter of voices, chance thunderstorms boom. Yet in *Berlin Alexanderplatz* there is less use of style than in either *Bolwieser* or *Chinese Roulette* with their roving camera movement. The cinematic style in the television series is more subservient to the telling of the story than one would expect of a Fassbinder film.

But on another level, the sound track assumes the greatest self-consciousness. Each of the major characters is assigned a musical motif that varies in style and tempo depending on the emotional state of its subject. Franz's theme—a simple series of harmonica chords—parallels Franz's emotional state. A soaring refrain of Franz's music often marks the end of a scene, but these optimistic chords begin to strike a false note over the course of the film as we realize that the hand of fate will fall again in the next episode.

All Hollywood genres use music to add emotional texture, but such self-conscious use of musical motifs to underscore the obvious has been conventionalized by the film melodrama. A good example is Max Steiner's score for *Mildred Pierce,* in which he assigns different motifs to Mildred and her children and weaves them for maximal emotional effect at her child's death scene.[21] Similarly, the up-and-down renditions of Franz's harmonica motif in episode after episode repeat the cyclical highs and lows in the protagonist's life. Franz's music telegraphs the fated nature of his actions.

Unlike classical narration, which poses a world that can be adequately explained and represented, melodramatic narration utilizes such classical narrational strategies to reveal the limits of the will of the protagonist. Specifically, melodrama attests to a deeper level of experience—a world beyond rational knowledge. Here human actions are driven by forces, desires, and fears that operate without rational explanation. Such a world allows for the logical motivation of Franz's contradictory personality as both brute and child. But this character-centered motivation slowly recedes as the objective narration disappears. Replacing the protagonist as the center of plot, the invisible hand of a larger narrational presence slowly steps out of the shadowy world of *Berlin Alexanderplatz*: the *Autor.*

Self-Consciousness: Melodrama and Modernism

Although they are often seen as stylistic and ideological opposites, Hollywood melodrama and the modernist art cinema share an important antirealist bias—an overt self-consciousness. Classical Hollywood narration attempts to present an unproblematic concept of realism. Its art "imitates" life—a fundamental principle of nineteenth-century aesthetics before modernism. Although melodrama does not challenge the classical view that one can adequately represent reality, it attacks the principle that our world can be understood through rational explanation. Rather, melodrama presents a world directed by emotional and metaphysical logic outside the character's self-willed actions—"something lost, inadmissible, repressed ties to its atavistic past."[22] On the other hand, the modernism of the art cinema also attacks the adequacy of representation to depict "reality." The art cinema assumes modernism's relativistic notion of "reality," in which, according to

David Lodge, "denotation is swamped by connotation, in which there are no narratives or logical climaxes but instead vibrant, suggestive, ambiguous images and symbols."[23]

So far, my analysis of *Berlin Alexanderplatz*'s classical and melodramatic narrational procedures has purposely omitted the role that the art cinema narration plays in the film's interpretation. I did this in order to reveal the degree to which much of the series can be read without recourse to the director/author as the principal organizing figure. Although there are moments within the film that can only be read as ethereal comment, it is important to point out how the film's melodrama and art film narrations share an unusual degree of character subjectivity, and therefore the stylized extremes of the film can be read as internally consistent.

Fassbinder marginalizes the irony and distance of both the Döblin novel and the art cinema's narrational techniques, but he retains the narrational depth of melodrama and the art cinema. In so doing, he combines the role once played by fate and history with that of the art film director. As a result, the film wavers between character subjectivity and directorial authority as sources of the film's extreme emotional directness. Here Fassbinder's statement that he is the protagonist takes on a narrational context. Franz Biberkopf's slow loss of self-will and narrational presence is paralleled by Fassbinder's growing presence. By comparing the series to the art cinema, we see how the film produces an unprecedented tension between the protagonist and the director as the center of the film's logic.

Nevertheless, *Berlin Alexanderplatz* as an art film has an ambivalent relationship with the art cinema's use of objective realism. First, the series does not share the art cinema's interest in "real" or topical subject matter. Although the Fassbinder series does revolve around the current issue of social and interpersonal repression, its emphasis is on the Weimar period and on the quirky emotional nature of Franz's reactions, which weakens the film's ties to contemporary reality. The violence and sexual explicitness are outgrowths of the conventions of the art cinema's postwar realism (reaction to Hollywood's code) and the traditional extremes of the melodrama genre. The film also undercuts this objective realism with its classical studio-style sets and acting performances. It sheds much of the verisimilitude of on-location shooting and favors professional actors placed in a controlled environment similar to the sets of Hollywood films.

Highlighting the chaotic realities of day-to-day existence, the art cinema and *Berlin Alexanderplatz* share a basic interest in loosening the causal link of events. On this level, the film's construction stands as a modernist structure—fragments of Biberkopf's life. There is no particular reason for the choice of episodes other than to present slices of Franz's life. In fact, the film tends to highlight scenes that have no apparent importance for the narrative's movement other than to reveal a facet of Franz's personality. Clearly *Berlin Alexanderplatz* shares the art cinema's interest in characterization as opposed to Hollywood's interest in plot movement. Fassbinder's film supports the modernist open-ended sense of causality. It emphasizes the indeterminacy of Franz's life, as the film's primary goal becomes reaction, not action—the study of the protagonist's character.

Although the Fassbinder series shares a similar analysis of the vagaries of character, it employs many elements of a more classical portrayal of character. For all his inconsistent behavior, Franz has clear, albeit contradictory, traits: childlike simplicity and a violent temper. Unlike Thomas's goal in Antonioni's *Blowup*, Franz's is a bit broad, but clear: to remain upstanding. As a result, his attempt to stay out of trouble forms a plot line. However, the breadth of his goal fits the art cinema's more existential or passive concept of motivation than is typical of classical or even melodramatic narration, which depends on a decisive act or event to end the film. Franz Biberkopf becomes more of a reactive than an active figure as the outside world motivates his actions and thus the narrative.

The film is constructed around a classic art cinema plot: the biography of an individual. And like Thomas's race around London pop culture in *Blowup*, Franz's movement from episode to episode exposes Berlin's underworld; this survey form is common to the art cinema. But unlike the passive itinerary of the art film character, Franz's movement is directed—from without. Whether it be an individual nemesis such as Lüders or Reinhold, a historical economic or political force (the state in the form of a legal directive or unemployment), or an even larger and more amorphous force such as fate, it is the goal-directed actions of others, not Franz, that move *Berlin Alexanderplatz*'s plot. Franz careens through Berlin like a pinball, flying violently from one catalytic event to another. Our interest is sustained by the "roulette" of the outside world's goals coinciding with Franz's passivity. Significantly, it is at moments of conflict with the goals of women that Franz attempts to assert control. His brutal actions come not from his own plans, however, but from a fear of feminine passivity.

The art cinema character is typically too ambiguous to be the simple melodramatic victim that Franz portrays. Taking their inspiration from the literature of the first quarter of the twentieth century, these modernist characters usually are exceptionally astute observers of the human condition. Often they have unusual insights into the inconsistencies of modern existence: consider the long philosophical monologues endemic to Bergman films, particularly *Cries and Whispers,* or even Fellini's oddly knowing simpletons. In contrast, Franz Biberkopf—a simple proletarian—spends his time confused about how the world around him functions. Each bit of bad news shocks him. Even after his dream and his stay in the mental hospital, Franz does not grow in awareness of the fundamental issues of life. He lacks the distance, the knowingness, of the modern man.

This refusal to offer Biberkopf even a moment of insight becomes evident when one considers how Fassbinder altered Döblin's intent. I have already discussed how Berlin recedes in importance as a parallel to Franz's character in the Fassbinder version. More importantly, Döblin's playful use of language and associational structure loses much of its modernist distance by being put into the mouth and reveries of Franz Biberkopf, thus creating a logical source. For example, when Franz throws water at Lüders, what is read in the novel as a nonsensical ethereal interjection—"Our little hands go clap clap clap, our little feet go tap tap tap"—becomes the confused and frustrated words of Biberkopf as he plays in a puddle in the film.[24] Additionally, odd factual information inserted into Döblin's whimsical narration often becomes a newspaper item that a character reads aloud: consider Lina's announcement of the unemployment figure for Berlin or the whore's reading of a scientific description of the causes of male impotence. Döblin's language in the mouths of Franz and the others loses much of its original iconoclastic linguistic anarchy.

When Franz speaks these nonsensical and dislocated statements, the film gives them logical motivation. They are either the result of a change in Franz's emotional state or examples of his childlike perspective on the world. For example, as Franz gets up with great enthusiasm after forced sex with Minna, Döblin comments ironically, "Franz Biberkopf is back again! Franz is discharged! Franz is free!"[25] In the film, these statements are made by Franz as he innocently celebrates his own pleasures without any consideration of their ramifications. Fassbinder's Biberkopf is a less ironic figure than Döblin's. Indulging in the sentimentalism of melodramatic typing, Fassbinder created a more tragically innocent figure. Again, the knowingness that Döblin's humorous language plays in the novel recedes. Even Fassbinder's infrequent voice-over use of the novel's ironic commentary and his insertion of titles, equations, and quotations do not overwhelm the melodrama to the degree that Döblin's language does in the novel. Fassbinder integrates

the novelist's modernist interjections into characters' utterances as part of
the fiction.

Finally, the series' boundary situation — Biberkopf's dream — does not
function as art cinema does. Typically, art films are built around a causality
based on a character's (or a narrator's) growing awareness of the human condition. This structure comes to fruition in the boundary situation, when "a
presented persona, a narrator, or an implied reader becomes aware of meaningful as against meaningless existence."[26] But in the Fassbinder series, the
dream functions as Franz's lobotomy. The result is Franz's long-sought-after
respectability. In the end, he is an obedient servant of the middle class —
the tragic ending of Franz's melodramatic existence.

Franz's flaw is that he is too simple and too much a victim to see
clearly. But because the sources of his repression keep changing, it is hard
to say whether the film posits a "correct" reality or point of view. Only with
the dream and the end of the film does the narrator's presence clearly appear. It is in "My Dream of Franz Biberkopf's Dream" that the narrator finally establishes the series' perspective. Here the play of the series' three
levels of narration — objective realism, subjective realism, and authorial commentary — fall into the ambiguous motivational play of objective realism,
character subjectivity, and ethereal commentary — the hallmark of art cinema narration.

Given the possible sources of character subjectivity in *Berlin Alexanderplatz,* one can understand most of the film's atmospheric touches without
recourse to the director as a controlling agent. Most of the nonobjective
techniques — dreams, hallucinations, stylized mise-en-scène, the emotion-
filled sound track — can be traced to an embodiment of Franz's or another
character's mental state, fate, or history. Since the hallmark of both melodrama
and the art cinema is a focus on the character's psychology, Fassbinder's
specific mixture of the two forms puts greater weight on character subjectivity as the source of the film's self-consciousness. With a normal art cinema film, one would look for a systematic use of stressed devices as an indication of authorial commentary.

"My Dream of Franz Biberkopf's Dream": Authorial Commentary, Autobiography, and the Epilogue

For all my efforts to deny a reading of the series as art cinema in favor of a
classic melodramatic form, *Berlin Alexanderplatz* is "a Fassbinder film." But
one can understand most of the series without recourse to Fassbinder as a

structural agent. It is only with the abrupt change in narrational form and content in the epilogue that Fassbinder—the *Autor* and autobiographical figure—comes forward to determine our reading.

The marks of authorship prior to the epilogue—the voice-over, the episode titles, the superimposed titles—can all be directly linked to the Döblin novel. Although the voice-over is Fassbinder's, the text he reads is verbatim from the novel. The ironic style and content of the words are in direct opposition to the film's tragic and straightforward narration. Fassbinder's recitation is marked by the slow and even tone of someone reading aloud. In fact, the quoting of Döblin's ironic modernist pronouncements is at the beginnings and ends of episodes—a privileged position reserved for the original work's authority.

The novel as the source of the voice-over's ironic content is underscored by the fact that the title of each episode contains the same formal irony. For example, episodes three and eight are entitled "A Hammer to the Head Can Hurt the Soul" and "The Sun Warms the Skin Which Sometimes Burns." Additionally, these titles are printed over an opening montage of documentary photographs from the 1920s, reiterating that the novel is a historical retelling. The series employs German script—Fraktur—for all the titles from the Döblin novel and the superimposed words within the narrative. The use of script indicates Döblin's own writing in that the novel, published in the 1920s, was printed in Fraktur. Fassbinder also signals Döblin's written original by printing all superimposed words and symbols on a white background, suggesting a book page.

At best, Döblin's modernism is marginalized in the film. Its cyclical use calls attention to the constructed nature of only part of the film. The modernist source is more literary than filmic. The irony is reserved for written or spoken language—not cinematic language such as editing or the mise-en-scène. It calls attention to the issue of Döblin's authorship more than Fassbinder's. In fact, the film's serious melodramatic content and style are in direct opposition to the irony and playfulness of the novel. This creates two parallel works held together by an interest in the character's subjectivity.

As a result, Fassbinder's auteur role is suppressed for most of the series. His signature is more evident in the choice of genre and the excesses of violence and sex than in a set of formal principles that run throughout the series. The heavily laden camera work of *Bolwieser* and especially *Chinese Roulette* disappears in favor of continuity editing. However, there are still select uses of camera movement, such as when the camera moves behind a fish tank to film the rape of Minna through the murky water, or when, as

Eva and Mieze discuss Eva's having a baby by Franz, the camera leaves its focus on the two women to film through a monkey cage. Such overt visual commentary is infrequent, but over the almost-fifteen-hour series, a pattern does develop. Such obscuring of our vision distances us from some of the film's intense moments of emotional expression. This visual commentary does not come often, and the pattern becomes evident only halfway through the series. It is the series' reward to the cinephile — similar to an art cinema viewer's recognition of a signature across an auteur's oeuvre.

Fassbinder's most overt assertion of his presence comes with the abrupt change in narrational mode in the epilogue. Subtitled "From the Death of a Child to the Birth of a Useful Person," the epilogue breaks away from the straightforward melodramatic narration into modernist narration. After Franz's nervous breakdown brought on by Mieze's murder, the film becomes a surrealistic nightmare. The episode intercuts seemingly objective scenes of Franz's stay in prison and the mental hospital with his subjective nightmare.

The film cuts quickly through numerous short scenes that review Franz's life, but in altered form: they are part of a madman's dream and Fassbinder's private symbolism. The epilogue opens in a cemetery populated by a majority of the film's characters, who are taunting Franz for his fatal flaws. This scene changes to a jail, where Reinhold makes love with a fellow inmate. From this scene we cut to a replay of Franz losing his arm as he is run over, only this time his friends Eva and Herbert are in the car. Then we see Franz and Reinhold meeting in jail, and as Franz passes Reinhold a knowing look passes between them. This is replaced by a scene in the forest where Reinhold, Ida, and Franz consecutively lie in the spot where Mieze was killed. This scene is interrupted by the image of an underground train station and a marching Nazi storm trooper, quickly intercut by communists tracing the same pattern.

Next we are greeted with an "objective" scene in the mental hospital, where a young doctor takes an interest in the catatonic Biberkopf. The doctor force-feeds him while he defends Franz's sanity. The logic of this scene is replaced by scenes of Reinhold in drag and the straitjacketed Franz eating out of a bowl on the floor as hundreds of rats encircle him. The Jewish sausage vendor is reintroduced, now selling concentration camp dolls. These short scenes lead to scenes of a slaughterhouse (an image introduced earlier in the film) where human beings are killed and hung like meat. Throughout these scenes two angels, Terah and Serug, guide Franz. The Döblin novel's commentary (earlier Fassbinder's voice-over) becomes their conversation. We can easily understand these sections resulting from character psychology — they are the fragmented dream of a madman.

The entire episode culminates in an apocalyptic scene of Franz's crucifixion, which is intercut by an image of an atomic bomb exploding to a 1960s tune. Anachronisms abound. On a self-consciously theatrical stage, Franz is slowly lifted up on a cross; the backdrop is Hieronymus Bosch's *Garden of Earthly Delights*. In the foreground is the Holy Family: Franz's landlady as the Virgin Mary, holding a baby Jesus doll with Franz's visage. Encircling this quasi-biblical scene are nude couples having an orgy. The characters pray before the crucifix. Cases of Coca-Cola, classical statues, and palm trees are interspersed on the stage. Simultaneously, a group of young people carry out a nude orgy — a "love-in" — on the stage. Intercut into this pop passion play are shadowy close-ups of Fassbinder, half-obscured, watching. During the scene the narrator comments on the crucifixion, Franz's death, and his rebirth as a new man.

The kaleidoscopic nature of these quickly cut scenes superficially reflects the energy of Döblin's style, but it also asserts Fassbinder's previously suppressed presence. The most obvious assertion is the post-Döblin iconography. From the concentration camp dolls to the atomic bomb to the 1960s references, the director not only comments on the series but also draws a causal line between prefascist Weimar culture and the youth culture of the 1960s and 1970s.

In his art films Fassbinder was always more directly concerned with the relation of West Germany to its fascist past. Anton Kaes argues that, like Walter Benjamin, Fassbinder "wanted to deal with the 'constellation' of past and present, with the moment of recognition in which the past and present mutually illuminate each other."[27] The conclusion of *The Marriage of Maria Braun,* where Fassbinder shows a series of portraits of every German chancellor from Hitler to the present (except Willy Brandt), stands as a classic metonymy for this "constellation." The abrupt change in style and narration in the conclusion, however, indicates that Fassbinder breaks with his depiction of the linearity of the past and the present.

Rather, the epilogue functions more as a usurpation of the history, aesthetics, and cultural authority of modernism by a new generational aesthetic and a new spokesman, as announced in Fassbinder's title: "My Dream of Franz Biberkopf's Dream." Significantly, the epilogue's style harks back to Fassbinder's theater work. The multimedia assault of music, filmed inserts, and mise-en-scènes from different periods is related to the direct action method of demonstration theater. The epilogue intersperses pop music sung by Janis Joplin ("Me and Bobby McGee"), Elvis Presley ("Santa Lucia"), the Velvet Underground ("Candy Says"), Leonard Cohen ("Chelsea Hotel"), Donovan ("Atlantis"), and Dean Martin ("Silent Night") with classical music by Handel (Organ Concerto no. 10), Richard Strauss (*Der Rosenkavalier*), Schubert (*Der Tod und das Mädchen*), and Wagner (*Tristan und Isolde*). There is no attempt at logical transitions between historical styles; it is like a modern-day battle of the bands.

In fact, most of the scenes have a presentational quality as the actors play to the camera and audience. Also, the epilogue presents metacabaret performances about Franz and the series. The style as well as the theatrical violent and sexual content serve as a visceral assault distancing the viewer from the fiction — similar to the Living Theater model for Fassbinder's Action Theater.

More importantly, the juxtaposition of the sacrosanct and the taboo — the Holy Family, the Third Reich, Wagner's music, Bosch's *Garden of Earthly Delights* — with pop iconography — Coca-Cola, the bomb, and rock music — owes its impetus to shock pop. It is as if under the weight of popularizing a modernist "great work" in a melodrama, Fassbinder bursts through in the epilogue to take over Döblin's authorial role. Not only does Fassbinder rewrite the form and content of the series around the priorities of his countercultural generation, he unmasks the authority of the text as the personal confession of an artist and a homosexual.

Inserted into this subjective malaise are classic Fassbinder melodramatic objective scenes. Marked by melodramatic moments — knowing glances between Franz and Reinhold or the pathetic image of a half-dead Franz being force-fed — these scenes repeat Fassbinder's visual style of the late 1970s. They serve to anchor our "objective" understanding of Franz's recovery for the final scenes, in which we see him as a car attendant, but they are dominated by the multitude of causally unconnected modernist scenes. In fact, when the film returns to the final scenes of classical narration after Franz's cure, the change in style seems abrupt after the extremes of the epilogue. The self-consciousness of Fassbinder's guiding hand lingers over the final resolution of Franz as a broken but useful man — as the episode's subtitle, "From the Death of a Child to the Birth of a Useful Person," telegraphs to us.

Finally, the epilogue allows Fassbinder to state his own interpretation of Franz's fatal flaw: repressed homosexual desire for Reinhold. Instead of Döblin's faceless authorial interjections, Fassbinder finally removes the veil of authorial authority and interjects his biography. Up to this point, the series has set up a clear heterosexual opposition between masculine violent aggression and feminine passive suffering—a classic Fassbinder dichotomy. Franz's attraction to Reinhold has been a more generalized, biblical temptation—sexual or material—as the title of the episode of their initial meeting emphasizes: "A Reaper with the Power of God."

Reinhold's presence throughout has had a homoerotic sexual ambiguity. With his stutter and his long skinny body, he exudes a satanic sensuality as he spits out his first words in the film. In fact, the film underscores Reinhold as a visual embodiment of the tempter of Eden. His first encounter with Franz is more flirtation than fraternal: the two coyly stare at each other as dangerously evocative pipes play. After this initial meeting, Reinhold's friendship exerts an "unnatural" hold on Franz; Franz dissolves love affairs for Reinhold, does not "rat" on Reinhold when Franz loses his arm, and finally does not recognize Reinhold's essential evilness, which results in the death of Franz's one true love, Mieze. Franz's power ends as the narration moves away from his point of view; Reinhold's power takes over. It is a symbolic transition in the series' focus, from the potential of a self-willed protagonist to the failure of a passive "controlled" individual—victim of his own desires and a society that forced him to repress them.

In the epilogue, the underlying homosexual theme is made explicit—a solid break from the novel. The overt homosexual nature of this bond appears only in the montage of Franz's dream. The sources of Franz's failure are both his unhealthy attraction to Reinhold and a society that forces him to repress his feelings. The sex scene between Reinhold and a cell mate explicitly introduces the issue of homosexuality, but whether Franz's attraction to Reinhold is purely homosexual is never directly stated. Rather, it is inferred. As Reinhold makes love to the young man, he speaks of his anger at Franz, for whom, he protests, "I basically feel nothing."

The ambiguity of this attraction between the film's protagonist and its antagonist is carried through a series of surreal encounters between them. First, they exchange glances of odd recognition as they pass each other in a jailhouse hall. These glances are repeated throughout their various interactions. Then Reinhold in drag whips Franz with a feather boa. He then punches Franz repeatedly in the stomach, yelling, "Yet another goal." Later, Franz appears made up to look like a woman. He discusses his suffering with Reinhold, now in a crown of thorns, who passes judgment on Franz's mortal suffering. This image of sacrifice is repeated in yet another scene as the Pums gang prepares to cut out his heart. As Franz begs for mercy and screams in agony as he is cut into, Reinhold smiles coyly in the foreground.

The encounters of these fatally attracted men culminate in a boxing match. As the scenes grow shorter, images of slaughter, of Franz's victims, and of Nazis become tightly intertwined, establishing a metaphoric comparison between the different victims. Juxtaposing these scenes with the boxing match ties Germany's historical victimization of the Jews to the failings of the Germans in the twenties and particularly to the unresolved sexual repression of German prefascist society. The two men battle while a whirl of larger-than-life people sit in judgment. The rear-screen-projected audience begins to spin and scream in a deafening roar. As pulsing electronic music reaches a crescendo, Reinhold pummels Franz to the ground and taunts Franz angrily: "I was not your taste. I know all of that. But wait, soon another one will come along." Franz, in near collapse, answers, "I am not the victor, I know that. I have not won." In this final encounter, Fassbinder leaves us with an ambiguous game of interference. As the director of a television series, he is as repressed as his protagonist, even in stating the issue of homosexual attraction directly.

Obviously, when Fassbinder proclaimed, "I am Biberkopf," he confessed and made Franz's unrequited homosexual desire explicit. It was a clever intertextual move for a television film that was to be an epic adaptation of a sanctioned work of German culture. The Fassbinder legend was read directly into the series. Fassbinder made Döblin's work his own, bringing to light what Foucault calls "the fragments of darkness" that empower the confessional.

Nevertheless, such a reading ignores the more complex history of how this ursurpation came about: the history of the *Autor* and how Fassbinder constructed a filmic form that questioned such authority. He transformed Döblin's protagonist into his own image and challenged the sanctity of official culture. *Berlin Alexanderplatz* remains a struggle between two German *Autoren* and their respective generational aesthetics: Döblin's modernism and Fassbinder's "pop"-ularized confession. This controversial battle began with the contradictions of a German film *Autor* who for television must be both an original individual and a representative of the German people. Fassbinder fulfilled this impossible responsibility with *Berlin Alexanderplatz* by publicly being both extraordinary and ordinary. He became the absent star of the series.

7 / The Popular Reception of *Berlin Alexanderplatz*

I read the novel five years later.... [I realized] that an enormous part of myself, my attitudes, my reactions, so many of the things I had considered all my own, were none other than those described by Döblin. I had ... unconsciously made Döblin's fantasy my own life.   Rainer Werner Fassbinder[1]

The adaptation from literature—especially when it contains expressionist passages—into a visual version is never unproblematic. This is where the ideas and the creativity of the director are demonstrated. Seen in this way Berlin Alexanderplatz *is a work that thoroughly carries the signature of the director, Rainer Werner Fassbinder. And for many viewers he did a good adaptation of the novel.*

WDR response to letters protesting
the broadcast of *Berlin Alexanderplatz*[2]

Fear and self-censorship.... [WDR is] simply saying [by rescheduling] that it is too pornographic.   Rainer Werner Fassbinder[3]

The broadcast of *Berlin Alexanderplatz* (October 1980–January 1981) is considered a failure within West Germany. From April 1980 to after its airing, the series was the focus of public controversy. There was a marked split between an overwhelmingly positive response from professional critics and a uniformly critical response from the viewing public. This occurrence offers an important case study in viewer reception or "the popular response" to an art film. The split between the press and the public contradicts the assumption that critics can and do condition the public reception of television and film. But can we then conclude that this controversy was a popular response by the German people who wanted to determine their culture?

On a certain level, we cannot. Much of the conservative condemnation was orchestrated. The tabloid press began prebroadcast attacks on the director and the rumored blasphemous content of the series in April. The Catholic Church spearheaded a six-month campaign of public denouncements and viewer letters to stop broadcast of the series. This expected conservative backlash, however, cannot fully account for the degree of division between the critics' and the viewing public's responses, which crossed political and religious allegiances. As Kristina Zerges points out, "Never before had the chasm been so great between professional critics, who enthusiastically praised the series, and the public, who rejected it."[4]

Berlin Alexanderplatz offers a remarkable opportunity to understand the relationship of cultural class to individual response. In addition to the ten months of intensive media coverage and the public debate, the response to the series was extensively surveyed by German researchers, led by Kristina Zerges, at the Technische Universität in Berlin. First the researchers analyzed the audience's social makeup—regional, professional, class, sex, and age differences—based on information provided by telejour, a West German equivalent of the Nielsen ratings. Then they constructed a survey based on the viewers' "subjective" response to the series for a selected region—the Nürnberg area. Finally, they analyzed viewer letters to Westdeutscher Rundfunk, the producing station.

Zerges and her colleagues wanted to understand why *Berlin Alexanderplatz* had failed in the public eye. As quantitative researchers, they were guided by a concept of "truth" as expressed in the "regularities" of their data. This "content analysis" has been defined as "a research technique for the objective, systematic, and quantitative description of the manifest content of communication."[5] Quantitative analysis looks at what is explicitly "there," or "the facts." Although the limitations of empirical analysis are too complex to cover here, the central problem, as stated by Robert Allen, is that "the principles of laboratory science greatly limit its ability to account for the complexities and subtleties of our engagement with those constructed worlds we see on television."[6]

Because Zerges was limited to manifest content of viewer mail and the letter campaign of the Catholic Church, her conclusions focused on how a "zealous minority" (the church hierarchy) could influence the "normal" reception of a television film or program.[7] Her content analysis does provide the data on who was watching and the degree to which they understood what they saw. The Catholic Church's letter campaign did fuel the anger against the series, but it cannot account for the array of responses.

As one reads over Zerges's results, an important qualitative pattern emerges: a debate about the role of high and low culture, and especially the rights of authorship or of the *Autor.* This chapter reconceptualizes reception analysis by balancing the quantitative analysis with a qualitative or interpretative analysis of "latent" content—the less "objective" issues of cultural codes and meanings. As in chapter 3, the application of Michel Foucault's discursive method allows the historian to interpret the more complex responses of the letters and the press. One still looks for the "regularities" that underlie empirical analysis, only they are wrapped in the complex cultural play of language, which calls for some interpretation. This chapter stems from, in addition to the data Zerges gathered, an analysis of over two hundred articles written about Fassbinder's *Berlin Alexanderplatz* in West Germany.

This perspective reveals sharp cultural divisions that structure perception of the social world and designate the objects of aesthetic enjoyment in West Germany. In fact, the controversy surrounding the Fassbinder film revolved more around a group's "cultural competence" with art cinema traditions (and particularly *Autorenfilme*) than around religious blasphemies. Pierre Bourdieu argues that these divisions come from social class differences in education, social origins, and exposure to "art."

This argument returns us to his notion of cultural capital, which I discussed in the introduction. As opposed to economic capital, cultural capital creates a class division based on not only knowledge of, but also the ability to define and produce, culture. Bourdieu writes, "When invested in the exercise of taste, cultural capital yields both a 'profit' in distinction, proportionate to the rarity of the means required to appropriate [cultural products] and a profit in legitimacy, the profit *par excellence* which consists in the fact of feeling justified in being (what one is), what it is right to be."[8] The class antagonisms brought out by *Berlin Alexanderplatz* began to expose the class bias or bourgeois underpinnings of the concept of *Autor.* But unfortunately, because of the ideology of aesthetic individualism within the *Autor* discourse, the debate was removed from the class and institutional context and displaced onto the individual artist. Not only the individual *Autor,* but also the homosexual Fassbinder, became its victim.

Major Events in the Production and Reception of *Berlin Alexanderplatz*

The *Berlin Alexanderplatz* television series was a coproduction of the Bavaria Atelier, Italian television (RAI), and the central sponsor, Westdeutscher Rundfunk (Cologne). Fassbinder's ten-year collaborator at WDR, Peter Märthesheimer, functioned as its producer. At a cost of 13 million marks (between $6 million and $7 million dollars), the series was West German television's most expensive undertaking to date. Nevertheless, the cost per minute for the epic series was less than that of the average television program.

Fassbinder completed the series in a relatively short time — between July 1979 and April 1980 — filming primarily at the Bavaria Atelier (the famed "Berlin" backlot) and in Berlin. The speed and economy of the production resulted from the fact that Fassbinder used a highly detailed script. Most of the primary actors had worked with Fassbinder before, and most of the scenes were filmed in one take. The film came in under budget. The series was unusual for a Fassbinder television film in that it was shot on thirty-five-millimeter film. The original plan was to film a feature version as well, but this never materialized because they received funding only for the television series.

Its fourteen parts and epilogue aired on Monday evenings between October and December 1980.[9] The series was initially to be televised at 8:15 p.m, West German television's most popular prime-time slot, but was pushed to the less-viewed 9:30 p.m. slot by the station in August 1980 as a result of the outcry over the content.[10] Although the series met with strong opposition within West Germany, it was sold to Sweden, Denmark, Finland, the Netherlands, and Yugoslavia by December 1980 — before it had completely aired on German television. Only Austria rejected it, based on the grounds that it violated Austrian pornography laws.

The series had been rumored for years by Fassbinder. Not only did he frequently use "Franz" as a pseudonym for his role as the film's editor and a character within his earlier films, but he began to speak of the projected filming of the novel as early as 1976. One can see Fassbinder dictating its script in his segment of *Germany in Autumn* in 1978. Explicit evidence of its production came from a series of articles published during filming. The first major promotional article appeared in the influential cultural weekly *Die Zeit* on March 3, 1980. In this article, Fassbinder admitted his aesthetic and autobiographical relation to the novel. Then two sensational articles on the filming of the epilogue appeared. The popular illustrated magazine

Quick reported inaccurately that the Holy Family was to appear nude in the epilogue.[11] These statements were then repeated in the Catholic weekly *Neue Bildpost* on September 7. By mid-September — three weeks before the airing of *Berlin Alexanderplatz* began — the series was already steeped in controversy.

The Quantitative Reception of *Berlin Alexanderplatz*

The 1983 analysis by Kristina Zerges documents the loss of viewership that the series experienced during the weeks it was broadcast by analyzing data provided by the ratings service telejour (see Appendix H).[12] The series began with 27 percent of the audience, or approximately 8.5 million viewers — an unprecedented audience share given the late viewing hour.[13] For episode two, the audience size shrunk to 22 percent. Episodes three and four continued the decline, with 18 and 11 percent of the potential viewership. This rapid drop was reversed by episode Five. Viewership then held steady through episodes ten, after which there was a slow loss of viewers until the epilogue.

The decline was fueled by a number of factors unrelated to content, according to Zerges. First, the large initial audience resulted from curiosity created by the extraordinary prepublicity. And ZDF, the Second Channel, competed with the Fassbinder series by offering a popular criminal series, *Tatort,* that ended in the evening before the Fassbinder series ended. This ZDF strategy drew away a number of working people who after their initial curiosity could not stay up for the late-night viewing.

The liberal-to-left North Rhine Westphalia region (WDR's homeland) had the highest regional viewership; Bavaria, West Germany's most conservative state, had the lowest. Despite the even later viewing hour for the epilogue (11:00 p.m.), the final segment drew 8 percent of the audience. The viewers, according to Zerges, tuned in to examine whether the epilogue was as blasphemous as the tabloids had reported.[14]

Significantly, the age of *Berlin Alexanderplatz* viewers ran counter to the art cinema's audience. Viewers over fifty were the largest group, undercutting the generalization that the art cinema and Fassbinder appeal primarily to a young "cineaste" audience. The smallest share of the audience was viewers between the ages of fourteen and twenty-nine. Viewers who were part of the countercultural movement — people ages thirty to forty-nine — fell in between the other two generations in terms of viewership.[15] The study concluded that the dominance of older people resulted partly from the fact that the series was moved into the late viewing hours (ending weekly at 11:30 p.m.); the viewer who was bound by a work or school schedule was less able to view the series.[16] On the whole, men and women watched the series in equal numbers.

Relationship of Socioeconomic Factors to the Aesthetic Reception of *Berlin Alexanderplatz*

In order to understand why the broad West German reception was negative, Zerges constructed a more specific regional study based on a questionnaire that was placed in the major newspapers of Nürnberg (*Nürnberger Nachtrichten*) and Berlin (*Berliner Morgenpost*). Although the survey was admittedly nonrepresentative (covering only two cities and aimed at viewers who read the newspaper), the response from Nürnberg revealed a significant pattern in what viewers found objectionable in *Berlin Alexanderplatz*.[17]

Of the respondents, 52.4 percent were male, 55 percent professed an Evangelical faith, 28.4 percent were between the ages of forty-seven and sixty-four, and 61.3 percent had a high school or better education. They were housewives, retired people, and white-collar workers. Of the 1,930 Nürnberg respondents, 87.4 percent had seen episode one and 96 percent had continued beyond the initial episode. The 4 percent who stopped watching the series gave, in descending order of importance, "sexually offensive," "boring," and "too poorly lighted" as their reasons for quitting. Among those who watched six or more episodes, the common denominator was age: viewers between thirty-five and forty-four made up 25.7 percent and those between forty-five and sixty-four 24 percent of the long-viewing audience.[18] The older the viewer, the more likely she or he watched the entire series.

Significantly, the decision to watch the series emanated more from the fact that it was adapted from a great German literary work than from Fassbinder's fame. A significant number of viewers (612) watched because of their acquaintance with the Döblin novel. Only one-eighth (241 respondents) of the Nürnberg audience was motivated by an interest in Fassbinder as a director. This statistical evidence supports the assertion that literary authorship plays a dominant role in West German culture.

The biggest impact on the viewers' choices came from newspapers and magazines (897 respondents), which ran numerous articles about production of the series; several published the novel in sections before the broadcast began. Other reasons given for watching the series were advice from friends (134), an example of world literature (127), television advertisement (76), "I am a Berliner" (50), the actors (47), and an interest in comparing the series to the 1929 Heinrich George film of the same title (32).

The viewer's age, sex, education, and social status also played a role. Men between the ages of nineteen and thirty-four made up the biggest segment of the audience: 52.1 percent. They were white-collar workers (25.5 percent), students (17.7 percent), pensioners (17.4 percent), and bureaucrats (17.2 percent). Television magazine articles influenced almost all the viewers who were forty-five to sixty-four years old, and more so the men (57.2 percent) than the women (42.8 percent). The service workers depended more on television magazines for their inspiration than did the more profession-oriented classes (bureaucrats, self-employed people, and students). Newspaper and magazine articles also influenced the younger female viewers.[19]

Viewer Evaluation of *Berlin Alexanderplatz*

Viewers were asked to evaluate the series by choosing six elements from a list that included boredom, sex, illumination/lighting conditions, violence/aggressiveness, medium comparison/adaptation/script, finances, relation to reality, relation to present, direction/camera work, emotional effect on the viewer, actors/casting, music/conversation, epilogue, and comparison with the 1929 George film.[20]

Boredom was the most common negative response: "too little forward movement," the bored viewers said; the narrative was "artificially noticeable"; there was too much introspection, too much thinking about action and not enough action. These problems were magnified by the viewers' response to the atmospheric lighting, which, according to Zerges, was "not recognized as an artistic element."[21]

Researchers correlated the negative response data with the socioeconomic characteristics of the audience. The older viewers were more likely to be negative about the series; viewers under thirty-four were more likely to be positive. Men more often judged the series as "good" or "very good." Women were more negative but differentiated parts of the series as good or bad. Religious affiliation played no part in the viewers' judgment of the series.[22]

The survey also found that the more educated the viewer, the more likely he or she was to like *Berlin Alexanderplatz*. The most negative responses came from workers, housewives, the self-employed, and retired people. Of

Table 1. Nürnberg viewer survey: evaluation of *Berlin Alexanderplatz*

Ranking of negative comments	Ranking of positive comments
1. Boredom (616)	1. Actors (521)
2. Lighting (509)	2. Direction/camera work (164)
3. Sex (477)	3. Relation to reality (155)
4. Violence (aggressiveness) (203)	4. Medium comparison (111)
5. Special reasons (189)	5. Special reasons (58)
6. Direction/camera work (121)	6. Emotional effect (54)
7. Relation to reality (109)	7. Lighting (14)
8. Finances (93)	8. Music/sound (13)
9. Medium comparison (86)	9. Relation to present (12)
10. Emotional effect (81)	10. Epilogue (8)
11. Music/sound (58)	11. Comparison to1929 film (5)
12. Comparison to 1929 film (33)	12. Violence (4)
13. Actors (28)	13. Sex (3)
14. Epilogue (13)	
15. Relation to the present (8)	

Source: Reprinted from Kristina Zerges, "Die TV-Series 'Berlin Alexanderplatz' von Rainer Werner Fassbinder, Dokumentation und Analyse eines Rezeptionsprocesses," *Spiel* 1 (1983): 156.

all the groups, viewers who were still in school most often responded positively. Not surprisingly, the older viewers found sex to be a problem, whereas the younger viewers tended to see boredom as the more important issue.[23]

Viewer Letters about *Berlin Alexanderplatz*

WDR and ARD received an unprecedented number of viewer letters protesting the series. On May 14, 1980, the tabloid *Die Illustrated Quick* published one of the first reports on *Berlin Alexanderplatz,* complete with text and scene photos, entitled "The Holy Family and Their Fool Fassbinder." The article reported:

> The director Rainer Werner Fassbinder breaks all records. Television gave a record sum of 13 million marks for his film of Döblin's novel "Berlin Alexanderplatz." . . .
> Crazed visions from the director: In his Bethlehem scene the hat-wearing Fassbinder wants to "show everything that one really should not do." Because of him, the Three Kings are reduced to thieves and the Holy Family is shown shockingly naked.[24]

This article caused the Catholic prelate for West Germany to publicly protest the making of the series to the ARD (the First Network) in June. Simultaneously, a letter campaign against the series began. The campaign was further fueled by the publication of a front-page article in the Catholic *Neue Bildpost* in early September that reiterated the statements of the *Quick* article. The ARD and WDR, the producing station, received 3,100 letters and postcards, which took a number of forms: individually formulated and signed letters and postcards; individually formulated and signed letters with preformulated petitions; photocopied, printed, or duplicated protests with lists of signatories and red, yellow, and white postcards preprinted with evaluative statements about the television program and the preformulated text of the protest organizers.

The Preprinted Postcards

Those who sent preprinted postcards had only to write in the title of the program and check the appropriate items on a preprinted list of objections to the broadcast. The opposite side of the postcard had a preprinted blank for the sender's name, birthdate, profession, and address. Most of these cards cited the *Quick* article as the source of their information.

The standardized text read: "This broadcast performs a terrible mockery of the resurrection of Christ, blackens the religious feelings of Christians; it is blasphemous. The broadcast should be banished."[25] Almost all of these postcards were sent between August and December 1980. Individually written protest postcards paraphrased the standardized texts. There was a pattern discernible in when the cards were sent: red postcards with individualized text were sent at the end of September; yellow postcards with standardized text were sent in December; yellow cards with individualized text all went out during the week of September 19; and normal white postcards with individualized texts were generally sent in November and December. These patterned waves of cards and letters indicated a structured campaign.

Analysis of the various cards reveals the characteristics of the senders. The primary group was women who were either housewives or retirees and over fifty years old. They were for the most part sent from the Munich area.

Standardized Protest Letters

Generally, the standardized postcards, letters, and petitions came from members of the Catholic Church and its social organizations. Individual priests initiated the campaigns in certain areas (e.g., a priest in Berlin garnered 450 petition signatures).

Letter One / In June 1980 a preformulated protest letter was sent to Catholics with the following cover letter:

> To All Catholics and Christians:
> For Your Information,
> So that no one will say: I did not know of this
> blasphemy.
> Who stands up for the *honor of God* today?
> Who fights against the mockery of God?
>   against the "Jesus" jeans,
>   against "Jesus' wedding,"
>   against the Fassbinder film (See *Quick* nr. 21, pp.
>   140–44) which shows the Holy Family
>   naked in a shocking manner?
> Who is silent, agrees with them! Please decide for yourself!
> Ez. 34:2: Woe to the shepherds who only tend to themselves.
> June 1980 (.............)

The preprinted protest letter was sent with a list of adjectives for the sender to circle. The letter read as follows:

> Your planned television broadcast with the title "The Holy Family and the Fool" from October to December in the premiere broadcast position,
> Fassbinder
> is
> factually wrong
> biased and tedentious
> unreasonable
> irresponsible
> It is blasphemous — offends also the religious convictions of millions of Christians, violates the Basic Law, works destructively, and calls down God's judgment.
> The work should be in no way broadcast!!!
> Sincerely,

The ARD received 201 of these preprinted protest cards.

Letter/Petition Two (769 Signatures) / From the end of November until the end of December, another text variation was sent from the Frankfurt area. The preprinted letter read as follows:

> The undersigned argue against Part 14 of the television film "Berlin Alexanderplatz" in which the biblical events of Bethlehem are seized

and mocked in an obscene manner. We ask *urgently* that this made-for-TV film not be broadcast on the network and to respect the 1954 Westdeutscher Rundfunk law in which the basic tenet is embodied in "The moral and religious convictions of the population are to be respected."

Letter/Petition Three (2,308 Signatures) / These petitions, more varied in text than the second letter/petition, were sent to WDR as early as June 6, 1980. The basic text can be summarized as:

> We, the undersigned, have learned of your plan to broadcast the last part of the TV series "Berlin Alexanderplatz" and the epilogue entitled "The Naked Mockery of Bethlehem."
> We are deeply indignant and ask you urgently to give up this broadcast.
> The broadcast is not only tasteless, but also is a huge insult to Christ and all Christians.
> If you do not respect our request, you should not be surprised when protests against your station flood in from a large percentage of the population.

Single Letters

Individually formulated and signed letters played a minor role in the protest against the series; there were only fifty-three. These personal letters resulted in part from the publication of the *Quick* article and the later *Neue Bildpost* articles. Their main criticism was the epilogue. Some threatened legal action if their request for cancellation of the series was not honored.

Negative Comments from Viewers

The negative reactions in the letters protesting the content of the series were directed at the sex, the violence, the brutality, the aggression, and the lack of morality. The dark lighting was the single major formal complaint. Many viewers wrote that they had had positive expectations because of the favorable criticism in the cultural press and were disappointed by the series. Letter writers praised the good acting in spite of its being "part of such a [bad] film." They complained that the series had wasted their money through license fees.

The letters variously characterized the series as "proletarian pornography," "expensive pissoir-and-bordello work that was botched," "a primitive dirty film," "a sadistic pornfilmstrip," "a dark chamber/mumbled ballad," "a fourteen-part film history about mire and smut," "a film full of fornication, murder, and manslaughter," "a film to make one vomit," "shit," and "a trash [*Schund*] film." The viewers were "disgusted." They found the film "unappetizing," "boring," "dirty," "ordinary," "greasy," "obscene," and "loathsome." One viewer described Franz Biberkopf as "an asocial type who stank right through the TV screen."[26]

Only a few letters dealt with specific formal points in the professional reviews. One viewer wrote: "The images are too dark, the facial expressions of the actors are not recognizable, they move like marionettes, the language is the opposite of the famed 'Berlin style' — primitive, clumsy, and heavy."[27] A letter complained about Peer Raben's music: "The nerve-wracking strumming as musical accompaniment was horrible." Berliners commented that it was not "their" Berlin Alexanderplatz that they saw in the series.

Again, there were genre divisions in the viewer letters. Women disliked the violence toward women, yet in the same breath they spoke against Fassbinder's homosexuality. In fact, so great was their frustration with the series that many female viewers said this was the first time they had written a letter to the network.

Of those who had read the novel, some reported that the Fassbinder series was a good adaptation of it. Others offered criticism — particularly about how the novel did not describe Ida's murder as graphically as the Fassbinder film did. One viewer argued that the novel was not better than the film series, but was somehow "more decent."

Positive Comments from Viewers

Admittedly, the letters that supported *Berlin Alexanderplatz* were the exception. Some letters complained about the late scheduling of the series and that television should not be "the moral guardian" of the world. In fact, a number of letter writers argued that reality was still more brutal than the film series. But the majority of positive comments were congratulatory of the film as "artwork." Viewers wrote that they were "impressed," "captivated," that they "experienced the oppression of the milieu" or were "possessed by the film's depiction of history for the entirety of the film." A less common statement was that the viewers had experienced a deep personal change as a result of the film's emotional depth. Some viewers supported the right of a minority to see something out of the ordinary on television.

In fact, some complained about the immaturity of the common citizen who could not enjoy film art.[28]

WDR's Reaction to the Letter Campaign

WDR was affected by both the letters and the *Quick* article. The German press and academic researchers generally accept that the letters along with the prelate's public complaint were responsible for the network's scheduling the series at such a late hour. WDR responded to the protest letters with its own letter:

> WDR and Rainer Werner Fassbinder have been accused of making an adaptation of the novel *Berlin Alexanderplatz* in which violence, sex, and brutality are the dominant elements. This is not true. The director was for the most part faithful to the source, transposing the dialogue almost word for word. Thus, it is a faithful adaptation. On the other hand, the adaptation from literature—especially when it contains expressionist passages—into a visual version is never unproblematic. This is where the ideas and the creativity of the director is demonstrated. Seen in this light, *Berlin Alexanderplatz* is a work that thoroughly carries the signature of the director, Rainer Werner Fassbinder. And for many viewers he did a good adaptation of the novel.
>
> Neither the author Döblin nor the director Fassbinder was primarily concerned to capture sex and violence as central narrative elements. On the other hand, one must say that the television film does provoke the objective viewer and possibly contains shocking passages. For this reason and especially in view of the discussion of violence on TV that took place two years ago and the laws to protect the youth, WDR set the viewing time at 9:30 p.m. The life and fate of Franz Biberkopf, the content of the novel and television series, are a piece of history that has been elevated to art. This work is one of the great novels of German literature, as is, for example, [Thomas Mann's] *Buddenbrooks*. The theme of both these novels is clearly the German past, which is also the case for both television series, even if *Berlin Alexanderplatz* was certainly less comfortable to watch.[29]

Zerges comments that the logic of this letter was to indicate that WDR has been able to contain the religious protest. Yet she does not address the letter's major rhetorical strategies—high culture, the rights of authorship, and the role of adaptation.[30]

Limitations of the Content Analysis of the Series and the Viewer Letters

The empirical analysis indicates that *Berlin Alexanderplatz* was an unusual event for a Fassbinder art film. The data indicate that the initial episode of the series reached one of the largest and broadest audiences ever for a Fassbinder film. In fact, the series reached an older and less-educated audience, one that typically did not see Fassbinder's films.

Viewer interest in the series was sparked more by the adaptation of a canonized literary work than by the role of West Germany's most renowned director. In fact, interest in Fassbinder and his style played a small role. Significantly, the audience analysis reveals that although the less-educated classes had access to and to a degree saw the series, those who enjoyed the series most were drawn from the educated classes. This result lends support to the assertion that the art cinema and *Autoren* works in general depended on a cultural competence of bourgeois education — thereby establishing a cultural class system for the reception for the film.

But the study also reveals significant limitations for understanding the reception of the series in relation to Fassbinder's role. The survey's preconceived categories evaluated the film's content and to a lesser extent its form. The category "direction/camera work" ranked as the sixth most frequent negative response and the second most frequent positive response, revealing a significant awareness of film form and a directorial presence. The survey was constructed in order to investigate the role of the write-in campaign by religious groups, however, and therefore eschewed questions that might touch on potentially more problematic content issues such as adaptation. A survey of the entire controversy shows that the Catholic write-in campaign was only a small, albeit vocal portion; even Zerges's survey of Nürnberg viewers reveals how minor a role religion played in the responses.

In the press reception of *Berlin Alexanderplatz,* the emphasis is on Fassbinder as a central element in the film's public reception. The violence, sex, and blasphemous content recede into the background. The importance of newspapers and magazines is evident from the degree to which Zerges's respondents resorted to them for their evaluative language. Nevertheless, the question still remains: Why did the broad public choose to reject the series in spite of the positive reception in the printed media?

Not all the press praised the series. The positive criticism came from the liberal cultural press, not the tabloid press. In fact, the series' public reception had much more to do with Fassbinder as an *Autor* and individual than the empirical research indicates. Three major themes were central in the popular and cultural reception of *Berlin Alexanderplatz*: the institutional split between the art cinema and television, the relationship of adaptation to authorship, and Fassbinder as both an artist and an individual. Once we establish the complex interrelationship of these three discourses, we can understand how *Berlin Alexanderplatz*'s failure was based primarily not on its sexual and violent explicitness and religious blasphemies, but on a class backlash against the cultural strategies of the art cinema.

Berlin Alexanderplatz's Relationship to Fassbinder's Television and Art Cinema Work

A central press issue was the conflict between Fassbinder and Westdeutscher Rundfunk over the station's decision to move the series from prime time to the less-viewed late evening hours. In an August press conference with representatives of the station, Fassbinder declared that the decision was a form of "censorship and patronizing treatment." The station representatives argued that the move was necessitated by laws that protect children from violence and sex on television. Fassbinder pointed out that the country's most popular crime series aired at the same time and contained equally pornographic and violent scenes.[31]

On the surface, all the major newspapers realized that the decision to move to the night hours denied the "mass audience" (*die breite Masse*) access to this difficult work.[32] But on a more complex level, the problem for the press became the role of television in relation to art, and particularly Germany's newly established art cinema — New German Cinema. In general, detailed descriptions of *Berlin Alexanderplatz* as art came from the established press; the tabloids examined the series in relation to "a realistic depiction." The cultural establishment received the Fassbinder television work almost unquestioningly as a major work of art.[33] Teleschau, as a news service for television, described it as "brilliant, with an epic depth. Already one can speak of it as a masterwork."[34] The *Süddeutsche Zeitung* reviewer wrote: "This film is a stroke of luck. All the imponderables that an artwork captures and can sometimes ruin have turned out for the best in this case. . . . Truth and beauty fit together seamlessly like nothing before."[35] Recognizing the inordinate amount of critical praise for the series, Ulrich Greiner wrote in *Die Zeit*:

One says that the critic has to guard against superlatives. However, Rainer Werner Fassbinder's adaptation of Alfred Döblin's "Berlin Alexanderplatz" is not only the longest and most expensive German television series ever, it is also Fassbinder's most important and beautiful work, a frightening and enchanting one, a wild and disciplined work without equal. It is to be counted among the very best programs ever to be shown on German television and among the best German films ever to be produced.[36]

Given all the praise, many of these established newspapers and magazines attempted to explain the film's controversy-ridden reception as a result of a central characteristic of art — to upset and teach. This same *Die Zeit* article took up the issue, asserting the rights of art based on its ability to "teach" the spectator:

> Fassbinder's film uses violence between human beings as a theme, but he makes its frightening nature less frightening because he shows the love and compassion. And because the violence is not accepted, it has its tragic reasons, which are shown as confusion and mistakes. He teaches us to see and conceive.[37]

This privileged educational function of art is reiterated in the *Frankfurter Allgemeine,* where the film is again described as a "masterwork" — a commonly used descriptive term — harking back to the apprenticeship concept (*Bildung*) underlying the German *Autor* process. As a result of this status, the article argues that "Fassbinder explains, bases, and arranges the violence in its social genesis."[38]

WDR, the producing station, attempted to legitimize the series and make it broadly acceptable based on its status as art while contradictorily changing its time slot and, therefore, its accessibility. The head of WDR's production staff compared the controversial content to a long line of art from "Bosch to Breughel to Barlach": "Art must provoke. And in this case, the film was a work of art and I am convinced that this film will be added to numbers of great and successful productions."[39] This statement echoes the strategy used previously in the WDR letter responding to the protest letters. The series was acceptable because it was already canonized as art: "The life and fate of Franz Biberkopf, the content of the novel and television series are a piece of history that have been elevated to literature." Significantly for the station as well as the established reviewers, the social importance and aesthetic disposition of the series were never questioned. Rather, the problem lay in the institutional differences between television and the art film.

From the standpoint of the "established" media, the rescheduling of the series resulted from the failings of television as a social institution. They posed the question of whether television should be in a position to decide what the public should see or be "headmaster," as the title of a *Frankfurter Allgemeine* article suggested.[40] One article pointed out how West German television had reached an impasse; it could not produce high art because it did not appeal to the tastes of the masses:

> The reproach of censorship may also be considered mindless, faddish attitude, and, as far as the politics of the media are concerned, it becomes completely fatal, when the zealous privatizers of the media join in on this chorus and hypocritically demand that the viewer have the right to choose a program for him/herself, a viewer who for the privatizers is otherwise only a figure in measuring the size of the planned commercial television industry.[41]

One can see here repetition of the postwar fear of mass taste falling victim to a preconceived agenda. In 1980 the menace had become commercialism, not fascism.

A variation of this view of the incompatibility of art with mass taste is articulated in an article from epd (a West German news service) that referred to the controversy as "the price of popularization" that the station had to pay to bring complex ideas and art to the broad masses.[42] Ultimately, these articles purveyed a complicated set of underlying assumptions: First, the public needs to be exposed to complex art. Second, mass tastes are by nature antagonistic to high art. And finally, high culture as an aesthetic disposition is a minority position. But many articles argued that high art must be produced to counteract the potentially destructive influence of commercial culture.

A number of popular magazines also focused on the issue of educational differences and cultural competence in the reception of *Berlin Alexanderplatz*. In a series of interviews of WDR executives by reporters for the popular but conservative boulevard presses *Quick* and *Neue Revue Aktuell*,[43] the question of the capability of the public surfaced again and again. For example, when the *Quick* interviewer asked whether the expensive series was not too demanding for the public, the television producer, Peter Märthesheimer, replied:

No. Television must offer a colorful palette and therefore such high-quality products. Döblin's novel is *the* representative German novel of the 1920s. Therefore it is the duty of television to make it accessible to the millions of the public.[44]

Here, Märthesheimer legitimized the series by alluding to West German television's original mandate for a democratic plurality of authorial points of view. And significantly, the reporter also asked if there was another country that could have realized such an expensive and sophisticated television production. Märthesheimer responded: "I can imagine that something similar would have been possible at the BBC at an earlier time when things were financially good." Not only the historical model but also the model of patrician-style broadcasting become clear: bourgeois culture and interests are disseminated as the highest priority for the broad audience.

The Role of Adaptation: Whose *Berlin Alexanderplatz*?

The subject of authorship of *Berlin Alexanderplatz* appeared in the press as an extension of the debates over the relationship of art to television. A September 1980 *Stuttgarter Zeitung* stated the problem succinctly: "This powerful work has created a German contest. Is the piece powerful because of Döblin's novel or Fassbinder's film?"[45] Significantly, the public analyses of authorship divided along lines of readership—to whom the newspaper or magazine was pitched. The cultural press agreed that Fassbinder had produced an "adequate" if not "exacting" adaptation of the Döblin work. In fact, the culturally powerful *Frankfurter Allgemeine* declared with unusual abandon: "It is conceivably the most exact adaptation."[46] The *Stuttgarter Zeitung* argued that "there is no discussion about the artistic meaning of Alfred Döblin's novel, nor the good translation of the novel into film by Rainer Werner Fassbinder."[47] Teleschau argued that the series read like a script from the novel, and therefore the source of the controversy lay at the television network's door:

> Although the book from Alfred Döblin was available for decades, although the script was available for years, although Fassbinder has held verbatim to the dialog and the facts, they [WDR] felt now that it is necessary to recommend to move it to a singularly bad scheduling placement after completion of production.[48]

These reviews also quoted Alfred Döblin's son, Claude Döblin, who at a WDR press conference affirmed that Fassbinder's *Berlin Alexanderplatz* was "an amazingly accurate rendering."[49] A number of newspapers accepted his relationship to the author and his status as a lawyer as evidence that he could judge the adequacy of the adaptation.

The cultural press did allow that the series reflected the influence of Fassbinder to some degree. The most commonly cited reason for Fassbinder's intercession into the novel's meaning was the problem of filming Berlin — the novel's central interest — when old Berlin had since been destroyed by World War II. *Fernseh Information* asked rhetorically whether "the film should better be called 'Franz Biberkopf.' " The article also argued that the limited access to Berlin was the reason for the undue emphasis on the interior action in the series.[50] In a similar vein, critic Wolfram Schütte, a leading advocate for New German Cinema, argued that the lack of a "filmable" old Berlin gave Fassbinder the right to greater creative freedom in interpreting the novel.[51] The *Die Zeit* reviewer felt that as a result of the lack of an authentic Berlin, Fassbinder had created "an example of how history is received [*Rezeptionsgeschichte*] and he reflects on that."[52]

Interestingly, the cultural press less often cited the American academic position that the translation of words into images is an important challenge in a filmic adaptation. In a rare example, the popular *Der Stern* argued that part of the problem emanated from Döblin's modernist formal method:

> Döblin's literary aesthetic — free association and temporal simultaneity of different actions — represents substantial difficulties for the translation of the novel into film. Fassbinder with his fourteen-part series finds an acceptable solution. He works dexterously with the monologue, which is foreign to a scene. Döblin's collage becomes the dialogue.[53]

The media journal *Kirche und Rundfunk,* however, argued that even though the changes were a result of the translation into film, the greater issue was the process of popularization:

> Film offers a different language, and any attempt to create an exactly copied adaptation out of an epic original is bound to encounter difficulties; additionally, Fassbinder was dealing with a television series (not with a mammoth film of fourteen hours as the series' subtitle suggests); so the formal dimensions of the film are a priori limited by the fact that a mass public (the whole world) has to be able to understand it.[54]

Die Zeit, Der Spiegel, and *Die Frankfurter Rundschau* — three central proponents of New German Cinema in the 1970s — argued that Fassbinder's faithfulness to the novel was not an exact reproduction of the original, but rather an aesthetic and emotional symbiosis between the two *Autoren*—a stance that the Haag book continued, as we saw in chapter 6. This position emanated from Fassbinder's much quoted statement, published in *Die Zeit* on March 14, 1980, in which he confessed his oeuvre-long relationship to the novel. In that article, Fassbinder had declared that the novel had been a seminal influence on his film work. In reading the novel for the first time, Fassbinder realized that "it reached the point where I was no longer reading, but rather living, suffering, despairing, fearing." Reading the novel again five years later, he became aware that "an enormous part of myself, my attitudes, my reactions, so many of the things I had considered all my own, were none other than those described by Döblin. I had ... unconsciously made Döblin's fantasy my own life."[55]

Given their respect for Fassbinder as an *Autor,* the "art cinema" critics accepted Fassbinder's statement as an insight into the relationship of the novel to the film. For all three reviews, Fassbinder's adaptation functioned as "a personal displacement of a literary text into the life's world of the interpreter."[56] In fact, Fassbinder's unusually personal relationship with the novel stood as proof of the film's faithful rendition of the novel. The *Frankfurter Rundschau* reviewer, Wolfram Schütte, simply quoted Fassbinder's *Die Zeit* statement in order to support his proclamation that the series was "the *great* confession, the settlement of a debt, the fulfillment of a dream, and a summing up of all his previous artistic efforts." Here the novel functions not only as a map of Fassbinder's early education or artistic *Ausbildung,* but also as an organizing influence on his career and oeuvre—both central determinants of an *Autor.*

Taking Fassbinder's identification with the novel one step further, Ulrich Greiner argued in his *Die Zeit* review that the power of the adaptation came from both Döblin's and Fassbinder's intense love for Franz Biberkopf: "Something very different occurs in this filmic adaptation of a work of literature. There is a new version of the novel—where both the film and its model appear as two faces of the same story."[57]

The parallel between the two *Autoren* received its most thorough treatment in a *Der Spiegel* article entitled "Stories of Power and Dependence." The essay compared Döblin's and Fassbinder's lives and works, even though a parallel article in the magazine was entitled "I am Biberkopf"—Fassbinder's statement. This article chose to quote other parts of Fassbinder's autobiographical statement about his relationship to the novel. The writer interpreted them as "a life in symbiosis with literature, a mystical union between a manic filmmaker and a writer who wrote out of passion."[58] In fact, the writer argued that the source of this "mystical union" between the two artists stemmed from Döblin's hatred of his father and how this disturbed relationship took on a sadomasochistic tone in his novel. The writer compared this with Fassbinder's own fatherless childhood "without an upbringing in non-middle-class surroundings in a nonfunctioning parental home." Relating this to Fassbinder's violent adaptation of the novel, the article states:

> This is the world that is rediscovered in Fassbinder's films. It is no wonder that *Berlin Alexanderplatz* hits like lightning; Franz Biberkopf and his march of pain were so alluring. There was a biographical parallel.

In the eyes of the *Spiegel* critic, the novel and therefore Döblin became Fassbinder's missing father figure, offering the filmmaker the special education that defined him as an *Autor.* The 1928 publication and the 1980 reproduction of *Berlin Alexanderplatz* are then unified by a hatred that the two artists had for their fathers and the need to express it — art as catharsis. Therefore, Fassbinder's adherence to and deviance from the original source resulted from a century-long Freudian psychodrama in which Döblin represents an object of both love and hate: father figure as well as cure. All three articles interpreted Fassbinder's ongoing use of "Franz," "Franz Biberkopf," and "Franz Walsch" in his films as examples of his career-long engagement with this film-as-therapy discourse. Within the rhetoric of the *Autor*/auteur, Fassbinder as an extraordinary individual and "art" filmmaker resulted from not only his anomalous childhood, but also the degree to which it corresponded to a canonized *Autor*'s biography. The parallel to Döblin's life, not to *Berlin Alexanderplatz,* then became the key to Fassbinder's status as an *Autor.*

The Relationship of *Berlin Alexanderplatz* to Fassbinder's Life

Fassbinder as absent star of the series figured prominently in all reviews. The written reception of *Berlin Alexanderplatz* was united in its interest in Fassbinder and his life as the central sources for interpreting the series. The cultural press's analyses isolated Fassbinder's relationship with the aesthetic traditions, and Döblin as the core of the series' power. In contrast, analyses in the popular newspapers and magazines were united on one major front: Fassbinder was the sole locus of the film's meaning. Almost every article agreed that *Berlin Alexanderplatz* was "Fassbinder's." Unlike the cultural press, the popular press did not discuss Döblin's role, out of either disinterest in the novel's standing as great literature or perhaps an unwillingness to attack its cultural standing. Additionally, description of the series' form and content receded into the background. As a *Quick* reporter so aptly put it, the question became: "Who is Fassbinder?"[59]

This emphasis in the popular press on Fassbinder as an extraordinary individual received its most significant treatment in the Springer Press campaign against him during the broadcast of *Berlin Alexanderplatz*. In over twenty articles, the Springer organs (*Das Bild, Die Welt, Hör zu, Bild am Sonntag,* and *Welt am Sonntag*) mounted a "personal" attack on Fassbinder and on the series' content. These articles were important to the popular reception of the series for a number of reasons. First, they reveal a highly structured rhetorical strategy through all the articles. Since these magazines and newspapers represented the most widely read news sources in West Germany, they stood as representative of the popular critical reception. Second, one can see the influence of their language and rhetorical strategies on non-Springer organs. And finally, this Springer campaign became the newest manifestation of the historical antagonism that Alex Springer had carried on with leftist arts in the late 1960s, and in particular with Fassbinder's Action Theater.

The most influential Springer articles were two companion pieces in the popular Sunday newspaper *Welt am Sonntag,* "The 13 Million Mark Thing of Rainer Werner Fassbinder" and "The Man Who Films the Million Mark Thing."[60] Timed nearly a month apart, the articles—the first a review of the film and the second a review of Fassbinder—paralleled each other in their anti-"high culture" bias. Step by step, they took apart the institutions and premises of high culture. The first article established the equation of Fassbinder's life with the film's narrative content; the second diminished the film's importance in favor of Fassbinder's life as narrative.

The major rhetorical strategy of the review was an attack on the "aesthetic disposition." The method was to create a conspiracy around the traditional institutions of the German art cinema. The article began by debunking the critical praise of the cultural press. Using short excerpts from reviews in *Frankfurter Allgemeine Zeitung, Die Zeit, Frankfurter Rundschau, Spiegel,* and *Süddeutsche Zeitung,* it turned their support of the series into a plan orchestrated by the cultural elite. The article opened thus: "The success seemed programmed and unavoidable. Never before had German television given out more money for a television production then for the fourteen-part series *Berlin Alexanderplatz.*" Posing the cultural press's reviews as not in touch with common viewers' reactions became a central opening conflict for many of the popular articles. *Gong*'s review, for example, was entitled "The Critics Exult. The Viewers Are Disappointed."[61]

The proposed elitist plot was extended to include the producing television station, Westdeutscher Rundfunk, and public television in general. The *Gong* reviewer quoted the head of WDR's programming: *Berlin Alexanderplatz* was "one of the most meaningful artworks of the century." Peter Märthesheimer, the series' producer, was quoted as legitimating the "artistic quality" of the lighting: "Any idiot can make a scene brightly lighted. But the fact that it remains dark is a sign of its complexity." This art-for-art's-sake aesthetic was further reinforced by the head of programming, who argued that some viewers would understand the complexity of the first episode only "after the fact." This article also blamed the television executives for their failure to own up to the series' content early on, before scheduling it in prime time. But unlike the cultural articles, this article argued that the fact that the "mass public" did not get to see the series in prime time was not an issue because the declining audience was proof of its negative vote.

This notion of "democratic choice" for the audience was further reinforced by other Springer Press articles that encouraged the audience to write to the magazines. And again, these letters mimicked the articles' antiaesthetic strategy and language, questioning the cost of what they thought to be of questionable worth.[62] In the letters to the press, the focus was significantly on the individual artist, as opposed to the letters about the series' content in the Catholic campaign. The Springer newspapers and magazines offered a viewer mail campaign as a subtle method of creating a sense of democratic participation. In this way they cleverly presented themselves as opposed to the nondemocratic, conspiratorial methods of the cultural elite of the press, the networks, and the directors that had fabricated New German Cinema as *German* film.

But the core of the Springer Press attack was aimed at Fassbinder the individual and at the concept of a state-supported artist as both representative and extraordinary. Even the first major *Welt am Sonntag* article — the review of the film — argued that the series resulted from Fassbinder's need to "press his obsessions." Other popular newspapers and magazines latched on to Fassbinder's statement that he was Biberkopf.[63] They overwhelmingly agreed that Franz Biberkopf's life, not Alfred Döblin's, paralleled Fassbinder's. Additionally, these reviews offered little description of the overall narrative or form of the film. In fact, the photographs that accompanied the popular articles were overwhelmingly of Fassbinder (usually caressing his genitals) and scenes of violence from the film. Given the small viewership of *Berlin Alexanderplatz* among the lower and less educated classes, these popular newspaper and magazine accounts of Fassbinder's autobiographical relationship to the series became the film's narrative or the center of their reception of the series. The *Welt am Sonntag* writer described the film thus:

> Instead of [Döblin's novel], Fassbinder brings an orgy of violence, perversion, and blasphemy onto the screen: manslaughter, rape, sweaty sex scenes and crucifixion of the protagonist in the middle of dancing naked people.... In the final analysis, "Berlin Alexanderplatz" becomes in Fassbinder's expert hands something that it wasn't in Döblin's novel: It is a homoerotic drama.[64]

Franz Biberkopf then became Fassbinder in all his violence and sexual promiscuity. In the opening lines of *Quick's* review, the reviewer isolated the epilogue as an example of Fassbinder's "murder of the father figure." Whereas the cultural press compared Fassbinder to Döblin as a biographical figure, popular reviews more often presented Döblin and the novel as substitute father figures. *Quick's* writer dissolved the distinctions between the film and Fassbinder's life as he argued that the epilogue was "a two-sided act of release"—his early childhood separation from and general lack of emotional support from his father.[65] Biberkopf's crucifixion allowed Fassbinder to cathartically end his own spiritual hell. *Funk Uhr* argued that Fassbinder totally falsified the novel and was led by his own personal "neurotic" obsessions—particularly Franz Biberkopf's homosexual desire for Reinhold.[66]

A variation of this equation of Fassbinder with Franz Biberkopf can be found in the description of the "conflict" between Fassbinder and the actor Günter Lamprecht. A number of articles posed the character of Franz Biberkopf as a battleground between Fassbinder's personal obsessions and his veteran actor's "knowledge" of a believable portrayal. The *Welt am Sonntag* reviewer argued that never before had a German actor been so embarrassed by a director. *Express* took on the theme and posed Lamprecht's established acting method against Fassbinder's single-take filming method. The article concluded that the actor suffered "torture" as a result of Fassbinder's fanatic directing style. *Fersehwoche* quoted Lamprecht as saying how obsessive the Fassbinder characterization had become: "I fall asleep as Biberkopf.... After a day of filming I fall in bed dead tired."[67] And upon seeing the first episode, they quoted the director: "All I saw was a three-and-a-half-hour monologue from Biberkopf. That's all." *TV Hören + Sehen* published a series of viewer letters dwelling on the scandal that divided the reception into two columns: the positive reception of Lamprecht ("beloved Lamprecht") and the negative reaction to Fassbinder and his film.[68] The extratextual conflict between actor and director substituted for the conflict of the two individuals over control of the Biberkopf character: Lamprecht as the popular figure of identification representing conservative values and Fassbinder as the artist representing the extraordinary or unidentifiable figure of nonnormative values.

As the series continued to lose viewers over its first month of broadcast, the popular press—and particularly the Springer Press articles—lost interest in the content. They homed in on the selection of Fassbinder as the "artist" and the criteria for that selection. The November 2 article in *Welt am Sonntag* represents the most concentrated example of the various arguments. After asking, "Who really is this man who constructed Fassbinder's most costly flop of the year?" the anonymous reporter announced that

> Fassbinder is a key figure in modern German culture. What Grass is for literature, Zadek is for theater, or Beuys is for fine art, Fassbinder is for film. Unattractive in his work and in his being, his impact is nevertheless enormous.

The article then proceeded to systematically assail once again all the major institutions of the German art cinema for their support—not of the series, but of Fassbinder during the 1970s. The object of this onslaught was the federal funding of the independent film:

> The 35-year-old Fassbinder has made over 40 films and television films. For them he has received state honors (at least five federal prizes), state financial support (at least 1.2 million DM [$470,000] from the Interior Ministry and 1.7 million DM [$670,000] for the Trade and Commerce Ministry).

Then the reviewer moved on to the cultural press for its critical praise of Fassbinder throughout his career:

> The liberal press cuddles him like the queen her lapdog. *Stern* calls him a "genius" and the *Süddeutsche Zeitung* called him "a hopelessly good human being." For *Twen* he was "the man of great action," for the *New York Times* he was "the messiah of new German film," and the *Mannheimer Zeitung* saw him as "the genial master of public popularity."

The article argued that honor and acclaim from these powerful cultural institutions were all Fassbinder needed to be considered "an acknowledged artist in our society."

In fact, the article took it upon itself to examine Fassbinder's life — the basis of his nomination as an artist or an expressive individual worthy of state support. Rarely has a New German Cinema, let alone a "German," artist been so publicly scrutinized. With a photograph of Fassbinder masturbating in leather clothing, sunglasses, and hat, the article started the personal attack by labeling him disturbed as a result of the anomalous nature of his middle-class childhood and his missing father.

The underlying middle-class concept of *Bildung* or education for an *Autor* was slowly dismantled. The criteria for what constitutes an art object receded as the issue was displaced onto the qualifications of the individual artist. Fassbinder was educated at an alternative school. He did not finish high school. At twenty he made his first film. His membership in Action Theater was related to German terrorism. The article also stated that his first film was "not a success." And for no apparent reason (in the writer's eyes) Fassbinder's second film, *Katzelmacher,* became an instant success and "federal prizes rained down."

Fassbinder's films served as proof of the autobiographical nature of his work as an *Autor.* "Many [of his films] come from autobiographical impulses. Fassbinder also said the same about the hero of *Berlin Alexanderplatz*: I am Biberkopf." Then the article listed the most sensational details of his private life: his homosexuality ("His proletarian homosexual characters whom he mimics are dream wishes"), his physical assaults on others, his public outbursts, his marriage to a member of his troupe, the suicides of two of his homosexual lovers, his sympathetic statements about German terrorism ("a few people who flipped out"), his teenage acne, the alleged anti-Semitism of his play *The Garbage, the City, and the Dead* and proposed film *Soll und Haben,* and finally his use of drugs, which the article intoned was the autobiographical source for his next film, *Cocaine.*

This constant baiting of Fassbinder's irregular films and private life in *Welt am Sonntag* as well as many of the popular press's articles was based on the belief that the artist must adhere to a normative role as a representative of German society. The article echoed this supposition when in the final lines the writer quoted a threatening Fassbinder statement: "One can destroy without throwing stones, one can destroy 'norms.' I believe that is the way to go." Yet his "publicly private" life was the extraordinariness that defined him and his films as "different" from the nonartist and the nonart object.

Around the time of this article, Fassbinder began to receive death threats and was put under police protection. The number of viewers for the series dwindled from 27 percent of the total viewing public for the first episode to a marginal 8 percent for the epilogue, even though the press continued to write about Fassbinder. After its defense, Westdeutscher Rundfunk slowly grew silent and hardly mentioned its biggest production to date in its year-end report.[69] The series was not rebroadcast until four years later, after the film's successful run in American art theaters. Then *Berlin Alexanderplatz* was shown on the educational channel that is reserved for "nonmainstream" tastes.

"One Can Destroy Without Throwing Stones, One Can Destroy 'Norms'"

The traditional academic wisdom in Germany is that Fassbinder's *Berlin Alexanderplatz* failed because of the concerted campaign by the Catholic Church to not only remove the series from prime time, but bar it from television altogether. This is the conclusion of the much-quoted Zerges study of the series' reception. Zerges sums up the issue thus: "It is shocking to see what the sectarian zeal of the representatives of the Catholic Church can do as the result of blind belief in the reports of the press. Even more shocking is the number of people who followed its lead." Zerges admits that this analysis is only one part of the reception, but for her it is the most important part. After her long analysis of the church's role, she concludes by saying that the role and function of the television critic needs to be re-defined. She speculates that the problem might also lie with an uneducated or unprepared public that does not understand the abstract language of such a series.[70] The *Autor* discourse is seemingly so ingrained in the German intellectual community that the problem of its authority remains an unexplored afterthought compared to traditional academic institutions of power such as the Church.

Berlin Alexanderplatz's controversial reception involved the status of the director within the art cinema as both a formal structural element within the work and an extratextual source of the film's logic. Because of the self-consciousness and ambiguity of the art cinema's form and content, Fassbinder served as a source of the series' operation for viewers who were informed or competent in the art cinema's reading strategies and knowledgeable about Fassbinder's other films. As Bordwell points out: "More broadly the author becomes the real-world parallel to the narrational presence 'who' communicates (what is the filmmaker *saying*?) and 'who' expresses (what is the artist's personal vision?)."[71] This author-within-the-text emphasis promotes an autobiographical element in many art films — Fassbinder's oeuvre as a confession. Many viewers were not prepared for the idiosyncratic nature of the series, nor for the primacy that the director played in understanding the film. Because of the extratextual emphasis on the author in the art cinema, Fassbinder became a central focus for those who did and did not watch the series — the director as star.

Admittedly, the printed campaign against the series and Fassbinder was orchestrated from above by the Springer Press, whose newspapers and magazines exerted a wider influence in the reception of the series than the church's private protest. Their opinions have the status of objective "news" and are mass circulated. The Springer Press does not mirror popular tastes; rather it exploits the fears, anger, and pleasures of the working class in a popular vernacular. Yet we cannot dismiss the tabloids' popularity with the German populace; their success is based on their ability to unmask inequalities in class and power.

Tabloids represent what Stuart Hall calls "an authoritarian populist mix." Their pleasure emanates from the fact that they are both ideologically confirmimg and formally accessible. Mark Pursehouse captures this tension in tabloids: "The popular interests in the individual, personalities, sex, scandal, violence, sport and amusement are presented in a lively, identifiable language and format." But this popular genre of newspapers "ideologically layers a heterosexual, male, white conservative capitalist, nationalist world view."[72] However, its appeal to the working class's distrust of authority cannot be discounted as a purely reactionary ethos; it represents an important site of resistance. Obviously, the Springer Press as a capitalist institution played on the individual's distrust of state power. But the tabloids still remain one of the few places where discussion of the inequalities of cultural power takes place.

Fassbinder traded on a similar popular aesthetic. His melodramatic rendition of *Berlin Alexanderplatz* focused on an individual working-class protagonist, sex, violence, and amusement. It provided just enough broad accessibility with its melodramatic highs and lows that it initially attracted a large audience. It was unusually inviting art film. Indeed, Fassbinder must have knowingly directed his public confession as much at the tabloids' pleasure in the sensational as at the bourgeoisie's tradition of the *Autor.*

But as the series turned increasingly negative, multilayered, and self-conscious across fifteen hours, the audience, in search of accessibility, switched to its *Autor* as the object of identification and source of meaning. The tabloids played on the audience's frustration with the series and directed it toward a biographical individual. They questioned the bourgeois discourse about artists being "extraordinary." The process of who and how an individual became anointed as an artist finally came to the forefront of West German popular discussion.

Quoting Foucault, Tim Corrigan argues that "the whole notion of an author of a text or film must obscure 'the legal and institutional systems that circumscribe, determine, articulate' it." For Foucault, it cannot "refer, purely and simply, to an actual individual insofar as it simultaneously gives rise to a variety of egos and a series of subject positions that individuals of any class may come to occupy."[73] More than any other recent director, Fassbinder brought this system to light. The popular reception led to a reactionary questioning of the representative nature of his homosexuality. Yet it opened up a powerful debate about power and culture.

Every community has its imaginary other. Nazi Germany had the Jew (as well as the homosexual and the communist). Postwar West Germany seems to offer enlightenment with its support of a plurality of aesthetic voices, yet real-life social differences are effaced through the title of author. And when that title comes to refer to an actual person such as Fassbinder — a homosexual and a cultural anarchist — the middle class had to contain the potential of other ways of living, as well as other ways of seeing. Since his death in 1982, Fassbinder has become a legend. For the working class, he has become a sign of the workings of cultural authority. For the middle class, he has become a genius.

8 / Conclusion

"The Canonization of a Monster"
Headline of *Der Spiegel* article commemorating
the tenth anniversary of Fassbinder's death[1]

In the end, did the viewer outcry over Fassbinder and *Berlin Alexanderplatz* fulfill Walter Benjamin's hopes for mass-produced art? Is it evidence of a public awareness of how the state produces a cultural class system through the title of *Autor*? Or did the response simply extend the reactionary bias that the general populace feels toward an unfamiliar or critical culture, which Fassbinder and his work represented? Benjamin predicted that the mass reproduction of art would finally give the noneducated access to art and that they would reject the power it held in the name of the bourgeoisie. "With regard to the screen," Benjamin proclaimed, "the critical and receptive attitudes of the public coincide." Of all the New German Cinema directors, Fassbinder created films dedicated to this accessibility; he attempted to undercut the traditional opposition between art and popular culture.

The popular failure of Fassbinder's *Berlin Alexanderplatz* did lead directly to a growing political conservatism in German television. The state institution was forced to reexamine what constituted "producible" programming in the 1980s. Egged on by a recessionary economy and the election of the conservative Christian Democratic government of Helmut Kohl in 1982, television by the mid-1980s lost much of the distinctive character that had marked its production of *Autorenfilm*. It produced and televised substantially fewer small-budget films characterized by the aesthetic individualism of their makers. *Autorenfilm* was already a misnomer by the late 1970s, as the filmmakers' own rhetoric about the artist's right to creative freedom caught up with them. Public funding was narrowed to those few directors who were "name artists" or the *Autoren* of New German Cinema. By the 1980s state support was reserved for the big-budget coproductions in which the filmmaker was reduced to directing what was in essence a "producer's film."

German television lost some of its German high-culture flavor by coproducing film spectacles with other European Community countries, and the new cable and satellite technologies reduced state television's hold on the German market and its ability to carry out its public service mandate in the 1980s. In the late 1970s Luxembourg proposed to use its satellite channel to beam commercial programming to West Germany and France; although the German government protested, it could not stop satellite transmission. The cabling of the nation began in 1985 after much furor over the influence of commercialization on German television.

Luxembourg's RTL Plus and Sat Eins (started by a consortium of West German publishers including Alex Springer) have made substantial inroads into public television's control of the spectrum of programming. These satellite stations have substantial financial clout; they offer an attractive medium for advertisers who want their advertisements interwoven into the programming, as opposed to public television's blocking of commercials into a two-hour period on weekday evenings. By 1993 satellite broadcast in Germany offered a number of additional commercial stations—Pro 7, MTV Europe, Vox, Premiere, and Eurosport—and American commercial series dominated satellite fictional programming: *Magnum PI, L.A. Law, Roseanne, General Hospital, Miami Vice, Charlie's Angels, Lassie, Flipper,* and *T. J. Hooker,* to name only a few. Satellite viewership is still small (less than 10 percent of the total television audience) in comparison to the ARD and ZDF, still the staples of German television, but Richard Collins notes that satellite's growing success in Germany "testifies to the vulnerability to commercial competition of public sector broadcasters that have lost contact with popular taste."[2]

German public television networks have responded to the competition with their own satellite channels (Eins Plus, 3 Sat, and a series of channels created by regional ARD stations), but the channels replicate the terrestrial service of their public-service networks: educational and high-culture programming. They legitimize the public service offering as part of their mandate to "balance" programming (*Ausgewogenheit*) with the commercial satellite offerings. This argument replicates their rationale for producing *Autorenfilm* as a counterweight to their own broadcast of American programming in the 1970s. Once again we see the continuation of the postwar distinction between high culture as German and popular culture as American. Commercial producers in European television shy away from buying German programming, which is known to have "the German touch" — a heavy-handed high-culture emphasis.[3] The major issue for German television in the 1980s and 1990s has been how to balance its public service mandate with the country's growing conservatism.

There is no better example of this shift in German television production than WDR's production of Edgar Reitz's popular epic series *Heimat* in 1984. The sixteen-hour saga of a provincial German family is the ideological and formal opposite of Fassbinder's *Berlin Alexanderplatz*. Reitz, a signer of the Oberhausen Manifesto, made this semiautobiographical account as a romantic fiction about his homeland (*Heimat*) along the Rhine. Like Fassbinder, Reitz was dedicated to popularizing German film with his series. He too used his own life and its relation to the *Autor* discourse to bolster his production's credibility.

But where Fassbinder balanced the melodrama of German big-city life against his personal confession, Reitz's series revealed a romantic nostalgia for the pure and simple life of his German rural origins. The series stands as a chronicle of "everyday" German history; the major political events of the twentieth century, whether in 1933 or 1983, seem far away. Its narrative is predicated on a boy's coming of age, his departure from and return to his homeland. In the final sentimental episode, Reitz's fictional persona, Paul, returns as a composer in the 1980s to discover the potential avant-garde music in the echoes of the caves of his homeland: the Romantic myth of the artist in harmony with his natural origins. But this myth has an uncomfortable German twist. As Anton Kaes cautions, "This interweaving of provincialism and homeland is a specifically German phenomenon where the historical dimension has continually been repressed and denied. Scenes of provincial life are never innocent in Germany."[4]

Heimat's theme and style harked back to the popular fiction and film of the early part of the century, which idealized provincial life as the essential German experience.[5] Love of motherhood, home, and nature were emphasized to the exclusion of the urban and the foreign. These values became the heart of fascist ideology in the 1930s. These conservative myths are what Döblin responded to when he wrote *Berlin Alexanderplatz,* his modernist vision of urban existence, in 1929. The Reitz series followed much of the original logic of the *Heimat* genre, marginalizing representations of non-Aryans and the Holocaust with the logic that in "historical reality" they did not have an impact on small-village life. Nevertheless, Reitz painted a complex mural of a popular German history that fuses all the styles and symbols of German film history while revealing the mutability and complexity of these historical representations.

Reitz's return to the values of the early *Heimat* films and literature struck a positive emotional chord in the West German public. Not only was *Heimat* a phenomenally popular series — 25 million Germans watched some portion of it — it launched a debate very different from that initiated by the Fassbinder series. The latter was a critical examination of the privilege of the *Autor,* while *Heimat* was seen as an affirmation of the German identity and caused a national outcry for a lost "good" Germany and the need for a positive history. In attempting to locate a popular culture, Reitz unwittingly created the old German alignment between the popular and nationalism.[6]

Must German popular culture always be aligned with nationalism? Two experiences speak against such a simple equation. First, the German broadcast of the American commercial series *Holocaust* in 1977 indicates the possibility of critical popular culture. Millions of Germans tuned in and watched the story of fictional Jewish protagonists during the Holocaust. Although the stereotypes and dramatics were dismissed by the left in Germany and America as a commercial vulgarization of a complex and sensitive historical event, the series opened up a national dialogue on the German responsibility for the Holocaust that had been repressed in West Germany since the war.

Equally important, the American series did what the leftist modernist plays and films about the Holocaust in the 1960s and 1970s could not do: it got Germans to identify with Jews. The series was a classical Hollywood melodramatic narrative that focused on an assimilated Jewish family; the drama and emotion of their experience of the Holocaust fueled the plot. The series' emotional impact in the German community caused Andreas Huyssen to suggest that artists, intellectuals, and political activists should rethink their high-culture bias and dependence on Brechtian aesthetics: "Documents, rational explanation, and social theory had been bypassed by the specific needs of spectators." In the end the left's rejection of *Holocaust* might represent a "rearguard struggle to hold on to an avantgarde aesthetic and politics of an earlier period which by now has become historical if not obsolete, in its claim to universality and rationality."[7]

Finally, the phenomenon of "Rainer Werner Fassbinder" offers the other historical moment of popular culture and critical awareness in recent German history. Fassbinder died more than a decade ago, in 1982, yet his legend lives. Five sensational biographies have been written. At the 1982 Venice Film Festival people tried to hawk copies of his supposed death mask. Two years later, in a film entitled *The Man Called Eva*, his former actress Eva Mattes played Fassbinder. In 1985 West Germany erupted over the attempted production of his play *The Garbage, the City, and the Dead* (*Der Müll, die Stadt und der Tod*) with its potentially anti-Semitic portrait of "the rich Jew." Not since *Holocaust* had Germans debated the "Jewish question" so openly, but now it became an issue of freedom of speech and the right to a German depiction of a Jew. This debate became so inflamed that *Die Zeit* proclaimed in a front-page headline: "Art Is Free and It Must Remain So."[8] Nevertheless, the play was never performed publicly. In the intervening years some of Fassbinder's co-workers gained international fame as artists; Kurt Raab and Brad Davis died of AIDS. A decade after his death, retrospectives popped up around the world, declaring Fassbinder a genius.

To sum up Fassbinder's legacy here would legitimize the myth of individual genius or the auteur theory, which this book seeks to refute. Fassbinder's success resulted from the historical circumstances of a German patrician notion of cultural democracy, the resulting *Autor* discourse, and the anarchical counterculture of the 1960s, which sought to break down hierarchies. These elements do not encompass the complexity of the West German reception of Fassbinder, but they do undercut the notion that Fassbinder appeared deus ex machina out of the Bavarian clouds to claim his rightful place among the likes of Goethe, Bach, and Brecht. Calling him a genius masks how a culture creates authority and power — the aura Benjamin had hoped would disappear.

Nevertheless, Fassbinder and "the Fassbinder film" do represent a unique historical period when these discourses, film genre traditions, and an individual's history united. Yet the West German bourgeois media has been frustrated in trying to canonize Fassbinder since his death. They are torn between praising him as a genius and condemning him as a monster. In 1992 the Fassbinder Foundation put on a retrospective of forty-two films under the motto "A Genius Never Dies." *Der Spiegel* responded with an article entitled "The Canonization of a Monster." *Die Süddeutsche Zeitung* wrote that "the Fassbinder phenomenon" contained all "the ingredients to elevate a profane existence to the height of near sacred veneration" but that these ingredients still could not be easily distilled.[9] And *Die Zeit Magazin* pronounced Fassbinder the "repulsive bloodhound genius" in the headline to a memoir by Armin Mueller-Stahl, a Fassbinder actor.[10] The Fassbinder legend has never rested easily in the political conscience of Germany.

That discomfort is his legend's "legacy": he is the country's most renowned filmmaker, yet German cultural authority has not been able to disarm what he represents politically through the empty category of the *Autor*. When the Allies replaced the authority of fascism with the new authority of the occupation and the *Autor* as its cultural discourse, they perpetuated a top-down notion of power. From an American perspective, because we live in the shadow of the homogeneity of conglomerate capitalism, the concept of a plurality of authorial voices may seem like an inspired democratic idea. And in light of recent incidents of German xenophobia, any governance that promotes plurality appears enlightened in a united Germany.

But we need to question whose plurality was promoted in the post-World War II period: the German educated class was disseminating its competence and tastes as a national culture. Sanctioned *Autoren* meant that the broad German public was once again denied participation in what constituted its culture. For the postwar generation of young Germans, this high culture was a repressive agency of social control. The cultural imperialism of Hollywood commercialism is obvious, but the cultural class imperialism exerted by the British Broadcasting Corporation—the other model for European televisual culture—has not been so apparent.

Fassbinder films played the two conquering cultures against each other, breaking the class-based dichotomy between high and low. They produced high art by popularizing (some said vulgarizing) canonical fiction and drama. They produced low art by melodramatizing an *Autor*'s life into an artist's public confession for the art cinema. In turn, his confession became a subject for the popular tabloids as they attempted to dismantle the power structure of the state's culture industry. Simultaneously, these films were attractive movies that not only invited identification as well as irony but also exposed the myth of the *Autor* by filling the category with a real person, not a model being.

In the end, critics may want to label Fassbinder's work postmodern because it broke traditional categories—especially in "pop"-ularizing modernism. But the Fassbinder film defies easy categorization. A comparison between Fassbinder films and the postmodern David Lynch films illuminates the difference. Both directors combine modernist and Hollywood style and content. Lynch deals with the surrealistic underbelly of small-town American existence. Fassbinder melodramatizes the lives of the German bourgeoisie and the vagaries of the underclass with a hint of authorial self-consciousness. Both are equally at home in the art cinema and popular culture. As a result, they were allowed to produce epic television series (*Berlin Alexanderplatz* and Lynch's *Twin Peaks*) that were promoted as "art television" and elevated through the directors' authority as auteurs.

But Lynch's films hold nothing sacred; his works are ironic celebrations of American commercial culture. They offer no more hint of moral truth than Agent Cooper's refrain, "Damn! That's good coffee."[11] Fassbinder's films also reveal an admiration for American commercial culture and popular culture in his choice of melodrama and pop culture iconography, but they chronicle the clear injustices of class and gender inequalities, even if Franz Biberkopf and other characters victimize themselves.

Lynch reveals himself as an artistic presence through his stylized irony. Although Fassbinder's voice can be quite ironic, his voice mixes with the other agencies of melodramatic fate and history to produce less-distanced and more emotionally accessible films. Lynch's personal history (he is the child of a middle-class Montana family who was educated through the American Film Institute and remains apolitical as a libertarian) fits comfortably within an American bourgeois myth of the artist as aesthetic individualist.[12] Fassbinder films, on the other hand, turn on their maker's authority, which makes his anomalous biography a narrative issue. They make an unusual concession as art films: they expose the tradition of authorial presence to criticism, revealing the politics of the art cinema. Lynch's postmodernism thumbs its nose at any such earnest aim.

Fassbinder's films and television work represent the art and political aims of the German counterculture in the 1960s. In many ways the Fassbinder film was the creation of his countercultural collective, which was held together well beyond the sixties by its playful mixture of pop culture and art cinema. Fassbinder the historical individual became the public locus of the troupe's cultural authority. His co-workers' role in the construction of the Fassbinder myth and films continues after his death. Julianne Lorenz, his editor, and Harry Baer, his production assistant, coordinated all his actors, writings, and films to produce not only the major restropective "A Genius Never Dies" in Berlin and Paris in 1992, but also a foundation to perpetuate the Fassbinder legend for Germany.[13]

Even as this book goes to press, his colleagues fight to control their version of the Fassbinder legend for America. In a *New York Times* article announcing a potential American retrospective of his work, Julianne Lorenz maintained angrily that "people talk about him and not his film.... If people need him to be a homosexual, OK.... He was also a bisexual, but I can't make people change their minds about that. He was not a monster." His cameraman for fifteen films, Michael Ballhaus, disagreed: "I think his reputation is not exaggerated, but I also think you don't have to know all this to understand and appreciate his work." Actress Hanna Schygulla said: "His life was at least as extreme as his films. He was a poet *maudit*."[14] As they did during his life, his troupe continues to construct the text called Fassbinder. They maintain the ambiguous relationship of his sensational life to his films, either directly or through protestation. Fassbinder's life continues to be "good copy" as the popular narrative.

This play between Fassbinder's life and his films still owes much to the aesthetics of the sixties—a movement perched between modernism and postmodernism. According to Richard McCormick, the German counterculture shared the utopian vision of dada modernism with the destruction of the elitism of art through Fassbinder's fusion of art with the everyday. And Fassbinder's work, like the counterculture, attempted "to overthrow a technocracy of elite managers by fusing individual emancipation with democratic mass politics."[15] In contrast, German postmodern experience began as a response to the failure of the sixties as a cultural revolution. In the reactionary climate of the *Tendenzwende,* artists and activists retreated from a global and confrontational vision of change and discovered the personal, subjective, and marginal as the material of political change. Yet the personal was not a new subject for a Fassbinder film in the 1970s. From the beginning in 1967, Fassbinder films looked forward to the subjectivity of the postmodern with the utopian logic of modernism. They used the personal as a site of confrontation, created a popular culture to represent the marginal, and undercut a technocratic culture with personal confession.

Fassbinder may have been made into a caricature of excess by the German tabloid press, as suggested by the reception of *Berlin Alexanderplatz.* The cultural press and the Fassbinder Foundation will continue to attempt to make him into a genius. Yet neither the bourgeois nor the tabloid press has been able to dismiss the power of his disquieting presence as Germany's leading postwar director. This power is not a new version of what Benjamin called "aura," where the artist becomes the site of originality and mystification. Rather, in regard to Fassbinder, "the critical and receptive attitudes of the public" do coincide. The public's curiosity about him always engenders questions about artists and art. His work played into and exposed this cultural power through the language of popular culture. This anarchistic populism will ensure that the legend of Rainer Werner Fassbinder will remain an uncomfortable memory in any future plan to engineer a German national culture.

Works by Rainer Werner Fassbinder

Abbreviations:
d = director
sc = screenwriter
c = cameraperson
ed = editor
m = music
ac = actors
r = running time
p = production company

Der Stadtreicher (1965)
(*The City Tramp*)
d/sc: Fassbinder—c: Josef Jung—ac: Christoph Roser, Susanne
Schimkus, Michael Fengler, Thomas Fengler, Irm Hermann, Fassbinder—
r: 10 min.—p: Roser-Film

Das kleine Chaos (1966)
(*The Little Chaos*)
d/sc: Fassbinder—c: Michael Fengler—ac: Marite Greiselis, Christoph
Roser, Lilo Pempeit, Greta Rehfeld, Fassbinder—r: 9 min.—p: Roser Film

Liebe ist kälter als der Tod (1969)
(*Love Is Colder Than Death*)
d/sc: Fassbinder—c: Dietrich Lohmann—ed: Franz Walsch (RWF)—m:
Peer Raben—ac: Ulli Lommel, Hanna Schygulla, Fassbinder, Hans
Hirschmüller, Katrin Schaake, Peter Berling, Ingrid Caven, Yaak
Karsunke, Peter Moland, Kurt Raab—r: 84 min.—p: antiteater-X-film

Katzelmacher (1969)
d/sc: Fassbinder (based on his play)—c: Dietrich Lohmann—ed: Franz
Walsch (RWF)—m: Franz Schubert—ac: Hanna Schygulla, Rudolf
Waldemar Brem, Lilith Ungerer, Elga Sorbas, Irm Hermann, Harry Baer,
Hans Hirschmüller, Fassbinder—r: 88 min.—p: antiteater-X-film

Götter der Pest (1969)
(*Gods of the Plague*)
d: Fassbinder, Michael Fengler — sc: Fassbinder — c: Dietrich Lohmann —
ed: Franz Walsch (RWF) — m: Peer Raben — ac: Harry Baer, Hanna
Schygulla, Margarethe von Trotta, Günther Kaufmann, Carla Aulaulu,
Ingrid Caven, Yaak Karsunke — r: 91 min. — p: antiteater

Warum läuft Herr R. amok? (1970)
(*Why Does Mr. R. Run Amok?*)
d/sc: Fassbinder, Michael Fengler — c: Dietrich Lohmann — ed: Franz
Walsch (RWF), Michael Fengler — m: Christian Anders — ac: Kurt Raab,
Lilith Ungerer, Amadeus Fengler, Harry Baer, Hanna Schygulla, Peer
Raben, Irm Hermann, Ingrid Caven — r: 88 min. — p: antiteater/Maran

Rio das Mortes (1970)
d/sc: Fassbinder (based on an idea from Volker Schlöndorff) — c: Dietrich
Lohmann — ed: Thea Eymesz — m: Peer Raben — ac: Hanna Schygulla,
Michael König, Günther Kaufmann, Katrin Schaake, Joachim von
Mengershausen, Lilo Pempeit, Ulli Lommel, Harry Baer, Hanna Axmann-
Rezzori — r: 84 min. — p: Janus Film und Fernsehen (for
ARD)/antiteater-X-film

Das Kaffeehaus (1970)
(*The Coffeehouse*)
d/sc: Fassbinder (based on a play by Carlo Goldoni) — c: Dietbert Schmidt,
Manfred Förster — m: Peer Raben — ac: Margit Carstensen, Ingrid
Caven, Hanna Schygulla, Kurt Raab, Harry Baer, Hans Hirschmüller,
Günther Kaufmann, Peter Moland, Wil Rabenbauer — r: 105 min. — p:
Westdeutscher Rundfunk (WDR)

Whity (1970)
d/sc: Fassbinder — c: Michael Ballhaus — ed: Franz Walsch (RWF), Thea
Eymesz — m: Peer Raben — ac: Günther Kaufmann, Hanna Schygulla,
Ulli Lommel, Harry Baer — r: 95 min. — p: Atlantis Film/antiteater-X-
film

Die Niklashauser Fahrt (1970)
(*The Niklashaus Trip*)
d: Fassbinder, Michael Fengler — sc: Fassbinder — c: Dietrich Lohmann —
ed: Thea Eymesz, Franz Walsch (RWF) — m: Peer Raben, Amon Düül II —

ac: Michael Künig, Fassbinder, Hanna Schygulla, Walter Sedlmayer, Margit Carstensen, Franz Maron, Kurt Raab—r: 86 min.—p: Janus Film und Fernsehen/Westdeutscher Rundfunk (WDR)

Der amerikanische Soldat (1970)
(*The American Soldier*)
d/sc: Fassbinder—c: Dietrich Lohmann—ed: Thea Eymesz—m: Peer Raben—ac: Karl Scheydt, Elga Sorbas, Margarethe von Trotta, Hark Bohm, Ingrid Caven, Fassbinder, Ulli Lommel, Irm Hermann—r: 80 min.—p: antiteater Munich

Pioniere in Ingolstadt (1970)
(*Pioneers in Ingolstadt*)
d/sc: Fassbinder (based on the play from Marieluise Fleisser)—c: Dietrich Lohmann—ed: Thea Eymesz—m: Peer Raben—ac: Hanna Schygulla, Harry Baer, Irm Hermann, Rudolf Waldemar Brem, Walter Sedlmayer, Klaus Löwitsch, Günther Kaufmann, Carla Aulaulu—r: 84 min.—p: Janus Film und Fernsehen/antiteater/Zweites Deutsches Fernsehen (ZDF)

Warnung vor einer heiligen Nutte (1970)
(*Beware of the Holy Whore*)
d/sc: Fassbinder—c: Michael Ballhaus—ed: Franz Walsch (RWF), Thea Eymesz—m: Peer Raben, Gaetano Donizetti, Elvis Presley, Ray Charles, Leonard Cohen, Spooky Tooth—ac: Lou Castell, Eddie Constantine, Hanna Schygulla, Marquard Bohm, Fassbinder, Ulli Lommel, Margarethe von Trotta, Werner Schroeter—r: 103 min.—p: antiteater-X-film/nova International

Der Händler der vier Jahreszeiten (1971)
(*Merchant of the Four Seasons*)
d/sc: Fassbinder—c: Dietrich Lohmann—ed: Thea Eymesz—ac: Hans Hirschmüller, Irm Hermann, Hanna Schygulla, Gusti Kneissl, Kurt Raab, Klaus Löwitsch, Karl Scheydt, Ingrid Caven—r: 89 min.—p: Filmverlag der Autoren/Zweites Deutsches Fernsehen (ZDF)

Die bitteren Tränen der Petra von Kant (1972)
(*The Bitter Tears of Petra von Kant*)
d/sc: Fassbinder (based on his play)—c: Michael Ballhaus—ed: Thea Eymesz—m: the Platters, the Walker Brothers, Giuseppe Verdi—ac: Margit Carstensen, Hanna Schygulla, Irm Hermann, Eva Mattes, Karin

Schaake, Gisela Fackeldey—r: 124 min.—p: Tango (R. W. Fassbinder
and Michael Fengler)

Wildwechsel (1972)
(Jailbait)
d/sc: Fassbinder (based on the play by Franz Xaver Kroetz)—c: Dietrich
Lohmann—ed: Thea Eymesz—m: Beethoven—ac: Jörg von Liebenfels,
Ruth Drexel, Eva Mattes, Harry Baer, Hanna Schygulla, Kurt Raab, Karl
Scheydt, Klaus Löwitsch—r: 102 min.—p: Intertel

Acht Stunden sind kein Tag (1972)
(Eight Hours Are Not a Day)
Five-part television series—d/sc: Fassbinder—c: Dietrich Lohmann—
ed: Marie Anne Gerhardt—m: Jean Geponint—ac: Gottfried John,
Hanna Schygulla, Luise Ullrich, Kurt Raab, Werner Finck, Renate
Roland, Irm Hermann, Herb Andres—r: 101 min. (part 1), 100 min. (part
2), 92 min. (part 3), 88 min. (part 4), 89 min. (part 5)—p: Westdeutscher
Rundfunk (WDR)

Bremer Freiheit (1972)
(Bremen Freedom)
d/sc: Fassbinder and Dietrich Lohmann—c: Dietrich Lohmann—ed:
Friedrich Niquet, Monika Solzbacher—ac: Margit Carstensen, Ulli
Lommel, Wolfgang Schenck, Walter Sedlmayer, Wolfgang Kieling, Kurt
Raab, Hanna Schygulla—r: 87 min.—p: Telefilm Saar/Saarländer
Rundfunk (SR)

Welt am Draht (1973)
(World on a Wire)
d: Fassbinder—sc: Fritz Müller-Scherz, Fassbinder (based on the novel by
Daniel Galouye)—c: Michael Ballhaus—ed: Marie Anne Gerhardt—m:
Gottfried Hüngsberg—ac: Klaus Löwitsch, Mascha Rabben, Adrian Hoven,
Ivan Desny, Barbara Valentin, Karl-Heinz Vosgerau, Günter Lamprecht,
Margit Carstensen, Wolfgang Schenk, Joachim Hansen, Rudolf Lenz, Kurt
Raab, Karl Scheydt, Ulli Lommel—r: 99 min.—p: Westdeutscher
Rundfunk (WDR)

Nora Helmer (1973)
d: Fassbinder—sc: a play by Henrik Ibsen—c: Willi Raber—ed: Anne-
Marie Bornheimer, Friedrich Niquet—ac: Margit Carstensen, Joachim

Hansen, Barbara Valentin, Ulli Lommel, Klaus Löwitsch, Lilo Pempeit, Irm Hermann — r: 101 min. — p: Telefilm Saar/Saarländer Rundfunk (SR)

Martha (1973)
d/sc: Fassbinder (inspired by a short story by Cornell Woolrich) — c: Michael Ballhaus — ed: Liesgret Schmitt-Klink — m: G. Donizetti — ac: Margit Carstensen, Karlheinz Böhm, Barbara Valentin, Ingrid Caven, Günther Lamprecht, Peter Chatel, Gisella Fackeldey — r: 112 min. — p: Westdeutscher Rundfunk (WDR)

Angst essen Seele auf (1973)
(*Ali/Fear Eats the Soul*)
d/sc: Fassbinder — c: Jürgen Jürges — ed: Thea Eymesz — ac: Brigitte Mira, El Hedi Ben Salem, Barbara Valentin, Irm Hermann, Fassbinder, Marquard Bohm, Walter Sedmayr — r: 93 min. — p: Tango (R. W. Fassbinder and Michael Fengler)

Effi Briest (1974)
d/sc: Fassbinder (based on the novel by Theodor Fontane) — c: Dietrich Lohmann, Jürgen Jürges — ed: Thea Eymesz — m: Camille Saint-Saëns — ac: Hanna Schygulla, Wolfgang Schenck, Karlheinz Böhm, Ulli Lommel, Ursula Strätz, Hark Bohm, Irm Hermann — r: 141 min. — p: Tango

Wie ein Vogel auf dem Draht (1974)
(*Like a Bird on the Wire*)
d: Fassbinder — sc: Fassbinder, Christian Hohoff — c: Erhard Spandel — m: Ingfried Hoffman, Kurt Edelhagen Orchestra — ac: Brigitte Mira, Evelyn Künnecke — r: 44 min. — p: Deutsche Film und Fernsehakademie Berlin

Faustrecht der Freiheit (1975)
(*Fox and His Friends*)
d/sc: Fassbinder — c: Michael Ballhaus — ed: Thea Eymesz — m: Peer Raben — ac: Fassbinder, Peter Chatel, Karlheinz Böhm, Rudolf Lenz, Karl Scheydt, Kurt Raab, Harry Baer — r: 123 min. — p: Tango/City (1977)

Mutter Küsters Fahrt zum Himmel (1975)
(*Mother Küster's Trip to Heaven*)
d: Fassbinder — sc: Fassbinder, Kurt Raab — c: Michael Ballhaus — ed: Thea Eymesz — m: Peer Raben — ac: Brigitte Mira, Ingrid Caven,

Karlheinz Böhm, Margit Carstensen, Irm Hermann, Gottfried John, Armin Meier, Kurt Raab—r: 120 min.—p: Tango Film

Angst vor der Angst (1975)
(*Fear of Fear*)
d/sc: Fassbinder (based on an idea from Asta Scheib)—c: Jürgen Jürges/Ulrich Prinz—ed: Liesgret Schmitt-Klink, Beate Fischer-Weiskirch—m: Peer Raben—ac: Margit Carstensen, Ulrich Faulhaber, Brigitte Mira, Irm Hermann, Kurt Raab, Ingrid Caven, Lio Pempeit—r: 88 min.—p: Westdeutscher Rundfunk (WDR)

Ich will doch nur, dass Ihr mich liebt (1975/76)
(*I Only Want You to Love Me*)
d/sc: Fassbinder (based on a case study)—c: Michael Ballhaus—ed: Liesgret Schmitt-Klink—m: Peer Raben—ac: Vitus Zeplichal, Elke Aberle, Alexander Allerson, Ernie Mangold, Johanna Hofer, Katharina Buchhammer, Wolfgang Hess, Armin Meier, Erika Runge—r: 104 min.—p: Bavaria Atelier/Westdeutscher Rundfunk (WDR)

Satansbraten (1975/76)
(*Satan's Brew*)
d/sc: Fassbinder—c: Jürgen Jürges—ed: Thea Eymesz, Gabi Eichel—m: Peer Raben—ac: Kurt Raab, Margit Carstensen, Helen Vita, Volker Spengler, Ingrid Caven, Marquard Bohm, Ulli Lommel, Y Sa Lo—r: 112 min.—p: Albatros/Trio

Chinesisches Roulette (1976)
(*Chinese Roulette*)
d/sc: Fassbinder—c: Michael Ballhaus—ed: Ila von Hasperg, Julianne Lorenz—m: Peer Raben—ac: Anna Karina, Macha Meril, Ulli Lommel, Brigitte Mira, Alex Allerson, Margit Carstensen, Andrea Schober, Armin Meier—r: 86 min.—p: Albatros Film (Michael Fengler)/Les Films du Losange Paris

Bolwieser (1976/77)
d/sc: Fassbinder (based on the novel by Oskar Maria von Graf)—c: Michael Ballhaus—ed: Ila von Hasperg, Juliane Lorenz—m: Peer Raben—ac: Kurt Raab, Elisabeth Trissenaar, Bernhard Helfrich, Udo Kier, Volker Spengler, Armin Meier—r: 201 min. (two-part television version)—p: Bavaria Atelier GmbH for Zweites Deutsches Fernsehen (ZDF)

Frauen in New York (1977)
(*Women in New York*)
d/sc: Fassbinder (based on play by Claire Boothe Luce) — c: Michael
Ballhaus — ed: Wolfgang Kerhutt — ac: Christa Berndl, Margit
Carstensen, Anne-Marie Kuster, Eva Mattes, Angela Schmidt, Heidi
Grübl, Ehmi Bessel, Irm Hermann, Gisela Uhlen, Barbara Sukowa — r:
111 min. — p: Norddeutscher Rundfunk (NDR)

Eine Reise ins Licht (1977)
(*Despair*)
d: Fassbinder — sc: Tom Stoppard (based on a novel by Vladimir
Nabokov) — c: Michael Ballhaus — ed: Reginald Beck, Juliane Lorenz —
m: Peer Raben — ac: Dirk Bogarde, Andrea Ferreol, Bernhard Wicki,
Volker Spengler, Klaus Löwitsch, Peter Kern, Roger Fritz — r: 114
min. — p: NF Geria II/Bavaria Munich(WDR)/SFP Paris

Deutschland im Herbst (1978)
(*Germany in Autumn*)
d: Alf Brustellin, Fassbinder, Alexander Kluge, Maximiliane Mainka,
Edgar Reitz, Katja Ruppe Hans, Peter Cloos, Bernhard Sinkel, Volker
Schlöndorff — sc: Fassbinder, Heinrich Böll, Peter Steinbach — c: Michael
Ballhaus, Jürgen Jürges, Bodo Kessler, Dietrich Lohmann, Jörg Schmidt-
Reitwein — ed: Beate Mainka-Jellinghaus — ac: Fassbinder, Hannelore
Hoger, Katja Ruppe, Angela Winkler, Heinz Bennent, Helmut Griem,
Vadim Glowna, Enno Patalas, Horst Mahler, Mario Adorf, Wolf
Biermann — r: 116 min. — p: Pro-Ject Film Production/Filmverlag der
Autoren/Hallelujah Film/Kairos Film

In einem Jahr mit 13 Monden (1978)
(*In a Year of Thirteen Moons*)
d/sc/c/ed: Fassbinder — m: Peer Raben — ac: Volker Spengler, Ingrid
Caven, Elisabeth Trissenaar, Gottfried John, Eva Mattes — r: 124 min. —
p: Tango Film/Pro-Ject Film

Die Ehe der Maria Braun (1978)
(*The Marriage of Maria Braun*)
d: Fassbinder — sc: Peter Märthesheimer, Pea Fröhlich, Fassbinder (based
on an idea by Fassbinder) — c: Michael Ballhaus — ed: Juliane Lorenz,
Franz Walsch (RWF) — m: Peer Raben — ac: Hanna Schygulla, Klaus
Löwitsch, Ivan Desny, Gottfried John, Günter Lamprecht, Gisela Uhlen,

Elisabeth Trissenaar — r: 120 min. — p: Albatros (Michael Fengler)/Trio (Hans Eckelkamp)/Westdeutscher Rundfunk (WDR)

Die dritte Generation (1979)
(*The Third Generation*)
d/sc/c: Fassbinder — ed: Juliane — m: Peer Raben — ac: Harry Baer, Hark Bohm, Margit Carstensen, Eddie Constantine, Günther Kaufmann, Udo Kier, Bulle Ogier, Lilo Pempeit, Hanna Schygulla, Volker Spengler, Y Sa Lo, Vituz Zeplichal — r: 111 min. — p: Tango/ Filmverlag der Autoren

Berlin Alexanderplatz (1980)
d/sc: Fassbinder (based on the novel by Alfred Döblin) — c: Xaver Schwarzenberger — ed: Juliane Lorenz — m: Peer Raben — ac: Günter Lamprecht, Barbara Sukowa, Hanna Schygulla, Ivan Desny, Gottfried John, Ingrid Caven, Brigitte Mira — r: 81 min. (part 1), 59 min. (parts 2-13), 111 min. (epilogue) — p: Bavaria/RAI for Westdeutscher Rundfunk (WDR)

Lili Marleen (1980)
d: Fassbinder — sc: Manfred Purzer, Fassbinder — c: Xaver Schwarzenberger — ed: Juliane Lorenz, Franz Walsch (RWF) — m: Peer Raben — ac: Hanna Schygulla, Giancarlo Giannini, Mel Ferrer, Christine Kaufmann, Hark Bohm, Karin Baal, Udo Kier, Gottfried John — r: 121 min. — p: Roxy Film (Luggi Waldleiter)/Rialto-Film (Horst Wendlandt)/Bavaria Rundfunk (BR)/CIP

Lola (1981)
d: Fassbinder — sc: Peter Märthesheimer, Pea Frölich, dialogue by Fassbinder — c: Xaver Schwarzenberger — ed: Juliane Lorenz, Franz Walsch (RWF) — m: Peer Raben — ac: Barbara Sukowa, Armin Mueller-Stahl, Mario Adorf, Matthias Fuchs, Helga Feddersen, Karin Baal, Ivan Desny, Hark Bohm — r: 113 min. — p: Rialto-Film (Horst Wendlandt/Trio-Film/Westdeutscher Rundfunk (WDR)

Die Sehnsucht der Veronika Voss (1981)
(*Veronika Voss*)
d: Fassbinder — sc: Peter Märthesheimer, Pea Fröhlich — c: Xaver Schwarzenberger — ed: Juliane Lorenz — m: Peer Raben — ac: Rosel Zech, Hilmar Thate, Cornelia Froboess, Armin Mueller-Stahl, Elisabeth Volkmann, Rudolf Platte, Doris Schade — r: 105 min. — p: Tango Film/Rialto-Film/Trio-Film/Maran-Film

Querelle (1982)

d: Fassbinder—sc: Burkhard Driest, Fassbinder (based on the story by Jean Genet)—c: Xaver Schwarzenberger—ed: Juliane Lorenz—m: Peer Raben—ac: Brad Davis, Franco Nero, Jeanne Moreau, Laurent Malet, Hanno Pöschl, Günther Kaufmann—r: 107 min.—p: Bavaria/Pro-Ject

Appendix A

Feature films on West German television by network and country of origin, 1977

Country of origin	Total number	%	ARD number	ZDF number
German remakes	25	7.5	12	13
West Germany	34	10.2	9	25
East Germany	2	0.6	1	1
Austria	4	1.2	1	3
Switzerland	1	0.3	1	—
United States	157	47.3	80	77
Great Britain	23	6.9	11	12
France	16	4.8	6	10
France/Italy	21	6.4	8	13
Italy	15	4.6	5	10
Czechoslovakia	8	2.4	4	4
Australia	4	1.2	3	1
Canada	4	1.2	1	3
Poland	3	0.9	—	3
Sweden	3	0.9	2	1
Soviet Union	3	0.9	2	1
Spain	2	0.6	1	1
Hungary	2	0.6	2	—
Belgium	1	0.3	1	—
Denmark	1	0.3	1	—
Greece	1	0.3	1	—
Brazil	1	0.3	1	—
Iran	1	0.3	1	—
Total	332	100.0	154	178

Source: *Filmstatistisches Taschenbuch* (Wiesbaden: Spitzenorganisation der Filmwirtschaft, 1977)

Appendix B

Portion of literary adaptations in relation to total television drama/films

Year	Television drama/ films (total	Literary adaptations	Percentage
1951–52	9	4	44.4
1953	47	28	59.6
1954	62	45	72.6
1955	88	78	88.6
1956	79	65	82.3
1957	90	82	91.1
1958	93	80	86.0
1959	96	77	80.2
1960	93	70	75.3
1961	158	123	77.8
1962	151	127	84.1
1963	240	177	73.8
1964	244	167	68.4
1965	262	167	63.7
1966	257	155	60.3
1967	248	149	60.1
1968	211	121	57.3
1969	241	129	53.5
1970	243	101	41.6
1971	240	100	41.7
1972	223	82	36.8
1973	216	92	42.6
1974	208	87	41.8
1975	191	94	48.9
1976	192	93	48.4
1977	218	89	40.8

Source: Knut Hickethier, *Das Fernsehspiel der Bundesrepublik: Themen, Form, Struktur, Theorie und Geschichte*

Appendix C

Types of literary sources for television drama adaptations

Year	Total adaptations	Theater No.	%	Prose No.	%	Radio No.	%	Other No.	%
1951–52	4	3	75.0	—	—	—	—	1	25.0
1953	28	21	75.0	3	10.7	4	14.3	—	—
1954	45	29	64.5	8	17.8	6	13.3	2	4.4
1955	78	59	75.6	14	18.0	4	18.0	1	1.3
1956	65	53	81.5	7	10.8	4	6.2	1	1.5
1957	82	64	78.1	11	13.4	6	7.3	1	1.2
1958	80	69	86.2	9	11.3	2	2.5	—	—
1959	77	66	85.7	9	11.7	2	2.6	—	—
1960	70	56	80.8	8	11.4	6	8.6	—	—
1961	123	104	84.6	17	13.8	1	0.8	1	0.8
1962	127	101	79.5	22	17.3	2	1.6	2	1.6
1963	177	137	77.3	35	19.8	4	2.3	1	0.6
1964	167	131	78.5	28	16.7	6	3.6	2	1.2
1965	167	116	69.4	40	24.0	6	3.6	5	3.0
1966	155	105	67.7	41	26.5	5	3.2	4	2.6
1967	149	101	67.8	44	29.6	2	1.3	2	1.3
1968	121	69	57.0	45	37.2	4	3.3	3	2.5
1969	129	70	54.2	50	38.8	7	5.4	2	1.6
1970	101	43	42.5	54	53.5	2	2.0	2	2.0
1971	100	52	52.0	43	43.0	5	5.0	—	—
1972	82	38	46.4	37	45.1	6	7.3	1	1.2
1973	92	38	41.3	52	56.5	1	1.1	1	1.1
1974	87	33	37.9	51	58.6	3	3.5	—	—
1975	94	45	47.9	48	51.1	1	1.0	—	—
1976	93	37	39.8	55	59.1	1	1.1	—	—
1977	89	58	65.2	29	32.6	1	1.1	1	1.1

Source: Knut Hickethier, *Das Fernsehspiel der Bundesrepublik: Themen, Form, Struktur, Theorie und Geschichte*

Appendix D

Feature films broadcast on national television, 1966–77

Year	Total number	ARD portion[a]	ZDF portion
1966	222	91	131
1967	272	115	157
1968	277	126	151
1969	282	136	146
1970	304	141	163
1971	335	158	177
1972	341	163	178
1973	317	144	173
1974	327	155	172
1975	346	167	179
1976	324	149	175
1977	332	154	178

Source: *ARD & ZDF Jahrbücher 1966–67*
[a]Gemeinschaftsprogramm

Appendix E

Coproduction and prepurchase (1974–79) under the
1974 Film/Fernseh-Abkommens

	Coproduction (ARD)		
Film and coproduction network/station	Production company	Director	Coproduction expenditure (DM)
Umarmungen ARD-BR released	I. Richter	I. Richter	350,000
Sommergaste ARD-SFB released	R. Ziegler	P. Stein	450,000
Nordsee ist Mordsee ARD-SDR released	Hbg. Kino-Komp.	H. Bohm	280,000
Die verlorene Ehre der Katharina Blum ARD-WDR released	Bioskop/Param. Orion	V. Schlöndorff	510,600
Mitgift ARD-WDR released	Sentana	M. Verhoeven	400,000
Der Sternsteinhof ARD-BR released	Roxy	Geissendorfer	550,000
Ansichten eines Clowns ARD-WDR released	Independent	V. Jasny	750,000
Die Marquise von O. ARD-HR released	Janus/Artemis	E. Rohmer	400,000
Der amerikanische Freund ARD-WDR released	Wenders	W. Wenders	600,000
Der Fangschuss ARD-HR released	Bioskop	V. Schlöndorff	300,000
Angst ist ein zweiter Schatten ARD-SWF released	FFAT	Kuckelmann	350,000
Das Tal der tanzenden Witwen ARD-SDR released	Albatros	V. Vogeler	200,000
Mein Onkel Theodor ARD-NDR/HR released	Ehmck	G. Ehmck	670,000
Die Standarte ARD-NDR released	Runze	O. Runze	1,000,000
Gefundenes Fressen ARD-BR released	Sentant	M. Verhoeven	400,000
Kreutzer ARD-BR released	Sunny Point	K. Emmerich	701,500

215

Coproduction (ARD) (continued)

Film and coproduction network/station	Production company	Director	Coproduction expenditure (DM)
Heinrich ARD-WDR released	R. Ziegler	H. Sanders	433,000
Elixiere des Teufels ARD-BR released	Roxy	M. Purzer	900,000
Johnny West ARD-HR released	Sunny Point	R. Koller	400,000
Finsternis bedeckt die Erde ARD-NDR not released	Independent	R. Hadrich	1,200,000
Die Jugendstreiche des Knaben Karl ARD-BR not released	Roxy/Seitz	F. Seitz	650,000
Halbe Halbe ARD-NDR released	Brandner/ DNS-Film	U. Brandner	400,000
Die Frau gegenüber ARD-BR released	DNS-Film	H. Noever	340,000
Die Brandstifter ARD-NDR/HR released	Ehmck	G. Ehmck	760,000
Wildlaufen (Taugenichts) ARD-WDR released	ABS	B. Sinckel	700,000
Der Mann im Schiff ARD-BR released	Roxy	M. Purzer	950,000
Winterspielt ARD-SFB/HR released	Ullstein AV	E. Fechner	924,600

Title Sponsoring TV station Theatrical standing	Production company	Director	DM from television
Geschichten aus dem Wiener Wald ARD-BR released	MFG-Film	M. Schell	500,000
Die gläserne Zelle ARD-BR released	Roxy-Film	Geissendorfer	950,000
Gotz v. Berlichingen ARD-BR released	Regina Film	W. Liebeneiner	950,000
Die Ehe der Maria Braun ARD-WDR released	Albatros	R. W. Fassbinder	600,000
Zwischengleis ARD-BR released	Artus Film	W. Staudte	550,000
Die Blechtrommel ARD-HR released	Seitz/Artemis	Schlöndorff	1,000,000
Der Preis fürs Überleben ARD-BR not released	DNS	H. Noever	700,000

Title Sponsoring TV station Theatrical standing	Production company	Director	DM from television
1 + 1 = 3 ARD-SDR released	Genee/v. Furstenberg	H. Genee	300,000
Die wunderbaren Jahre ARD-SWF not released	Seitz	R. Kunze	800,000
Theo gegen den Rest der Welt ARD-WDR not released	Tura-Film	P. S. Bringmann	850,000
Gibbi West Germany ARD-WDR not released	Bioskop Film	C. Buschmann	600,000
Lili Marleen ARD-BR not released	Roxy Film	N. Gessner	1,300,000
Carnapping Bestellt- *Geklaut-Geliefert* ARD-HR not released	Geissler	W. Wicker	500,000
Berlinger ZDF released	Independent	Sinkel/Brustellin	700,000
Warum bellt Herr Bobikow? ZDF released	Corona	A. Lattuada	415,000
Bomber und Paganini ZDF released	Perakis	N. Perakis	540,000
In Gefahr und grösster Not *bringt der Mittelweg den Tod* ZDF released	Kairos	A. Kluge	200,000
Also es war so ZDF not released	Thome	I. Thome	486,500
Der starke Ferdinand ZDF released	Kairso	A. Kluge	650,000
Gruppenbild mit Dame ZDF released	Geissler	A. Petrovic	700,000
Grete Minde ZDF released	Solaris	H. Genee	800,000
Tatarenwuste ZDF released	Corona	V. Zurlini	750,000
Das Schlangenei ZDF released	Rialto	I. Bergman	1,100,000
Stroszek ZDF released	Herzog	W. Herzog	650,000
Der Schneider von Ulm ZDF released	Reitz	E. Reitz	900,000
Der Schimmelreiter ZDF released	Albis/Studio	A. Weidenmann	700,000
Moritz, lieber Moritz ZDF released	Hbg. Kino-Komp.	H. Bohm	600,000
Jeder für sich und Gott gegen alle ZDF released	Herzog	W. Herzog	544,000

Title Sponsoring TV station Theatrical standing	Production company	Director	DM from television
Coproduction (ARD) (continued)			
Viktoria ZDF released	Corona	B. Widerberg	500,000
Die Hamburger Krankheit ZDF released	Halleluja	P. Fleischmann	800,000
Tod oder Freiheit ZDF released	Ziegler/Param. Orion	W. Gremm	700,000

Title Sponsoring TV station Theatrical standing	Production company	Director	DM from television
Coproduction (ZDF)			
Die Faust in der Tasche ZDF released	Basis-Film	M. Willutzki	430,000
David ZDF released	v. Vietinghoff	P. Lilienthal	800,000
Neues vom Rauber Hotzenplotz ZDF released	Ehmck	G. Ehmck	400,000
Nosferatu — Phantom der Nacht ZDF released	Herzog	W. Herzog	800,000
Milo, Milo ZDF released	Vietinghoff Perakis	N. Perakis	800,000
Eine einfache Geschichte ZDF released	Rialto	C. Sautet	400,000
Der Verkauf des Bruders ZDF not released	Linda-Film	C. Sautet	400,000
Die Patriotin ZDF released	Kairos-Film	A. Kluge	280,000
Bericht über Samur ZDF not released	Ziegler Schaubuhne	P. Stein	1,200,000
So weit das Auge reicht ZDF not released	Prokino	E. Keusch	800,000
Arabische Nachte ZDF released	Albatros	C. Lembke	500,000
Mortenhoe ZDF not released	TV 13	B. Tavernier	500,000
Im Herzen des Hurricans ZDF not released	Hbg. Kino-Komp.	H. Bohm	600,000
Die Geburt der Hexe ZDF not released	Jochen Richter	W. Minks	700,000
Palermo oder Wolfsburg ZDF not released	Th. Mauch	W. Schroeter	560,000
Gladow ZDF not released	v. Vietinghoff	T. Brasch	800,000
Fitzcarraldo ZDF not released	Herzog	W. Herzog	980,000

Prepurchased Films (ARD)			
Title	Production company	Director	Theatrical standing
Das Messer im Rucken	O. Runze	O. Runze	released
Mutter Küsters Fahrt zum Himmel	Tango-Film	Fassbinder	released
Im Laufe der Zeit	W. Wenders	W. Wenders	released
Fluchtversuch	Tatjuna	V. Jasny	released
Malou	R. Ziegler	J. Meerapfel	not released
Verlorenes Leben	O. Runze	O. Runze	released
Die Vertreibung aus dem Paradies	N. Schilling	N. Schilling	released
Rheingold	Visual	N. Schilling	released
Im dunklen Herz des Nachmittags	Albatros	W. Schroeter	not released
Transamazonica-Phantastische Reise	Jura-Film	F. Kalden	not released
. . . als Diesel geboren	Road Movies	P. Przygodda	not released
Radio on	Road Movies	Chris Petit	not released
Ein Portrait des Yangtse-Kiang	Durniok	Lorenzen/ Durniok	not released
Nick	Road Movies	W. Wenders	released

Prepurchased Films (ZDF)			
Title	Production company	Director	Theatrical standing
Potato-Fritz	Schamoni	P. Schamoni	released
Unordnung und frühes Leid	Seitz	F. Seitz	released
Eierdiebe	Albatros	M. Fengler	released
Herz aus Glas	Herzog	W. Herzog	released
Jacobine	Gauer	Gauer/Bodansky	released
Das fünfte Gebot	Oase	D. Tessari	released
Kneuss	Brechbuhl/Meili	G. Meili	Schweitz
Wassilissa	R. v. Praunheim	R. v. Praunheim	not released
Die Anstalt	Common-film	R. Minow	released
Das Land, wo Milch und Honig fliessen	Simba-Film	N. Jariv	not released
Beschreibung einer Insel	Moana-Film	R. Thome	released
Woyzeck	Herzog	W. Herzog	released
Henry Angst	Kratisch	I. Kratisch	not released

Appendix F

The Film/TV Abkommen

Films of New German Cinema directors

ARD or WDR coproduced or prepurchased

R. W. Fassbinder	*Die Ehe der Maria Braun* (*The Marriage of Maria Braun* [1978/WDR])
	Mutter Küsters Fahrt zum Himmel (*Mother Küster's Trip to Heaven* [1975/ARD prepurchased])
E. Rohmer	*Die Marquise von O.* (*The Marquise of O.* [1976/BR])
Helma Sanders	*Heinrich* (1976/WDR)
Volker Schlöndorff	*Die verlorene Ehre der Katharina Blum* (*The Lost Honor of Katharina Blum* [1975/WDR])
	Die Blechtrommel (*The Tin Drum* [1979/WDR])
Wim Wenders	*Der amerikanische Freund* (*The American Friend* [1977/WDR])
	Im Lauf der Zeit (*Kings of the Road* [1976/ARD prepurchased])
	Nick's Film (1979/ARD prepurchased)

ZDF coproduced or prepurchased

Ingmar Bergman	*Das Schlangenei* (*The Serpent's Egg* [1978])
H. Bohm	*Moritz, lieber Moritz* (*Moritz, Dear Moritz* [1979])
	Im Herzen des Hurricans (*In the Eye of the Hurricane* [19795])
Werner Herzog	*Stroszek* (1977)
	Jeder für sich und Gott gegen alle (*Kasper Hauser* [1974])
	Nosferatu (1978)
	Fitzcarraldo (1979)
	Herz aus Glas (*Heart Out of Glass* [1976/prepurchased])
	Woyzeck (1978/prepurchased)
A. Kluge	*In Gefahr und grösster Not bringt der Mittelweg den Tod* (*The Middle of the Road Is a Very Dead End* [1974])
	Der starker Ferdinand (*The Strongman Ferdinand* [1975])
	Die Patriotin (*The Patriotic Woman* [1979])
W. Schroeter	*Palermo oder Wolfsburg* (*Palermo or Wolfsburg* [1980])
	Im Dunklen Herz des Nachmittags (*In the Heart of Darkness in the Afternoon* [1977/ARD prepurchased])
B. Tavernier	*Mortenhoe* (*Deathwatch* [1979])

Appendix G

Appendix H

Audience share for the *Berlin Alexanderplatz* episodes

Episode	Date of broadcast	Percent and number of viewers
One	Sun. 10/12/80	27 or 5.65 million
Two	Mon. 10/13/80	22 or 4.62 million
Three	Mon. 10/20/80	18 or 3.88 million
Four	Mon. 10/27/80	11 or 2.25 million
Five	Mon. 11/3/80	16 or 3.42 million
Six	Mon. 11/10/80	16 or 3.28 million
Seven	Mon. 11/17/80	16 or 3.37 million
Eight	Mon. 11/24/80	16 or 3.37 million
Nine	Mon. 12/1/80	15 or 3.21 million
Ten	Mon. 12/8/80	18 or 3.70 million
Eleven	Mon. 12/22/80	14 or 2.99 million
Twelve	Mon. 12/29/80	13 or 2.72 million
Epilogue		8 or 1.65 million

Source: Kristina Zerges, "Die TV-Series 'Berlin Alexanderplatz' von Rainer Werner Fassbinder. Dokumentation und Analyse eines Rezeptionsprocesses."

Notes

1 / The Melodrama of Fassbinder's Reception

1. Walter Benjamin, *Illuminations* (New York: Schocken, 1978), 234.

2. In the summer of 1984 West German television produced Edgar Reitz's *Heimat,* an eleven-part TV series that cost 35 million marks (see the conclusion of this book). For an in-depth analysis of the series, see the special issue on *Heimat, New German Critique* 36 (Fall 1985): 3–90. In 1993 West German television produced a mammoth thirteen-part, or twenty-six-hour sequel to *Heimat: The Second Heimat* (*Zweite Heimat*).

3. ARD (Arbeitsgemeinschaft der öffentlichrechtlichen Rundfunkanstalten der Bundes-republik Deutschland) is the first channel of three possible West German television networks. The actual producer of *Berlin Alexanderplatz* was Westdeutscher Rundfunk in Cologne.

4. Tony Bennett, *Formalism and Marxism* (New York: Methuen, 1979), 148.

5. Judith Mayne, "Fassbinder and Spectatorship," *New German Critique* 12 (Fall 1977): 65.

6. John Sandford, *The New German Cinema* (Totowa, N.J.: Barnes and Noble, 1980), 64.

7. Timothy Corrigan, *New German Film: The Displaced Image* (Austin: University of Texas Press, 1983), 45.

8. Eric Rentschler, *New German Film in the Course of Time* (Bedford Hills, N.Y.: Red-grave, 1984), 84.

9. Early influential writing on the ideological nature of melodrama includes Paul Wil-lemen, "Distanciation and Douglas Sirk," *Screen* 12, no. 2 (Summer 1971): 63–67; *Douglas Sirk,* ed. Laura Mulvey and Jon Halliday (Edinburgh: Edinburgh Film Festival, 1972); and Geoffrey Nowell-Smith, "Minnelli and Melodrama," *Screen* 2, no. 28 (Summer 1977): 113–18.

10. Thomas Elsaesser, "Tales of Sound and Fury: Observations on the Family Melo-drama," *Monogram* 4 (1972): 2–15.

11. Ibid.

12. See Willemen, "Distanciation and Douglas Sirk"; Steve Neale, "Douglas Sirk," *Framework* 5 (Winter 1976–77): 16–18; and Jon Halliday, *Sirk on Sirk* (New York: Viking, 1972), 7–13.

13. Laura Mulvey, "Notes on Sirk and Melodrama," in *Home Is Where the Heart Is: Studies in Melodrama and the Woman's Film,* ed. Christine Gledhill (London: British Film Insti-tute, 1987), 75–79.

14. Significantly, when Elsaesser later turns to his next academic interest, Fassbinder, he makes no attempt to apply his theories of melodrama's political potential to this more obvious use of melodrama and politics. Elsaesser's criticism on Fassbinder includes "A Cinema of Vicious Circles," in *Fassbinder,* ed. Tony Rayns (London: British Film Institute, 1980), 24–36; "*Lili Marleen,* Fascism and Film Industry," *October* 22: 120–40; and "Primary Identifica-tion and the Historical Subject: Fassbinder and Germany," *Cinetracts* 11 (Fall 1980): 43–52. In his recent survey, *New German Cinema: A History* (New Brunswick, N.J.: Rutgers University Press, 1989), Elsaesser argues that Fassbinder's use of melodrama refers more to film history than the genre's formal dissonance: "It is true that allusionism is part of a complex process

whereby film-making assures itself of its own history, and the New German Cinema progressively did just that" (122).

15. Fredric Jameson, "Reading Hitchcock," *October* 23: 17.

16. Sylvia Harvey, "Whose Brecht? Memories for the Eighties—A Critical Recovery," *Screen* 23, no. 1 (May/June 1982): 48.

17. Christian Braad Thomsen's statement that "Fassbinder does not begin where Godard began but where he ended" (*Take One* 4, no. 6 [1974]: 12) and George Morris's that "Fassbinder is arguably the most revolutionary figure to surface in film since Jean-Luc Godard" ("Fassbinder X 5," *Film Comment,* September/October 1981, 59–65) are typical.

18. Most of film theory's writings on Brecht have been rather slanted because they have depended on the limited English translations, in particular *Brecht on Theater: The Development of an Aesthetic,* ed. John Willett (New York: Hill and Wang, 1964).

19. Bennett, *Formalism and Marxism,* 104.

20. Introduction to *Popular European Cinema,* ed. Richard Dyer and Ginette Vincendeau (London: Routledge, 1992), 1.

21. Thomas H. Guback, "Hollywood's International Market," in *The American Film Industry,* ed. Tino Balio (Madison: University of Wisconsin Press, 1976), 400.

22. Ibid., 409.

23. Ibid., 408.

24. Joseph D. Phillips, "Film Conglomerate Blockbusters: International Aspects and Product Homogenization," in *The American Movie Industry,* ed. Gorham Kindem (Carbondale: Southern Illinois University Press, 1982), 335.

25. Richard Caves, *American Industry: Structure, Conduct, Performance* (Englewood Cliffs, N.J.: Prentice Hall, 1964), 55; and Paul A. Sammuelson, *Economics: An Introductory Analysis,* 7th ed. (New York: McGraw-Hill, 1967), 139–54.

26. In fact, Gustav Stolper wrote in the preface to his influential economic history of Germany in 1940 (before the Allied occupation) that "it is an economic, not a political history that is told here. The account of Germany's economic history probably reveals, however, a much closer interrelation between politics and economics than that of any other great European nation." Gustav Stolper, Karl Hauser, and Knut Borchardt, *The German Economy 1870 to the Present,* trans. Toni Stolper (New York: Harcourt, Brace, 1967), 323.

27. Nicos Poulantzas, *Fascism and Dictatorship* (London: New Left Books, 1974).

28. Paul Sweezy, *Theory of Capitalist Development* (New York: Monthly Review Press, 1942), 293.

29. Ephraim Nimni, "Marxism and Nationalism," in *Marxist Sociology Revisited,* ed. M. Shaw (London: Macmillan, 1985), 101–2.

30. Dyer and Vincendeau, *Popular European Cinema,* 7.

31. Roland Barthes, *Image-Music-Text* (London: Fontana, 1977), 145.

32. John Caughie, preface to *Theories of Authorship,* ed. John Caughie (London: British Film Institute, 1981), 2.

33. Elsaesser, *New German Cinema,* 74–85.

34. Jan Dawson, "A Labyrinth of Subsidies: The Origins of the New German Cinema," *Sight and Sound,* Winter 1980–81: 15.

35. Ibid., 19.

36. Elsaesser, *New German Cinema,* 43.

37. See Sheila Johnston, "The Author as Public Institution," *Screen* 32/33 (Autumn/Winter 1979–80): 67–78.

38. Elsaesser, *New German Cinema,* 40.

39. Pierre Bourdieu, *Distinction: A Social Critique of the Judgement of Taste* (Cambridge, Mass.: Harvard University Press, 1984), 68.

40. Ibid.

2 / Engineering a Democracy through *Autorenfilm*: The Political Context of Television's Support of Fassbinder

1. Quoted from *Völkischer Beobachter,* cited in David Welch, *Propaganda and the German Cinema 1933–1945* (Oxford: Clarendon Press, 1983), 39.

2. Lord William Strang, *Home and Abroad* (London: Deutsch, 1956), 234–35. I am grateful to Thomas Streeter in that a number of the ideas in this chapter emanate from conversations I had with him in 1984.

3. Raymond Williams, *Television: Technology and Cultural Form* (New York: Schocken, 1975), 24.

4. Joint Chiefs of Staff Directive (JCS 1067) issued on October 31, 1945, reprinted in James K. Pollack, *Germany under Occupation* (Ann Arbor, Mich.: Wahr, 1947), 78.

5. The Morgenthau plan adopted by the American zone as stated in the major governing statement of the immediate period after the German surrender promoted a theory of "collective guilt." The directive instructed the Allies to tell the Germans that they "cannot escape responsibility" for what they brought on themselves. The American forces were in those first months "to take no steps looking towards the economic rehabilitation of Germany or designed to maintain or strengthen the German economy." See Pollack, *Germany under Occupation,* 100–15.

6. Nicholas Pronay, "'To Stamp Out the Whole Tradition ...,'" introduction to *The Political Re-education of Germany and Her Allies,* ed. Nicholas Pronay and Keith Wilson (London: Croom Helm, 1985), 1–2.

7. The journal is *Functional Program, Information Control, Office of Military Government U.S. Zone,* part 2, February 22, 1946. The reference comes from William Arthur Rugh, "The Politics of Broadcasting after World War Two" (dissertation, Columbia University Press, 1967), 11.

8. This American sensibility is exemplified in the Universum Film Aktiengesellschaft (UFI) holding company law of 1949, by which the Americans dissolved the giant media conglomerate, disposing of motion picture property "in a manner best calculated to foster a sound, democratic and privately-owned motion picture industry in Germany organized so as to preclude excessive concentration of economic power."

A more modern version of this correlation is expressed by Arthur M. Okun: "The economist sees the competitive market and pricing mechanism as a particularly efficient way of expression to individual choices. ... Free choice and competition expressed through purchasing and selling decisions of individual competitors often have a remarkable property of yielding results that cannot be improved on by public action" (*Political Economy of Prosperity* [Washington, D.C.: Brookings Institution, 1970], 5–6).

9. David Childs and Jeffrey Johnson, *West Germany: Politics and Society* (London: Croom Helm, 1981), 148. William Rugh argues that broadcasting was not commercialized because of the lack of multiple frequencies necessary for competition and "the lack of anything to advertise in 1948" ("Politics of Broadcasting," 20). Although this seems a more likely explanation of the lack of private enterprise involved with early German broadcasting than Childs and Johnson's, I found no other corroboration of this position.

10. Hans Bausch, *Rundfunkpolitik nach 1945: Erster Teil: 1945–1962* (Munich: Deutscher Taschenbuch, 1980), 24–45.

11. Michael Balfour, "In Retrospect: Britain's Policy of 'Re-education,'" in *Political Re-education of Germany,* 147.

12. Secretary of State George Marshall's speech is quoted in *Germany 1947–1949: The Story in Documents,* Department of State Publication no. 3556 (Washington, D.C.: Government Printing Office, 1950), 154.

13. It should be mentioned that the English reeducation program slowly became motivated in some circles by an anticommunist fear similar to the Americans'. In 1948 the British regional commissioner for North Rhine Westphalia, General Sir Brian Robertson, argued that "it was clear ... that unless the German people were helped to transform the conditions then existing into a situation which would provide a bearable if modest standard of living it would be impossible to prevent the spread of communism through the whole country" (quoted in Michael Tracey, "The Illusive Ideal: An Essay on Hugh Greene and the Creation of Broadcasting in the Federal Republic of Germany" [dissertation, University of Leicester, 1980], 25).

14. John M. MacKenzie, *Propaganda and Empire: The Manipulation of British Public Opinion 1880–1960* (Manchester: Manchester University Press, 1984), 67–95.

15. Pronay, "To Stamp Out the Whole Tradition," 8–9.

16. Ibid., 8.

17. Arthur Williams, *Broadcasting and Democracy in West Germany* (Philadelphia: Temple University Press, 1976), 3.

18. Asa Briggs, *The Birth of Broadcasting: The History of Broadcasting in the United Kingdom*, 2 vols. (London: Oxford University Press, 1961), 2:37–106.

19. Sidney W. Head, *Broadcasting in America*, 4th ed. (Boston: Houghton Mifflin, 1982), 5.

20. Briggs, *Birth of Broadcasting*, 261.

21. Although the British did exert more influence on the course of West German broadcasting, the Americans had a profound influence in shaping Bayerischer Rundfunk (BR), which was to become the virulently anticommunist and conservative station in the ARD. See Barbara Mettler, *Demokratisierung und Kalter Krieg: Zur amerikanischen Informations- und Rundfunkpolitik in Westdeutschland 1945–1949* (Berlin: Volker Spiess, 1975).

22. Because the papers from this period by law could not be opened for examination for thirty years, they are only now coming to the surface for academic scrutiny. Pronay, "To Stamp Out the Whole Tradition," 16–23.

23. Ibid., 8–9.

24. Tracey, "Illusive Ideal," 40. It was, however, the task of the BBC's German Service to carry out the corrective or missionary service by substituting "democratic" culture for authoritarian or Nazi "propaganda." Bishop wrote that they must install "cultural programmes using every means provided by radio technique to reflect to the German audience the literature, art, scholarship, music, theatre, film and science of the outside.... Talks and discussions were intended to reintroduce Germans to the values and traditions of western Christian civilization, and to correct past German distortions of the facts of history" (Tracey, "Illusive Ideal," 41).

25. To be more exact, the constitution was written for the Hamburg station NWDR, which functioned as the central broadcast station for the British zone and later was partitioned into the Hamburg NDR (Norddeutscher Rundfunk) and Cologne's WDR (Westdeutscher Rundfunk), producer of the majority of Fassbinder's television work.

26. Tracey, "Illusive Ideal," 2.

27. Ibid., 86.

28. Ibid., 57–58.

29. Greene never hesitated in exercising his authority to select and keep broadcast personnel. Greene's administration at NWDR was racked with controversy over his hiring or firing of "suspected" communists and ex-Nazis. Many of these personnel changes were highly controversial in that the charges were not substantiated. Michael Tracey's glowing biography serves unwittingly to reveal the capriciousness of Greene's decisions in the name of British upper class propriety; see Michael Tracey, *A Variety of Lives: A Biography of Sir Hugh Greene* (London: Bodley Head, 1983).

30. Thomas Streeter, "German Broadcasting and the Legacy of the Allied Occupation," seminar paper, University of Illinois, 23.

31. Tracey, "Illusive Ideal," 136.

32. The American zone was by far the most decentralized with four institutions: Radio Frankfurt, Radio München, Radio Stuttgart, and Radio Bremen. The British and French zones were centralized into one station each. NWDR, based in Hamburg, covered all of the huge British zone; Südwestfunk in Baden-Baden covered the much smaller French zone.

33. The six broadcast institutions of ARD or the First Network, which correspond with *Land* boundaries, are: Bayerischer Rundfunk (Bavaria), Hessischer Rundfunk (Hesse), Radio Bremen (Bremen), Saarländischer Rundfunk (Saar), Westdeutscher Rundfunk (North Rhineland-Westphalia), and Sender Freies Berlin (West Berlin). Norddeutscher Rundfunk (Hamburg) serves three lands — Hamburg, Lower Saxony, and Schleswig-Holstein; Südwestfunk serves the Rhineland-Palatinate and part of Baden-Württemberg; and Süddeutscher Rundfunk serves the remaining part of Baden-Württemberg.

34. A. Williams, *Broadcasting and Democracy*, 17–18.

35. Arthur Williams takes apart the phrasing of the consortium's title in order to reveal how carefully chosen the words are. In particular, Williams argues that *Arbeitsgemeinschaft* "can mean simply a 'study group,' but more often than not means some form of joint association formed to achieve a common objective with the only link between the members and the achievement of the objective." In addition, the political choice of *öffentlichrechtlich* puts the emphasis "on their status as independent, sovereign bodies; ... the aim they share of providing the public with free broadcasting service, free of any predominant political or commercial interests" (*Broadcasting and Democracy*, 15–16).

36. According to Tracey, NWDR's main stations were located in Hamburg, Cologne, and Berlin. The Hamburg station provided 60 percent of the programming between 6:00 a.m. and 1:00 a.m., the Cologne station 25 percent, and the Berlin station 12 to 15 percent. When Hugh Greene left, the station had 2,000 employees ("Illusive Ideal," 63). Hans Bausch estimates a much larger NWDR audience: over 5 million listeners. He argues that over 53 percent of all broadcast listeners were in the British zone as opposed to 23 percent in the American zone and 10 percent in the French zone (*Rundfunkpolitik nach 1945*, 19).

37. Tracey, "Illusive Ideal," 64. The series of station governance boards was run by representatives of the stations and the community. The NWDR control structure had three levels: the Broadcasting Council (*Hauptausschuss*, later to become the *Rundfunkrat*), the Administrative Council (*Verwaltungsrat*), and the director-general (*Intendant*). The Broadcasting Council's sixteen members came from established West German society: the *Länder* presidents, the central judiciary, the educational system, the Catholic and Lutheran churches, the trade unions, the journalist union, theater management, the musical academy, and the trade association board. The council in turn elected the *Rundfunkrat*, the nonrepresentational, but most powerful and independent, tier of control, which administered the station's daily business and programming decisions and appointed the director-general. Of the West German television stations, all but two had instituted these three tiers of control by the 1970s. Other "socially relevant" groups were represented on at least the *Rundfunkrat*.

38. A. Williams, *Broadcasting and Democracy*, 102.

39. Anton Kaes, "Literary Intellectuals and the Cinema: Charting a Controversy (1909–1929)," *New German Critique* 40 (Winter 1987): 16.

40. Ibid., 23.

41. Robin Lenman, "Mass Culture and the State in Germany, 1900–1926," in *Ideas into Politics: Aspects of European History 1880–1950*, ed. R. J. Bullen et al. (London: Croom Helm, 1984), 51–59.

42. Originally published in English by Princeton University Press in 1947.

43. Siegfried Kracauer, *From Caligari to Hitler: A Psychological History of the German Film* (Princeton, N.J.: Princeton University Press, 1947), 8–9.

44. Ibid., 71.

45. Max Horkheimer and Theodor W. Adorno, "The Culture Industry: Enlightenment as Mass Deception," *Dialectic of Enlightenment* (New York: Continuum, 1987), 120–67. In relation to Kracauer's influence on Adorno and Horkheimer, John Gay has documented the postwar intellectual interchange between these influential critics in "The Extraterritorial Life of Siegfried Kracauer," *Salmagundi* 31–32 (Fall 1975–Winter 1976): 49–106, and "Adorno and Kracauer: Notes on a Troubled Friendship," *Salmagundi* 40 (Winter 1978): 42–66. Thomas Elsaesser has also referred to the relationship in "Film History and Visual Pleasure: Weimar Cinema," in *Cinema Histories/Cinema Practices,* ed. Patricia Mellencamp and Philip Rosen (Frederick, Md.: University Publications of America, 1984), 67.

46. Andreas Meyer, "Bausteine zu einer Situationsanalyse des bundesdeutschen Kinos: No. 2 Gremien-Kinos," *medium* 11 (November 1977): 16.

47. Elsaesser, "Film History and Visual Pleasure: Weimar Cinema," in *Cinema Histories/Cinema Practices,* ed. Patricia Mellencamp and Philip Rosen (Frederick, Md.: University Publications of America, 1984), 60.

48. Heinz Ungureit, "Ein aufsässiges Spiel-Fernsehen," in *Schöne neue Fernsehwelt. Utopien der Macher,* ed. Jochim Dennhardt and Daniela Hartmann (Munich: Kindler, 1984), 77.

49. Karl Holzamer, "Vor und Nachdenkliches über Fernsehen," *Rufer und Hörer* 5 (1951): 386.

50. The former British station, NWDR, was the first German television station to begin broadcasting, in November of 1950. The broadcast ran intermittently until Christmas 1952, when NWDR initiated the first regular program. The first ARD network program carried in common did not start until November 1954.

51. The German statistic comes from *ZDF Jahrbuch 1974,* 50, and the American statistic from Fredric Stuart's "The Effects of Television on the Motion Picture Industry: 1948–1960," in *The American Movie Industry,* ed. Gorham Kindem (Carbondale: Southern Illinois University Press, 1982), 266.

52. Knut Hickethier, *Das Fernsehspiel der Bundesrepublik: Themen, Form, Struktur, Theorie und Geschichte* (Stuttgart: Metzlersche, 1980), 17.

53. Dieter Stolte, "Trotz aller Unterschiede: Kino und Fernsehen sind auf einander angewiesen," in *Filmförderung 1974–1979: Der deutsche Film und das Fernsehen* (Frankfurt: ZDF, 1980), 9.

54. Klaus Keller, "Kino und Fernsehen-Keine Alternativmedien-Aber Konkurrenzmedien," *Funk Korrespondenz* 13, no. 28 (March 1979): 1.

55. Werner Hess, "Warnung vor unrealistischen Wünschen der Filmwirtschaft," *Kirche und Rundfunk* 58 (July 24, 1976): 3. Yet the studios and production companies welcomed television as a financially strong business partner. The 1957 jump in television licenses resulted in more capital for film personnel and studios. The late 1950s and early 1960s brought the first series of significant changes in the balance between the film and television industries. In 1957 the ARD and UFA created the first production agreement between the two industries to film three television films in Studio Eight of the old UFA Bavarian studio. By 1959 WDR and SDR (Süddeutscher Rundfunk) had bought the studio, turning it into Bavaria Atelier GmbH, yet 60 percent of its use was still devoted to German feature film production in these early years. In 1958 Hamburg's NDR and Cologne's WDR created a film production collective filming in Hamburg's Real Film studios. By 1960 NDR had bought the film studio, making it a commercial subsidiary, Real-Film GmbH. And in 1962 the Berlin Senate attempted to get Sender Freies Berlin, an ARD station and the second channel, to buy the bankrupt remaining Berlin studios.

56. Hickethier, *Das Fernsehspiel der Bundesrepublik.*

57. Richard Collins and Vincent Porter, *WDR and the Arbeiterfilm* (London: British Film Institute, 1981), 32.

58. Werner Waldmann, *Das deutsche Fernsehspiel: Ein systematischer Überblick* (Wiesbaden: Akademische Verlaggesellschaft Athenaion, 1977), 4.

59. E. M. Berger, "Dramaturgie des Fernsehen," *Fernsehstudio* 1 (1953): 18; quoted in Hickethier, *Das Fernsehspiel der Bundesrepublik,* 80.

60. There are some important exceptions to this rule, including the work of NDR producer Egon Monk, who was influenced by Bertolt Brecht and produced some of the most politically controversial television films (e.g., *Schlachtvieh*) of the Adenauer era. See Egon Netenjakob, "Der Fersehfilm ist-Film," *Film und Fernsehen* 7 (July 1970): 35, and Knut Hickethier, "Das Fernsehspiel in der Adenauer Ära," *TV-Courier/Dokumentation* 2 (January 19, 1981): 7.

61. Hickethier, *Das Fernsehspiel der Bundesrepublik,* 160–62.

62. Hickethier, "Das Fernsehspiel in der Adenauer Ära," 7–8.

63. Eric Rentschler argues that Group 47 represented an example to the Oberhausen group of artists who met collectively to discuss and lobby for their political rights. In fact, there was a meeting between the two groups that ended in a fiasco, neither side understanding the other. See Eric Rentschler, *New German Film in the Course of Time* (Bedford Hills, N.Y.: Redgrave, 1984), 32–33.

64. John Sandford, *The Mass Media of the German-Speaking Countries* (London: Oswald Woolff, 1976), 56–57, and *Die Spiegel-Affäre,* ed. Jürgen Seifert, 2 vols. (Freiburg: Olten, 1966).

65. Seifert, *Die Spiegel-Affäre,* 44.

66. Hickethier, *Das Fernsehspiel der Bundesrepublik,* 224.

67. Quoted in Hans C. Blumenberg, "Bildschirm contra Leinwand," *Die Zeit* 24 (June 23, 1978): 28.

68. Egon Monk, "Parteinahme als Notwendigkeit," *epd* 17, no. 30 (April 1966): 1.

69. Blumenberg, "Bildschirm contra Leinwand," 28.

70. Another example of the growing acceptance of the cultural importance of television was the willingness of West Germany's most renowned writers (Group 47) such as Schnurre, Böll, and Andersch to allow television to adapt their work.

71. Hickethier, *Das Fernsehspiel der Bundesrepublik,* 71.

72. The data on feature films in West Germany comes from Elisabeth Berg and Bernward Frank, *Film und Fernsehen: Ergebnisse einer Repräsentativerhebung 1978* (Mainz: Hase and Köhler, 1979), 20, 25. The *Fernsehspiel* statistic is from Hickethier, *Das Fernsehspiel der Bundesrepublik,* 74.

73. Alexandre Astruc, "The Birth of a New Avant-garde: *la camera-stylo,*" in *The New Wave,* ed. Peter Graham (London: Secker and Warburg, 1968), 17–23.

74. Quoted in David Bordwell and Kristin Thompson, *Film Art: An Introduction,* 2d ed. (New York: Knopf, 1986), 373. Emphasis in original.

75. Ibid.

76. Hickethier, *Das Fernsehspiel der Bundesrepublik,* 227.

77. Meyer, "Bausteine zu einer Situationsanalyse," 17.

78. Quoted by Sheila Johnston in "The Author as Public Institution: The 'New' Cinema in the Federal Republic of Germany," *Screen* 32/33 (Autumn/Winter 1979/80): 68.

79. Michael Dost, Florian Hopf, and Alexander Kluge, *Filmwirtschaft in der BRD und in Europa: Götterdämmerung in Raten* (Munich: Hanser, 1973), 129.

80. Günter Rohrbach, "Die verhängnisvolle Macht der Regisseure," *ARD Fernsehspiel* 3 (1983): 320.

81. A. Williams, *Broadcasting and Democracy,* 29. The court specified how these "socially relevant groups" were to be represented: "Article 5 of the Basic Law does, however, require that this modern instrument for the formation of opinion should surrender neither to the state nor to any one group in society. The promoters of broadcasting programmes must, therefore, be so organized that all relevant forces have an influence in the organs of control and a fair hearing in the overall programme which guarantee a minimum balance in content, impartial-

ity and mutual respect. This can be secured only if these organizational and material principles are made generally binding by law" (A. Williams, ibid., 30).

82. Elisabeth Berg and Bernward Frank, *Film und Fernsehen: Ergebnisse einer Repräsentativerhebung 1978*, 26.

83. Imported foreign television programs made up about 5 to 8 percent of West German public television in the 1980s, but American television progams were some of the most popular; *Dallas* and *Dynasty* were known as *Der Denver Klan*. German television tends to program American television series such as *Sesame Street*, *Hart to Hart*, *Lassie*, and *The Donna Reed Show* for the late afternoon to early evening. The lion's share of American culture comes from the showing of American feature films.

84. Under the new law, direct film subsidization gave way to an entertainment tax (*Filmgroschen*) of ten pfennig or five cents per ticket. This tax amounted to an operating budget of $2.25 million a year. In 1969 the board awarded 65 films approximately 150,000 deutsche marks ($37,000). Of the 65 films, 42 were counted as purely *German* films and 23 were co-productions with other European Community countries. This subsidy law, for all its contradictions and industry support, has remained until the present as the mainstay of direct governmental film support for independent filmmaking in Germany.

The end result of the 1967 act was a noticeable growth in production: new production profits jumped from 38,780,000 to 50,540,000 marks in 1968; 72 films were made in 1967, 110 in 1969, and an all-time-record 112 in 1971. But the subsidized productions in the years directly following passage of the act were the traditional litany of German cheap thrillers and sex films ("report" films). The seemingly small (by industry standards) grants encouraged commercial producers to go for low-budget "quickies" and short-term profits rather than more financially risky films.

85. In the 1960s, according to Gunther Witte, head of WDR's *Fernsehspiel* department in 1981, "the most talented and experienced filmmakers of our land worked for our programs. Moreover, we knew that new German film had found a home with us. However, this seeming identity between television and film could not last forever" (Gunther Witte, "Crux mit dem Kino: Szenen einer Ehe zwischen zwei Medien," *WDR Print*, December 1981, 5).

86. Hickethier, *Das Fernsehspiel der Bundesrepublik*, 233.

87. Ernest W. Fuhr, "On the Legal Position of Freelance Workers in Broadcasting Organizations in the Federal Republic of Germany," *European Broadcasting Union* 5 (September 1978): 39.

88. Quoted in Johnston, "The Author as Public Institution," 77.

89. Frieda Grafe and Enno Patalas, "Warum wir das beste Fernsehen und das schlechteste Film haben," *Filmkritik* 12 (1970): 473.

90. Hickethier, *Das Fernsehspiel der Bundesrepublik*, 36–37.

91. Anthony Smith, "The Relationship of Management with Creative Staff," in *Lord Annan's Report of the Commission on the Future of Broadcasting* (London: Her Majesty's Stationery Office, 1977), 82, 84.

92. The most well known of these are "The Old German Film from 1929 to 1933," "The Controversial Films," "The Great Silent Films," "Films out of East Germany," "Films of the Russian Revolution," and "Films out of Cuba."

93. These programs are *Filmforum* (1964), *Zehn Minuten für den Kinogänger* (*Ten Minutes for the Moviegoer*, 1965), which became *Ratschlag für Kinogänger* (*Advice for Moviegoers*, 1967), and in 1970 *Apropos Film*, a joint production with Austrian state television by two professional critics from *Wiener Magazin*. See Klaus Bruene, "Das ZDF und seine Spielfilme: Ein Blick zurück nach 20 Jahren," *ZDF Jahrbuch 1982*, 70–71.

94. John Ellis and Sheila Johnston, "The Radical Film Funding of ZDF," *Screen* 24, no. 4/5 (May/June 1982): 67.

95. Hajo Schedlich, "Sie alle lockte das Experiment," *Das kleine Fernsehspiel*, 1967–68: 3.

96. In an interview with Eckart Stein by John Ellis and Sheila Johnston in "Radical Film Funding," 72.

97. *Warum läuft Herr R. amok? (Why Does Mr. R. Run Amok?*, 1970), *Das Kaffeehaus (The Coffeehouse*, 1970), *Die Nicklashauser Fahrt (The Niklashaus Trip*, 1970), *Pioniere in Ingolstadt (The Pioneers of Ingolstadt*, 1970), *Acht Stunden sind kein Tag (Eight Hours Are Not a Day*, 1972), *Bremer Freiheit (Bremen Freedom*, 1972), *Welt am Draht (World on a Wire*, 1973), and *Martha* (1973).

98. Wenders produced his first two feature films as WDR *Fernsehspiele*: *Die Angst des Tormanns beim Elfmeter (The Goalie's Anxiety at the Penalty Kick*, 1971) and *Die scharlachrote Buchstabe (The Scarlet Letter*, 1972).

99. *Redakteuren* translates more closely as "editors," which again reveals historical and cultural differences: the film business is closer to its literary origins than the American *producer*, which emphasizes the industrial origins of the cultural object.

100. Falkenberg, director of cultural programming at WDR, studied at Göttingen, Zurich, and Harvard before receiving his doctorate. Günter Rohrbach had studied with Jürgen Habermas at Bonn University where he received his doctorate.

101. See Andreas Huyssen's essay "The Politics of Identification: *Holocaust* and West German Drama," in *After the Great Divide: Modernism, Mass Culture, Postmodernism* (Bloomington: Indiana University Press, 1986), 94–114.

102. Examples of Märthesheimer's essays and responses in English can be found in Collins and Porter, *WDR and the Arbeiterfilm*, 143–52, and in Huyssen, "Politics of Identification: *Holocaust* and West German Drama," 99.

103. For a discussion of this change in political climate in West Germany in the early 1970s, see Jack Zipes, "From the *Berufsverbot* to Terrorism," *Telos* 34 (Winter 1977–78): 136–37.

104. Stolte, "Trotz aller Unterschiede," 9.

105. The more exact title of the bill is Abkommen zwischen den Filmförderungsanstalten und den um der ARD zusammengeschlossen Rundfunkanstalten sowie dem ZDF vom 4.11 1974.

106. Elisabeth Berg, "Fernsehen — ökonomisches Standbein der Filmwirtschaft. Fernsehumsätze der Filmwirtschaft weiterhin steigend," *Media Perspektiven* 6 (1977): 333.

107. Andreas Meyer, "Auf dem Wege der Besserung: Anmerkungen zur Einigung über das Film/Fernseh-Rahmenabkommen," *medium* 10 (October 1974): 4–5. Heinz Ungureit, "Television Co-productions — On the International Level and with the Cinema," *European Broadcasting Union Review* 29, no. 3 (1978): 25–26.

108. Ungureit, "Television Co-productions," 26.

109. For example, by the latter half of the 1970s Fassbinder was able to invest over 700,000 marks ($200,000) from the Film Promotion Law monies in what was perhaps his most personal film, *In a Year of Thirteen Moons* (Harry Baer, *Schlafen kann ich, wenn ich tot bin* [Cologne: Kiepenheuer and Witsch, 1982], 120).

110. The forerunner "alternative" or non-American-affiliated distributors remain Atlas and Kirchner, which traded in the 1960s and 1970s on art films from other European countries. According to Helmut H. Diederich, the other firms can be divided into four kinds: (1) directors who represented their own films (Filmverlag der Autoren, Basis, and Robert van Ackeren's "Luxmeta"); (2) theater or chain owners who distributed films that would play well in their own theaters, typically art houses (die Arbeitsgemeinschaft Kino in Hamburg, Impuls, prokino, and Peter Vollman's theater chain); (3) distributors involved with political films (Neue Welt, Unidoc, Zentral, and Basis); and (4) distribution connected with West German archives ("Freunde der Deutschen Kinemathek"). For more comprehensive information, see Helmut H. Diederich, "Phantasie und Engagement gegen Kommerz. Filmwirtschaft: Alternativ-Verleiher in der BRD," *medium* 9 (September 1977): 12–17.

232 / Notes to pages 54–58

111. The thirteen founders of the Filmverlag der Autoren are Hark Bohm, Michael Fengler, Peter Lilienthal, Hans Noever, Peter Ariel, Uwe Brandner, Veith von Fürstenberg, Florian Furtwängler, Thomas Schamoni, Laurens Straub, Wim Wenders, Hans Geissendörfer, and Volker Vogeler.

112. This statement was first published in Barbara Bronnen and Corinna Brocher, *Die Filmemacher. Zur neuen deutschen Produktion nach Oberhausen 1962* (Munich: Bertelsmann, 1973), 151ff. It was published again in Helmut H. Diederich's "Fangschuss für furchtlose Flieger. Die Geschichte des 'Filmverlag der Autoren' von der Solidargemeinschaft bis Augstein," *medium* 3 (March 1977): 4.

113. The twenty-five productions included Wim Wenders's *Die Angst des Tormanns beim Elfmeter* (*The Anxiety of the Goalkeeper at the Penalty Kick*), and *Alice in den Städten* (*Alice in the Cities*); Hans Noever's *Zahltag* (*Payday*); Peter Raben's *Adele Spitzeder*; Helma Sander's *Erdbeben in Chile* (*Earthquake in Chile*); Hans Geissendörfer's *Perahin*; Volker Vogeler's *Verflucht von Amerika*; Michael Fengler's *Zwischenbericht* (*Interim Report*); Peter Lilienthal's *La Victoria* and *Shirley Chisholm for President*; Peter Ariel's *Das Kartenhaus* (*The House of Cards*); Wolfgang Limmer's *Manager-Haertekurs*; Erika Runge's *Ich bin Bürger der DDR* (*I Am a Citizen of the GDR*); Florian Furtwängler's *Little Big Horn* and *Paul Getty*; and Hark Bohm's *Ich kann auch 'ne Arche bau'n so wie Tschetan* (*I Can Also Build an Ark like Tschetan*). *Der Indianerjunge* (*The Indian Youth*) was the single *Verlag* film that was produced with television coproduction money.

114. During the expansion, Straub was accused by the less well known original members of neglecting their films and resigned under pressure.

115. Diederich, "Fangschuss für furchtlose Flieger," 4–9.

116. "I'd Rather Be a Streetsweeper in Mexico Than a Filmmaker in Germany," in *The Anarchy of the Imagination: Interviews, Essays, Notes by Rainer Werner Fassbinder,* ed. Michael Töteberg and Leo A. Lensing, trans. Krishna Winston (Baltimore: Johns Hopkins University Press, 1992).

117. Rohrbach, "Die verhängnisvolle Macht der Regisseure," 10–15, and Edgar Reitz, "Zurück zum Produzentenfilme?" in the same issue of *ARD Fernsehspiel* (3[1983]: 15–19).

118. The preface to this statement read: "The patron attitude which television takes toward film to be honest is in no way disinterested. Film needs television indeed for its economic existence. Conversely, the dependence of television on film is even much stronger and more lasting. A television schedule which would do without film broadcasts suffers an eminent loss of attractiveness. The viewer's evaluation of television through feature films occupies an important place. And television must have a vital interest in the fact that more feature films are produced. One cannot substitute television dramas at one's pleasure as some would like to say. Then the production of feature films without television participation is not only productive, there are also fewer and fewer television dramas being produced just for this medium" (Günter Rohrbach, "Das Subventions-TV. Ein Plädoyer für den amphibischen Film," *Kirche und Rundfunk* 34 [May 7, 1977]: 6).

119. Johnston, "The Author as Public Institution," 77.

120. Hickethier, *Das Fernsehspiel der Bundesrepublik,* 81.

121. Günter Rohrbach, "Kommt das Fernsehen in die Kinos? Die Finanzmisere und das Fernsehspiel der Zukunft/Ein Rettungsvorschlag," *Frankfurter Allgemeine Zeitung,* February 15, 1975, 22.

122. Claudia Lensen, "fragen an dr. günter rohrbach," *frauen und film* 15 (February 1978): 46.

123. The last noteworthy *Originalfernsehspiele*—films still made under the control of WDR's drama department—were successful not because of their popularity on television, but because they could be profitably released theatrically. In 1973 WDR's drama department

produced Wim Wenders's elliptical and idiosyncratic *Falsche Bewegung (False Move)*, which had cost the unusually large sum (for television) of 700,000 marks ($200,000). Instead of showing it in the scheduled television time slot, they tested it out in theatrical release. The film was a critical success and put the relatively unknown Wenders (with only two WDR *Fernsehspiele* previously seen by a broad public) in the public eye. It won the coveted Federal Film Prize in 1975. Wenders's success lent credence to Rohrbach's claim that there were no differences between a made-for-TV film and a feature film financed by television under the Abkommen.

124. The lists of WDR *Fernsehspiele* and the feature films come from WDR's yearly general reports. See *WDR Jahresbericht* 1975: 22–23; 1976: 31; and 1977: 47–48.

3 / Fassbinder as a Popular Auteur: The Making of an Authorial Legend

1. Wilfried Wiegand, "Interview with Rainer Werner Fassbinder," in *Fassbinder*, trans. Ruth McCormick (New York: Tanam, 1981), 76.

2. "Briefe," *Der Spiegel* 45 (October 3, 1980): 7.

3. Günter Rohrbach, Fassbinder's television producer, in a nationally broadcast obituary, " ' . . . Ich will doch nur, dass Ihr mich liebt.' Zum Tode Rainer Werner Fassbinders: Wüdigungen von Mensch und Werk," *WDR Print*, July 1982, 7.

4. David Bordwell, *The Films of Carl Theodor Dreyer* (Berkeley: University of California Press, 1981), 9.

5. Ibid.

6. Ibid.

7. For a discussion in English of these historical class divisions, see John Sandford's *The Mass Media of the German-Speaking Countries* (London: Oswald Woolff, 1976), 25–68.

8. Michel Foucault, *The Archeology of Knowledge*, trans. A. M. Sheridan Smith (New York: Harper Colophon, 1972), 38.

9. Richard Dyer, *Stars* (London: British Film Institute, 1979), 72–98.

10. Peter Handke, "Strassentheater und Kellertheater," *Theater heute*, April 1969, 6–12.

11. "Zerschlagt das bürgerliche Theater!" *Theater heute*, February 1969, 29.

12. Although the membership of the Action Theater collective changed often, the seven major participants were Fassbinder, Peer Raben, Ursula Strätz-Söhnlein, Hanna Schygulla, Irm Hermann, Ingrid Caven, and Kurt Raab. Except for Strätz-Sohnlein, all of them became part of Fassbinder's film troupe, as actors and sometimes as creative assistants. Raab often acted as the set designer and assistant director (twenty-four films), and Raben composed the music for no fewer than twenty-five of Fassbinder's films. This tight working/living collective was the central issue of much of the public reception of Fassbinder's work.

13. The small advertisement for the Action Theater's *Antigone* ran simply: "*Antigone* freely adapted from Sophocles" (*Süddeutsche Zeitung*, October 2, 1967, 18).

14. Ibid.

15. "Büchner im Münchner Action Theater," *Süddeutsche Zeitung*, October 9, 1967, 11.

16. Ibid.

17. In fact, Fassbinder's debut as a playwright, *For Example, Ingolstadt* (*Zum Beispiel Ingolstadt*), based on a novel by Marieluise Fleisser about the psychological world of the middle class, did not even receive a review in the Munich newspaper when it opened in late February 1968.

18. Yaak Karsunke, a biographer of Fassbinder's theater period, has pointed out that this positive review of Fassbinder's work may have resulted from the fact that for the first time the *Süddeutsche Zeitung* sent a film critic instead of a theater critic. He argues that the film critic had a clearer insight into Fassbinder's visual pop art style. See Karsunke, "History

of Anti-Teater: The Beginnings," in *Fassbinder,* trans. Ruth McCormick (New York: Tanam, 1984), 4.

19. Alf Brustellin, "Jenseits des Kulturbetriebs-Eine Uraufführung und eine Straub-Inszenierung im Action Theater," *Süddeutsche Zeitung,* April 9, 1968, 24. Brustellin became a filmmaker himself in the 1970s.

20. Ibid.

21. Ibid.

22. Karsunke, "History of Anti-Teater," 6.

23. "Enteignet Thoas! *Iphigenie* fern von Goethe, im Münchner antiteater," *Süddeutsche Zeitung,* October 31/November 1, 1968, 10.

24. Before his first feature, Fassbinder made two short "student" (his term) films: *Der Stadtreicher* (1965) and *Das kleine Chaos* (1966), filmed in 16 mm format and with black and white stock, lasted respectively ten and twelve minutes; they were exhibited only at student film clubs and only Irm Hermann of the theater collective took part in them. These two films are available in West Germany but not in the United States. The scripts of Fassbinder's first four films (*Katzelmacher* was the fourth) are published in Rainer Werner Fassbinder, *Die Kinofilme 1* (Munich: Schirmer/Mosel, 1987).

25. John Sandford characterizes *Die Frankfurter Allgemeine Zeitung* as "West Germany's most prestigious daily ... [with] the nearest thing to a national distribution among the 'quality' dailies" in *Mass Media of the German-Speaking Countries,* 211.

26. "Interview über *Liebe ist kälter als der Tod,*" *Frankfurter Allgemeine Zeitung,* June 26, 1969, 23, and "Interview mit R. W. Fassbinder," *Der Tagesspiegel,* September 29, 1969, 26.

27. *Film* 2 (1969): 34–55.

28. Peter Iden, "The Impactmaker," in *Fassbinder,* 13–14.

29. Harry Baer, *Schlafen kann ich, wenn ich tot bin* (Cologne: Kiepenheuer and Witsch, 1982), 254. Although the premiere of *Katzelmacher* elicited the first American review of Fassbinder's work, the German press did not respond fully until the film was shown as part of the "Showdown" series of Fassbinder works in Bremen.

30. A short review of Fassbinder's *Katzelmacher* in *Der Spiegel* appeared in November 1969 — the first national recognition of his position as a film director (*der Regisseur:* a term for a director that grew out of theater). The article heralded the film as "one of the most original German films in a long time."

31. Fritz Rumler, "Spass fördert das Bewusstsein," *Der Spiegel* 53 (December 1969): 82.

32. Ibid.

33. "Grosse Person," *Der Spiegel* 6 (November 1970): 143.

34. Ibid.

35. *Variety's* report of the Berlin film festival screening of *Liebe ist kälter als der Tod* stands as one of the first public recognitions in the United States of Fassbinder's work.

36. *Variety,* May 10, 1972, 43.

37. Richard Dyer, *Stars* (London: British Film Institute, 1979), 22.

38. "Der Boss und Sein Team," *Die Zeit,* July 31, 1970, 9.

39. Elizabeth Burns, *Theatricality* (London: Longman, 1972), 146–47. Quoted in *Stars,* 23.

40. Dyer, *Stars,* 49.

41. "Aussenseiter mit Herz," *Hör zu,* April 1970, 24.

42. "Der Boss und sein Team," 9.

43. "Mit 24 der grösste Macher," *Twen* 6 (June 1970): 115.

44. Ibid.

45. "Statt der 'Ware' — wahre Kunst machen," *Neue Westfälische Zeitung,* June 27, 1970, 9.

46. "Genie aus Zufall," *Stuttgarter Zeitung,* October 27, 1972, 12.

47. "Kraftwerk," *Die Welt,* July 23, 1975, 3.

48. Ibid.

49. "Ungeschichtlich ins Ungeschick," *Die Welt*, May 27, 1976, 3.

50. "Aussenseiter mit Herz," 24.

51. Rumler, "Spass fördert das Bewusstsein," 82.

52. "Zugunsten der Realität," *Frankfurter Rundschau*, March 12, 1974, 2.

53. "Filme zum Wegwerfen," *Stuttgarter Zeitung*, August 23, 1974, 12. The book is *Reihe Film 2: Rainer Werner Fassbinder*, ed. Peter W. Jansen and Wolfram Schütte (Munich: Hanser, 1975).

54. "Ungeschichtlich ins Ungeschick," 5.

55. Hans C. Blumenberg, "Schreie und Flüstern," *Die Zeit*, October 15, 1976, 33.

56. My criterion for describing a Fassbinder film as a television film or a theater film is based on where the film premiered.

57. This survey of the popular press in 1970 is culled from "Der Aussenseiter mit Herz," *Hör zu*, April 16, 1970, 24; "Statt der 'Ware'-wahre Kunst machen," June 27, 1970, 10; "Mit 24 der grösste Macher," 113–15; and "Der kleine Rebell hat ausgesorgt ... Schnellfilmer Rainer Werner Fassbinder und seine Erfolge," *Westdeutsche Allgemeine Zeitung*, July 4, 1970, 10. For analysis of the "culture press," I am using Wolf Donner, "Der Boss und sein Team," 9–10; "Das Gangster-Spiel," *Film und Fernsehen* 8, no. 7 (July 1970): 14–15; and Ekehard Pluta, "Die Sachen sind so, wie sie sind. Versuch über fünf Filme des Rainer Werner Fassbinders," *Film und Fernsehen* 8, no. 12 (December 1970): 15–19.

58. "Aussenseiter mit Herz," 24.

59. Eric Rentschler, *New German Film in the Course of Time* (Bedford Hills, N.Y.: Redgrave, 1984), 84.

60. "'Früher wollte ich immer nur drehen,'" *Aachener Nachrichten* 19 (May 1971): 5. Fassbinder also did a series of radio play adaptations in 1970–71: Goethe's *Iphigenie* and *Ganz in Weiss* (an eighteenth-century work). Oddly, in an interview about the adaptation of *Iphigenie*, he contrasts his position on the depersonalized nature of work in television to the intimacy of radio production. In radio adaptations, he argued, "Authors [*Autoren*] should always realise their own work. Direction and scriptwriting are the same thing for the radio play" ("Das Hörspiel hat Zukunft," *Kölnische Rundschau*, April 30, 1971, 5).

61. Vincent Collins and Richard Porter, *WDR and the Arbeiterfilm: Fassbinder, Ziewer and Others* (London: British Film Institute, 1981), 1–174.

62. Peter Märthesheimer, "Die Okkupation des bürgerlichen Genres," *Fernseh und Bildung* 13 (1974): 23. The translation of this article is from Collins and Porter, *WDR and the Arbeiterfilm*, 149.

63. W. Röhl, "Kommt die Proletwelle?" *Konkret* 13 (1973): 7. This section of the interview is translated in Collins and Porter, *WDR and the Arbeiterfilm*, 52.

64. Collins and Porter, *WDR and the Arbeiterfilm*, 52.

65. "Genie aus Zufall," *Stuttgarter Zeitung*, October 27, 1972, 23; "Rainer Werner Fassbinder-der kleine vermaledeite Teufel aus der Hosentasche," *Kölnische Rundschau*, December 19, 1972, 15; and "schön populär," *Der Spiegel* 44 (1972): 177. Collins and Porter declare that *Eight Hours* was a noticeable break from Fassbinder's previous "film" work, which "hitherto centered around his own autobiography and emotional economy." (*WDR and the Arbeiterfilm*, 53). But what they overlook is that the series fitted comfortably with Fassbinder's work as a television adaptor or a director who comfortably suppress her "artistic vision" to adapt others' works or forms for a broad audience.

66. Röhl, "Kommt die Proletwelle?" 34.

67. A position paper put out by a conservative watchdog group for the Christian Democratic Party (CDU) in 1975 surveyed all the "radical" WDR productions. In discussing the *Arbeiterfilme* ("a series pregnant with class conflict"), the report isolated Fassbinder's state-

ments about political film and the radical nature of the WDR staff. Its interest lay not so much in Fassbinder, but in proving the leftist sympathies of the station as demonstrated by their support of Fassbinder and the series ("Dokumente zu Sendungen des WDR" [Cologne: CDU des Rheinlandes, 1975], 1–56).

68. Wolfgang Ruf, "Acht Stunden ist ein langer Tag," *Kirche und Rundfunk* 79 (November 20, 1974): 6.

69. Wolf Donner, "Idyllen eines TV Juros," *Die Zeit,* December 23, 1972, 22.

70. W. Gast and Gerhard R. Kaiser, "Kritik der Fernsehspiel. Das Beispiel von Fassbinders *Acht Stunden sind kein Tag,*" in *Literatur, Medien, Kritik,* ed. Jörg Drews (Heidelberg: Quelle and Meyer, 1977). This article is translated in Collins and Porter, *WDR and the Arbeiterfilm,* 109.

71. Collins and Porter, *WDR and the Arbeiterfilm,* 110.

72. Peter Märthesheimer, "Ich will doch nur dass Ihr mich liebt. Aus einem Gespräch mit Rainer Werner Fassbinder," *Fernsehspiele* (Cologne: Westdeutscher Rundfunk, January-June 1976), 152–53.

73. The state monies as compared to the film cost that Fassbinder received for films between 1970 and 1975 are:

	State award	Film cost
Katzelmacher	250,000 DM	80,000 DM
Warum läuft Herr R. amok?	250,000 DM	135,000 DM
Der Händler der vier Jahreszeiten	450,000 DM	178,000 DM
Effie Briest	260,000 DM	750,000 DM
Die bitteren Tränen der Petra von Kant	200,000 DM	325,000 DM

74. This Fassbinder play has caused continued controversy as a result of its analysis of the growth of postwar building speculation in Frankfurt and the role that Jews played. Most problematic has been the play's potential stereotype of the rich Jew. *Die Welt,* West Germany's most popular daily, reacted to the play with an article with the subheadline "How Rainer Werner Fassbinder Came Under Suspicion for Anti-Semitism." The newspaper argues that Fassbinder's tendencies toward melodramatic figures and comic book clichés produced an anti-Semitic image of the postwar Jew in Germany ("Ungeschlictlich ins Ungeschick," *Die Welt,* March 27, 1976, 10). Wolfgang Limmer of the liberal *Der Spiegel* concluded that the play was not about hating the Jews, but "his general hate of humanity" ("Wem schrei ich um Hilfe?" *Der Spiegel* 41 [1976]: 236).

75. Rainer Werner Fassbinder, "The Third Generation," in *The Anarchy of the Imagination,* ed. Michael Töteberg and Leo Lessing (Baltimore: Johns Hopkins University Press, 1992), 128. Yet Fassbinder also denied that the film was a political statement. He argued for a much more ambiguous definition of *political*: "*The Third Generation* is not a so-called political film, except in the sense that film is political." See "documentation," in *Fassbinder,* ed. Tony Rayns (London: British Film Institute, 1979), 119.

4 / Shock Pop: Fassbinder and the Aesthetics of the German Counterculture

1. Andy Warhol, *Diaries,* ed. Pat Hackett (New York: Warner, 1989), 446. Entry dated June 8, 1982.

2. Thomas Elsaesser, *New German Cinema: A History* (New Brunswick, N.J.: Rutgers University Press, 1989), 292. Also see Manny Farber and Patricia Patterson, "Fassbinder," *Film Comment,* November/December 1975, 5.

3. In a letter to the author, Peter Märthesheimer (Fassbinder's producer for a number

of his international films) wrote that he plans to write a book exposing the fact that Fassbinder produced little of what is credited to him and that his artistic entourage is responsible for his "signature style." See the conclusion of this book.

4. "Happenings," in *Happenings. Fluxus. Pop Art. Nouveau réalisme,* ed. Jürgen Becker and Wolf Vorstell (Reinbek: Rowohlt, 1965), 45.

5. Richard W. McCormick, *The Politics of Self: Feminism and the Postmodern in West German Literature and Film* (Princeton, N.J.: Princeton University Press, 1991), 32.

6. Andreas Huyssen, *After the Great Divide: Modernism, Mass Culture, Postmodernism* (Bloomington: Indiana University Press, 1991), 32.

7. "Wenn man für ein grosses Publikum arbeitet, muss sich nicht nur die form ändern," in *Die Anarchie der Phantasie,* ed. Michael Töteberg (Frankfurt: Fischer, 1986), 41.

8. Christian Braad Thomsen, "Five Interviews with Fassbinder," in *Fassbinder,* ed. Tony Rayns (London: British Film Institute, 1976), 83.

9. Gordon Craig, *The Germans* (New York: Meridian, 1982), 185.

10. *Süddeutsche Zeitung,* May 26, 1967, 34.

11. *Süddeutsche Zeitung,* May 14, 1968, 12.

12. Knut Hickethier, *Das Fernsehspiel der Bundesrepublik: Themen, Form, Struktur, Theorie und Geschichte* (Stuttgart: Metzlersche, 1980), 188.

13. Henning Rischbieter, "Wie tot ist Brecht?" *Theater heute* 3 (March 1968): 26.

14. Peter Handke, "Strassentheater und Theatertheater," *Theater heute* 4 (April 1968): 7.

15. The Action Theater never produced a Brecht play, but the productions often made mention of him or incorporated his ideas, although neither he nor his ideas were privileged. For example, in the group's production of *Antigone,* Brecht's *Antigonemodell* was one of several sources that the troupe used, refusing to allow any one source to be the "correct" one. Additionally, with the production of *Axel Caesar Haarmann* (a political reference to the Roman dictator and the right-wing publisher Springer) the troupe's leaflet proclaimed: "This has to do with Springer ...! (and the rotten democracy which allows him power)." Referring to Brecht, the pamphlet explained that the performance's aim was "about what power is, and how it is endured as a perverted emotion with some people" (Rayns, "Documentation," in *Fassbinder,* 100).

16. "Against Lukács," *New Left Review* 84 (March/April 1974): 54.

17. Jost Hermand, *Pop Internationale* (Frankfurt: Athenaeum, 1971), 14.

18. *Süddeutsche Zeitung,* November 4–5, 1967, 11.

19. Hermand, *Pop Internationale,* 15.

20. Huyssen, *After the Great Divide,* 211–12.

21. Dick Hebdige, *Hiding in the Light: On Images and Things* (London: Routledge, 1988), 120.

22. Bertolt Brecht, *Brecht on Theater: The Development of an Aesthetic,* ed. and trans. John Willett (New York: Hill & Wang, 1964), 72–73.

23. Brecht, "A Short Organum for Theater," in *Brecht on Theater,* 198–99.

24. Dick Hebdige, *Subculture: The Meaning of Style* (London: Routledge, 1979), 100–112.

25. Andrew Ross, *No Respect: Intellectuals and Popular Culture* (London: Routledge, 1989), 139.

26. Hermand, *Pop Internationale,* 95.

27. A good example of this alternative culture sensibility is the "Nonprofit Festival" in Munich in the summer of 1968 (*Süddeutsche Zeitung,* August 30, 1968, 16).

28. *Andy Warhol* (Berlin: der deutschen Gesellschaft für bildende Kunst Kunstverein, 1978).

29. "Kino Schlechtlin: Andy Warhol's Underground-Film 'Chelsea Girls,'" *Süddeutsche Zeitung,* May 20, 1968, 13.

30. Wolfgang Längsfeld, "Der Untergrund—museumreif?" *Süddeutsche Zeitung,* June 20, 1968, 18.

31. Susan Sontag, "Happenings: An Art of Radical Juxtaposition," in *Against Interpretation* (New York: Farrar, Straus & Giroux, 1966), 265.

32. Peter Wollen, "Raiding the Icebox," in *Andy Warhol Film Factory,* ed. Michael O'Pray (London: British Film Institute, 1989), 16.

33. *Süddeutsche Zeitung,* February 23, 1967, 17.

34. C. W. E. Bigsby, *Confrontation and Commitment: A Study of Contemporary American Drama 1950–1966* (Columbia: University of Missouri Press, 1968), 61.

35. Paul Pörtner, "Psychodrama: Theater der Spontaneität," *Theater heute* 9 (September 1967): 19.

36. "Happening mit dem Living Theater," *Theater heute* 2 (February 1967): 67.

37. Michael Töteberg has written an excellent and comprehensive analysis of Fassbinder's debt to Antonin Artaud and the Living Theater: "Das Theater der Grausamkeit as Lehrstück. Zwischen Brecht und Artaud: Die experimentallen Theatertexte Fassbinders," *Text + Kritik* 103 (July 1989): 20–34.

38. "Anti-Gone," *Abendzeitung,* August 22, 1967, 7.

39. Alfred Brustellin, "Kriegstänze um Sophokles," *Süddeutsche Zeitung,* August 22, 1967, 18.

40. Alfred Brustellin, "Action Theater in München," *Theater heute* 6 (June 1968): 44.

41. *Süddeutsche Zeitung,* December 21, 1967, 17.

42. Quoted in Töteberg, "Das Theater der Grausamkeit," 23.

43. "Sprung auf die Strasse," *Süddeutsche Zeitung,* May 22,1968, 24.

44. *Satan's Brew* (1975–76) begins with the following Artaud quotation: "Ce qui difference / les païens de nous, / c'est qu'à l'origine / de toutes leurs croyances, / il y a un terrible effort / pour ne pas penser en hommes, / pour garder le contact / avec la creation entière, / c'est-à-dire avec la divinité."

45. Uri Nertz, "Brecht/Artaud," *Third Rail: Review of International Arts and Literature* 1982: 32.

46. *The Theater and Its Double* was written in 1936, at the end of his active theater involvement. The two theater companies he presided over dissolved quickly. And his most famous play, *The Cenci,* stopped being produced after seventeen performances.

47. This refusal to accept Western norms of representation offers for Jacques Derrida evidence of the problematic of representation or the "Artaud paradox"—the necessity to deny the laws of representation while simultaneously observing these laws to indicate that they have been denied. Derrida writes: "Artaud also desired the impossibility of the theater, wanted to erase the stage, no longer wanted to see what transpires in a locality always inhabited or haunted by the father and subjected to the repetition of murder." See "Theater of Cruelty and the Closure of Representation," *Theater* 9 (Summer 1978): 13.

48. Artaud, *The Theater and Its Double* (New York: Grove, 1958), 114.

49. "Antonin Artaud: Schluss mit den Meisterwerk," *Theater heute* 5 (May 1968): 16.

50. Martin Esslin, *Antonin Artaud* (New York: Penguin, 1972), 112.

51. See my "R. W. Fassbinder's Confessional Melodrama: Towards Historicizing Melodrama within the Art Cinema," *Wide Angle* 12, no. 1 (1990): 44–59.

52. See Kaja Silverman, *Male Subjectivity at the Margins* (London: Routledge, 1992), 214–496; Thomas Elsaesser, "*Berlin Alexanderplatz*: Franz Biberkopf /s/ Exchange," *Wide Angle* 12, no. 1 (1990): 30–33; and Eric Rentschler's "Terms of Dismemberment: The Body in/and/of Fassbinder's *Berlin Alexanderplatz,*" *New German Critique* 34 (Winter 1985): 194–208.

53. Silverman, *Male Subjectivity,* 253.

54. Rainer Werner Fassbinder, "Six Films by Douglas Sirk," in *The Marriage of Maria Braun,* ed. Joyce Rheuban (New Brunswick, N.J.: Rutgers University Press, 1986), 197. The article was first published in *Fernsehen und Film* 2 (February 1971): 9–13. Thomas Elsaesser

translated it into English and published it in *Douglas Sirk,* ed. Laura Mulvey and Jon Halliday (Edinburgh: Edinburgh Film Festival, 1972).

55. Fassbinder, "Six Films," 199.

56. Richard Dyer, "Reading Fassbinder's Sexual Politics," in *Fassbinder,* ed. Tony Rayns, 62; Jack Babuscio, "Camp and Gay Sensibility," in *Gays and Films,* ed. Richard Dyer (London: British Film Institute, 1977), 49–50; and Manny Farber and Patricia Patterson, "Fassbinder," *Film Comment,* November/December 1975, 4–5.

57. Andrew Ross, *No Respect,* 139.

58. Fassbinder, "Six Films," 197.

59. Richard Dyer, "Judy Garland and Gay Men," in *Heavenly Bodies: Film Stars and Society,* ed. Richard Dyer (London: St. Martin's, 1986), 183–84.

60. Fassbinder, "Six Films," 198.

61. Mark Booth, *Camp* (New York: Quartet, 1983), 18.

62. I owe a debt of gratitude for this section on camp to Ken Feil and his thoughtful ideas about the complexity of gay camp culture. See Kenneth J. Feil, "Male Sexuality in A[D]dress: Post Stonewall Gay Camp in Mainstream Film and Television" (master's thesis, Emerson College, 1991).

63. Jonathan Culler, *Roland Barthes* (New York: Oxford University Press, 1986), 92.

64. Fredric Jameson, *The Political Unconscious* (Ithaca, N.Y.: Cornell University Press, 1981), 281–99.

65. Richard Dyer, "Reading Fassbinder's Sexual Politics," in *Fassbinder,* ed. Tony Rayns, 55.

5 / The Textual Fassbinder: Two Institutional Genres

1. "Five Interviews with Fassbinder," in *Fassbinder,* ed. Tony Rayns (London: British Film Institute, 1979), 83.

2. Edward Said, *The World, the Text, and the Critic* (Cambridge, Mass.: Harvard University Press, 1983), 4.

3. Fredric Jameson, *The Political Unconscious* (Ithaca, N.Y.: Cornell University Press, 1981), 105, and "Magical Narratives: Romance as Genre," *New Literary History* 7 (1975): 157.

4. Thomas Schatz, *Hollywood Genres* (New York: Random House, 1981), 4.

5. John Fiske, *Television Culture* (London: Methuen, 1987), 110.

6. Pierre Bourdieu, *Distinction: A Social Critique of the Judgement of Taste* (Cambridge, Mass.: Harvard University Press, 1984), 3.

7. David Bordwell, *Narration in Fiction Film* (Madison: University of Wisconsin Press, 1986), 211.

8. Ibid.

9. Both of these films are available through the German government and are distributed in the United States by West Glen Film in New York City for a nominal fee.

10. The Fassbinder adaptations: *Das Kaffeehaus* (*The Coffeehouse,* 1970) from a play by Carlo Goldoni; *Pioniere in Ingolstadt* (*Pioneers in Ingolstadt,* 1970) from a play by Marieluise Fleisser; *Wildwechsel* (*Jailbait,* 1972) from a play by Franz Xaver Kroetz; *Welt am Draht* (*World on a Wire,* 1973) from a novel by Daniel F. Galouye; *Nora Helmer* (1973) from *A Doll's House* by Henrik Ibsen; *Martha* (1973) from Cornell Woolrich's short story "For the Rest of Your Life"; *Bolwieser* (American release title, *The Stationmaster's Wife,* 1976/77) from *Die Ehe des Herr Bolwiesers,* a 1933 novel by Oskar Maria von Graf; *Frauen in New York* (*Women in New York,* 1977) from *The Women,* a play by Claire Boothe Luce; and *Berlin Alexanderplatz* (1980) from a novel by Alfred Döblin.

11. Knut Hickethier, *Das Fernsehspiel der Bundesrepublik: Themen, Form, Struktur, Theorie und Geschichte 1951–1977* (Stuttgart: Metzlersche, 1980).

12. Michel Foucault, "What Is an Author," in *Theories of Authorship,* ed. John Caughie (London: British Film Institute, 1981), 286.

13. Bordwell, *Narration,* 49.

14. *The Oxford English Dictionary* (Oxford: Oxford University Press, 1970), 567–68.

15. Peter Brooks, *The Melodramatic Imagination* (New Haven, Conn.: Yale University Press, 1976).

16. Christine Gledhill, "Introduction," in *Home Is Where the Heart Is: Studies in Melodrama and the Woman's Film,* ed. Christine Gledhill (London: British Film Institute, 1986), 1.

17. Wilhelm Roth, "Annotated Filmography," in *Fassbinder,* trans. Ruth McCormick (New York: Tandam, 1981), 172.

18. Roth, "Annotated Filmography," 137.

19. An example of this critical reaction is Karl Prümm's "Aufwendiges Melodram, nicht kritischer Realismus, *Bolwieser* Fernsehfilm von Rainer Werner Fassbinder nach Oskar Maria Graf," *epd,* August 6, 1977, 13–15.

20. Christian Braad Thomsen, "Five Interviews with Fassbinder," in *Fassbinder,* ed. Tony Rayns (London: British Film Institute, 1980), 100.

21. Benjamin Henrichs, "*Pioniere in Ingolstadt,*" *Film und Fernsehen* 5 (1971): 51.

22. Hickethier, *Das Fernsehspiel der Bundesrepublik,* 199.

23. Oskar Maria von Graf, *Die Ehe des Herr Bolwiesers* (Munich: Feder, 1964).

24. For an example of this stance, see Annette Kuhn's discussion of the dominant cinema in *Women's Picture* (London: Kegan, Routledge, 1982), 21–65.

25. Jane Feuer, "Melodrama, Serial Form and Television Today," *Screen* 25, no. 1 (January/February 1984): 8.

26. Bordwell, *Narration,* 207.

27. Ibid., 70.

28. Thomas Elsaesser, "Cinema of Vicious Circles," in *Fassbinder,* ed. Tony Rayns (London: British Film Institute, 1980), 24–36.

29. Gledhill, *Home Is Where the Heart Is,* 14–22.

30. Fassbinder's confessional melodramas include *Katzelmacher* (1969), *Gods of the Plague* (*Götter der Pest* [1969]), *Whity* (1970), *The American Soldier* (*Der amerikanische Soldat* [1970]), *Beware of the Holy Whore* (*Warnung vor einer heiligen Nutte* [1970]), *Merchant of the Four Seasons* (*Der Händler der vier Jahreszeiten* [1971]), *The Bitter Tears of Petra von Kant* (*Die bitteren Tränen der Petra von Kant* [1972]), *Jailbait* (*Wildwechsel* [1972]), *World on a Wire* (*Welt am Draht* [1973]), *Ali/Fear Eats the Soul* (*Angst essen Seele auf* [1973]), *Fox and His Friends* (*Faustrecht der Freiheit* [1975]), *Mother Küster's Trip to Heaven* (*Mutter Küsters Fährt zum Himmel* [1975]), *Satan's Brew* (*Satansbraten* [1975–76]), *Chinese Roulette* (*Chinesisches Roulette* [1976]), *Germany in Autumn* (*Deutschland im Herbst* [1977–78]), *In a Year of Thirteen Moons* (*In einem Jahr mit 13 Monden* [1978]), and *The Third Generation* (*Die dritte Generation* [1979]). I have excluded *Despair* (1977) and *The Marriage of Maria Braun* (*Die Ehe der Maria Braun* [1978]) because they were made explicitly for an international export market.

31. Bordwell, *Narration,* 207.

32. Richard Dyer, "Fassbinder's Sexual Politics," in *Fassbinder,* ed. Tony Rayns, 2d ed. (London: British Film Institute, 1980), 55.

33. David Bordwell, "The Art Cinema as a Mode of Film Practice," *Film Criticism* 4, no. 1 (Fall 1979): 62.

34. Bordwell, *Narration,* 209.

35. Michel Foucault, *History of Sexuality,* vol. 1 (London: Penguin, 1978), 69.

36. Bordwell, *Narration,* 208.

37. Richard Combs, *"Chinese Roulette* and *Despair," Sight and Sound,* Autumn 1978, 259.

6 / *Berlin Alexanderplatz*: The Interplay of Fassbinder's Textual Voices

1. "I Am Biberkopf" was the *Der Spiegel* cover story headline on October 13, 1980.

2. "Die Städte des Menschen und seine Seele, Alfred Döblins *Berlin Alexanderplatz," Die Zeit,* March 14, 1980, 21.

3. Friedrich Nietzsche, *Beyond Good and Evil* (London: George Allen, 1967), 10.

4. Elizabeth W. Bruss's "Eye for I: Making and Unmaking Autobiography in Film," in *Autobiography: Essays: Theoretical and Critical,* ed. James Olney (Princeton, N.J.: Princeton University, 1980), 296–320, is one of the very few analyses of the role of autobiography in film.

5. Achim Haag, *"Deine Sehnsucht kann keiner stillen" Rainer Werner Fassbinders Berlin Alexanderplatz* (Munich: Trickster, 1992).

6. Ibid., 94–141.

7. See Kaja Silverman, *Male Subjectivity at the Margins* (London: Routledge, 1992), 214–496,; Thomas Elsaesser, *"Berlin Alexanderplatz*: Franz Biberkopf /s/ Exchange," *Wide Angle* 12, no. 1 (1990): 30–33; and Eric Rentschler, "Terms of Dismemberment: The Body in/and/of Fassbinder's *Berlin Alexanderplatz," New German Critique* 34 (Winter 1985): 194–208.

8. Rentschler, "Terms of Dismemberment," 208.

9. Silverman, *Male Subjectivity,* 215.

10. See John Ellis, *Visible Fictions: Cinema, Television, Video* (London: Routledge, 1982), 111–71, and Sandy Flitterman-Lewis, "Psychoanalysis, Film and Television," in *Channels of Discourse,* ed. Robert Allen (Chapel Hill: University of North Carolina Press, 1987), 172–210.

11. Within this model of ethereal intervention, Benveniste breaks down enunciation or the process that creates the speech act (*énoncé*) into subcategories: *histoire* (where explicit indicators of the enunciation are suppressed) and *discourse* (explicit marks of enunciation that acknowledge the conditions of the utterance). If *histoire* marks itself off as a form of impersonal speech or an objective account of an event, *discourse* utilizes first- and second-person pronouns and the aorist tense to call attention to the source of the verbal statement. The use of *discourse* calls attention to the ultimate subjectivity of language. Benveniste argues that "I" is the center of language, that "it is literally true that the basis of the subjectivity is in the exercise of language" (Emile Benveniste, *Problems in General Linguistics,* trans. Mary Elizabeth Meek [Coral Gables, Fla.: University of Miami Press, 1971], 195–230).

12. Christian Metz, "History/Discourse: A Note on Two Voyeurisms," trans. Susan Bennett, *Edinburgh Magazine* 1 (1976): 20–30, and Mark Nash, "*Vampyr* and the Fantastic," *Screen* 17, no. 3 (Autumn 1976): 29–67.

13. I am referring here to the paperback English language version translated by Eugene Jolas (New York: Frederick Ungar, 1983). This version was reissued with photographs from the Fassbinder television series as part of the American promotion for the series.

14. Döblin, *Berlin Alexanderplatz,* trans. Eugene Jolas (New York: Frederick Ungar, 1983), 253–54.

15. Ibid., 205, 171.

16. Ibid., 348.

17. Russell A. Berman, *The Rise of the Modern German Novel: Crisis and Charisma* (Cambridge, Mass.: Harvard University Press, 1986), 232–60.

18. Elsaesser, "Franz Biberkopf /s/Exchange," 31.

19. David Bordwell, *Narration in Fiction Film* (Madison: University of Wisconsin Press, 1986), 71.

20. *Webster's New Collegiate Dictionary* (Springfield, Mass.: Merriam, 1973), 417.

21. Claudia Gorbman, *Unheard Melodies: Narrative Film Music* (Bloomington: Indiana University Press, 1987), 93.

22. Christine Gledhill, ed., introduction to *Home Is Where the Heart Is: Studies in Melodrama and the Woman's Film* (London: British Film Institute, 1987), 32.

23. David Lodge, "Modernism, Antimodernism and Postmodernism," *New Review* 4, no. 38 (May 1977): 40.

24. Döblin, *Berlin Alexanderplatz,* 150.

25. Ibid., 40.

26. Bordwell, *Narration,* 208.

27. Anton Kaes, *From Hitler to Heimat: The Return of History as Film* (Cambridge, Mass.: Harvard University Press, 1989), 79.

7 / The Popular Reception of *Berlin Alexanderplatz*

1. "Die Städte des Menschen und seine Seele. Alfred Döblins Roman *Berlin Alexanderplatz*," *Die Zeit,* March 14, 1980, 13.

2. As quoted by Kristina Zerges, "Die TV-Series 'Berlin Alexanderplatz' von Rainer Werner Fassbinder. Dokumentation und Analyse eines Rezeptionsprocesses," *Spiel* 1 (1983): 175.

3. At an August 1980 press conference, responding to WDR's rescheduling of *Berlin Alexanderplatz* from prime-time to later viewing hours. *Kölner Stadt-Anzeiger,* August 27, 1980, 2.

4. Zerges, "Die TV-Series 'Berlin Alexanderplatz,' " 138–39.

5. Bernard Berelson, *Content Analysis in Communication Research* (Glencoe, Ill.: Free Press, 1952), 18.

6. Robert Allen, "Talking about Television," in *Channels of Discourse,* ed. R. Allen (Chapel Hill: University of North Carolina University Press, 1987), 11.

7. Zerges, "Die TV-Series 'Berlin Alexanderplatz,' " 174–75.

8. Pierre Bourdieu, *Distinction* (Cambridge, Mass.: Harvard University Press, 1984), 228.

9. The actual times and dates of the broadcast of *Berlin Alexanderplatz* are Sunday, October 12, 1980, at 9:00 p.m. and then Mondays at 9:30: October 13, 20, 27, November 3, 10, 17, 24, December 1, 8, 15, 22, and 29. The epilogue was broadcast December 29 at 11:00 p.m.

10. The decision was made on August 5 or 6, 1980, and announced at a press conference in Munich on August 25.

11. *Quick* 21 (May 14, 1980): 140–41.

12. Kristina Zerges states that her analysis of *Berlin Alexanderplatz* "concentrates more on the questions of the production and the aesthetics of the different media forms than on actual reception process." However, her conclusions are based on her extensive content analysis of the viewer mail and reception of the series. See Zerges, "Die TV-Series 'Berlin Alexanderplatz,' " 173–75.

13. By way of comparison, the audience size was 30 percent for the nightly news and 30 to 40 percent for the episodes of the American series *Holocaust* in 1979.

14. Zerges, "Die TV-Series 'Berlin Alexanderplatz,' " 147.

15. Ibid., 149.

16. Ibid., 174.

17. Given the financial limits of the study, Zerges admits, "the results of this kind of study can make no pretension to be representative through this data base form. Nevertheless,

the results delivered some important pieces of information about the reception of this controversial TV series. The choice of the two cities was based on nonsystematic criteria. Berlin was chosen based on the "special" relationship that Berliners have with the novel about their city and also the degree to which the newspaper had built up the series. The choice of Nürnberg was, according to Zerges, completely "accidental." Zerges, "Die TV-Series 'Berlin Alexanderplatz,'" 149.

18. Ibid., 151–52. Nearly half of the viewers (47.1 percent) watched the series with their spouses while 42 percent viewed it alone. The majority—58.4 percent—watched some of the episodes all the way through, whereas 10 percent watched the series intermittently. About a third of the viewers (29.1 percent) watched some episodes in their entirety and parts of others.

19. Zerges, "Die TV-Series 'Berlin Alexanderplatz,'" 152–53.

20. Ibid., 156–57.

21. Ibid., 158.

22. Ibid., 158–59.

23. Ibid., 159–60.

24. *Quick* 21 (May 14, 1980): 140

25. Zerges, "Die TV-Series 'Berlin Alexanderplatz,'" 164.

26. Ibid., 169–72.

27. Ibid., 170.

28. Ibid., 172.

29. Ibid., 173.

30. Ibid., 173–75.

31. "Für Fassbinder ist das Zensur," *Frankfurter Rundschau,* August 27, 1980, 12.

32. "Kommentar: Der Ärger um 'Berlin Alexanderplatz,'" *teleschau aktuell,* September 2–7, 1980, 2.

33. In West Germany there is a clear distinction between the bourgeois and the popular newspapers, and the class divisions of their respective readership are clear. Although various classes have access to and read bourgeois newspapers and magazines, I am categorizing them based on which class constitutes the majority of their audience. The "bourgeois" or "cultural" press includes: *Der Spiegel, Die Frankfurter Allgemeine Zeitung, Die Frankfurter Rundschau, Die Zeit, Die Süddeutsche Zeitung,* teleschau, and *Die Stuttgarter Zeitung.* I have also included the more professional television journals and newsletters (*Fernseh Information* and *Kirche und Rundfunk*) as part of the cultural press. For an English-language discussion of these historical class divisions, see John Sandford's *The Mass Media of the German-Speaking Countries* (London: Oswald Woolff, 1976), 25–68.

34. "Kommentar," 2.

35. "Gibt es ein Leben vor dem Tod," *Süddeutsche Zeitung,* October 11, 1980, 12.

36. Ulrich Greiner, "Die Schrecken der Liebe," *Die Zeit,* October 10, 1980, 45.

37. Ibid.

38. Michael Schwarze, "Das Fernsehen as Oberlehrer," *Frankfurter Allgemeine Zeitung,* August 27, 1980, 10.

39. "*Berlin Alexanderplatz*: nichts für Kinder," *Süddeutsche Zeitung,* August 25, 1980, 21.

40. Schwarze, "Das Fernsehen," 10.

41. Henrik Schmidt, "Verschiebung 'Berlin Alexanderplatz': Pro und Contra," *epd/Kirche und Rundfunk* 69 (September 3, 1980): 1.

42. Uwe Kammann, "Augenwischerei," *epd/Kirche und Rundfunk* 69 (September 3, 1980): 2.

43. The other interview was with WDR's program leader, Dieter Ertel. When asked whether Fassbinder was only for intellectuals, he responded: "Fassbinder needs above all aware

film viewers who bring set [film knowledge] prerequisites with them" ("Kurz-Interview mit WDR Programmleiter-Dieter Ertel," *Neue Revue Aktuell,* October 31, 1980, 7).

44. "Stolz aufs Fernsehen," *Quick* 44 (October 23, 1980): 9.

45. Ruprecht Skasa-Weiss, "Trübe Zeiten, trübe Bilder," *Stuttgarter Zeitung,* September 4, 1980, 11.

46. Schwarze, "Das Fernsehen," 12.

47. "Prolog für Fassbinders Superding," *Stuttgarter Zeitung,* August 28, 1980, 14.

48. "Kommentar," 2.

49. "*Berlin Alexanderplatz*: Nichts für Kinder," 21.

50. "Das grösste Serienprojekt des grössten Sender: 'Berlin Alexanderplatz,'" *Fernseh Information* 17 (September 1980): 413.

51. Wolfram Schütte, "Franz, Mieze, Reinhold, Tod & Teufel: Rainer Werner Fassbinder's 'Berlin Alexanderplatz,'" *Frankfurter Rundschau,* October 11, 1980, 34.

52. Ulrich Greiner, "Die Schrecken der Liebe," *Die Zeit,* October 10, 1980, 45.

53. "14 Folgen für 13 Millionen," *Stern* 41 (October 2, 1980): 258.

54. Hans Bachmüller, "Vom futuristischen Roman zum Melodram," *epd/Kirche und Rundfunk* 84 (October 25, 1980): 18.

55. Rainer Werner Fassbinder, "Die Städte des Menschen und seine Seele. Alfred Döblins Roman *Berlin Alexanderplatz,*" *Die Zeit,* March 14, 1980, 13.

56. Eric Rentschler, "Terms of Dismemberment: The Body in/and/of Fassbinder's *Berlin Alexanderplatz,*" *New German Critique* 34 (Winter 1985): 194–5.

57. Greiner, "Die Schrecken der Liebe," 45.

58. "Fassbinder: 'Der Biberkopf, das bin ich,'" *Der Spiegel,* October 13, 1980, 224, and "Geschichten um Macht und Abhängigkeit," *Der Spiegel,* October 13, 1980, 244.

59. "Fassbinder: 'Meine Arbeit ist erotisch,'" *Quick,* October 23, 1980, 52.

60. "Das Millionen-Ding des Rainer Werner Fassbinder," *Welt am Sonntag,* October 19, 1980, 3, and "Der Mann, der das Millionen-Ding drehte," *Welt am Sonntag,* November 2, 1980, 8.

61. *Gong* 6 (October 1, 1980): 8.

62. The theory that the diminishing audience share was a vote on the series' success was a central issue in much of the viewer mail published in these popular magazines. Examples of articles based on viewer responses are "Empörung über Fassbinders Alexanderplatz," *Funk Uhr,* October 1, 1980, 8, and "'Berlin Alexanderplatz'—schade um das viele verplemperte Geld," *Welt am Sonntag,* November 23, 1980, 27.

63. I am defining "popular" newspapers and magazines based on the breadth of their readership as reported by John Sandford in *Mass Media of the German-Speaking Countries,* 38–60, 210–17. In this category I include all the "illustrateds" (tabloids such as *Stern, Quick,* and *Express*), television magazines (*Hör zu, TV Hören + Sehen, Funk Uhr*), and *Das Bild* and *Die Welt* as the most widely read newspapers in West Germany.

64. "Das 13 Millionen-Ding des Rainer Werner Fassbinder," *Welt am Sonntag,* October 19, 1980, 3.

65. "Meine Arbeit," 52.

66. *Funk Uhr,* October 11, 1980, 4.

67. "Die Valentin k.o. geschlagen," *Express,* October 2, 1980, 1.

68. *TV Hören + Sehen,* October 15, 1980, 12.

69. *Westdeutscher Rundfunk Anstalt des öffentlichen Rechts Jahresbericht* (Cologne: Westdeutscher Rundfunk Presse, 1980), 48.

70. Zerges, "Die TV-Series 'Berlin Alexanderplatz,'" 174.

71. David Bordwell, *Narration in Fiction Film* (Madison: University of Wisconsin Press, 1986), 211.

72. Quoted in Jim McGuigan, *Cultural Populism* (London: Routledge, 1992), 181.

73. Timothy Corrigan, *Between Mirage and History: The Films of Werner Herzog* (New York: Methuen, 1986), 5.

8 / Conclusion

1. Urs Jenny, "Die Heiligsprechung eines Ungeheuers," *Der Spiegel* 24 (1992): 224.

2. Richard Collins, *Satellite Television in Western Europe* (London: John Libbey, 1992), 9.

3. German state televison has recently moved into commercial television via Norddeutscher Rundfunk's NDR International. ZDF has exploited the closest thing to a German popular genre, the detective series, and marketed its program *Derrick* in Italy and France. See Michael Hofmann, "Germany," in *The New Television in Europe,* ed. Alessandro Silj (London: John Libbey, 1992), 570.

4. Anton Kaes, *From Hitler to Heimat: The Return of History as Film* (Cambridge, Mass.: Harvard University Press, 1989), 164.

5. According to Eric Rentschler, the films of Peter Ostermayr and the *Wiener Kunstfilmgesellschaft* (Viennese Art Film Company) during the 1910s and 1920s represent the best examples of *Heimat-filme.* They were adaptations of the novels of Ludwig Ganghofer and Ludwig Anzengruber and their idealized visions of German country life and land. Leni Riefenstahl's *Das blaue Light* (1932) remains the best-known instance of how the Nazis took up the genre as part of their cultural output. See Eric Rentschler's discussion of the *Heimat* film in *New German Film in the Course of Time* (Bedford Hills, N.Y.: Redgrave, 1984), 105–8. And for discussion of the Nazi's use of the *Heimat* genre, see Rentschler, "The Elemental, the Ornamental, and the Instrumental," in *The Other Perspective in Gender and Culture,* ed. Juliet McConnell (New York: Columbia University Press, 1990), 161–88.

6. So popular was *Heimat* that in the summer of 1993 German television produced *The Second Heimat*—at twenty-six hours the biggest made-for-TV series in German television history.

7. Andreas Huyssen, "The Politics of Identification: 'Holocaust' and West German Drama," in *After the Great Divide: Modernism, Mass Culture, Postmodernism* (Bloomington: Indiana University Press, 1986), 114.

8. Theo Sommer, "Die Kunst ist frei und muss es bleiben," *Die Zeit,* November 8, 1985, 1. The controversy made the front page of almost all of the West German newspapers and was covered in the United States by the *New York Times* between September 23 and November 1, 1985. Two academic book-length studies have since appeared in German: Janusz Bodex, *Die Fassbinder-Kontoversen: Entstehung und Wirkung eines literarischen Textes: Zu Kontinuität und Wandel einiger Erscheinungsformen des Alltagsantisemitismus in Deutschland nach 1945, seinen künstlerischen Weihen und seiner öffentlichen Inszenierung* (Frankfurt: Peter Lang, 1991), and Heiner Lichtenstein, ed., *Die Fassbinder Kontroverse, oder, Das Ende der Schönheit* (Königstein: Äthenaum, 1986).

9. Peter Buchka, "Das Phänomen Fassbinder," *Die Süddeutsche Zeitung,* June 10, 1992, 18.

10. "Ekel Spürhund Genie," *Die Zeit Magazin* 24 (June 1992).

11. See my "Postmodern Misogyny in *Blue Velvet,*" *Genders* 13 (Spring 1992): 73–89.

12. See David Ansen, "The Kid from Mars," *Newsweek,* April 9, 1990, 66–71, and Lizzie Borden, "'Blue Velvet,'" *Village Voice,* September 23, 1986, 86.

13. See the Fassbinder Foundation's catalog for the exhibition *Rainer Werner Fassbinder: Werkschau 28.5–19.7 1992,* ed. Marion Schmid and Hebert Gehr (Berlin: Aragon, 1992).

14. Rebecca Lieb, "Fassbinder's Films Are Back, Maybe," *New York Times,* August 29, 1993, 12–13.

15. Richard W. McCormick, *Politics of Self* (Princeton, N.J.: Princeton University Press, 1991), 234.

Selected Bibliography

Archives

Museum for Broadcasting, New York
Westdeutscher Rundfunk Archiv, Cologne

Books and Scholarly Articles

Adelson, Leslie A. *Crisis of Subjectivity: Botho Strauss's Challenge to West German Prose of the 1970s.* Amsterdam: Rodopi, 1984.

Adorno, Theodor W., and Max Horkheimer. *Dialectic of Enlightenment.* New York: Herder and Herder, 1972.

Allen, Robert, ed. *Channels of Discourse.* Chapel Hill: University of North Carolina Press, 1987.

Alvarez, Luis, ed. "Homenaje a Rainer Werner Fassbinder." *Kinetoscopio* 16 (November–December 1992): 44–87.

Andrew, Dudley. "The Unauthorized Auteur Today." In *Film Theory Goes to the Movies,* edited by Jim Collins, Hilary Radner, and Ava Preacher Collins, 77–85. New York: Routledge, 1994.

Anell, Lars. *Recession: The Western European Economies and the Changing World Orders.* New York: St. Martin's, 1981.

Ang, Ien. *Watching Dallas: Soap Opera and Melodramatic Imagination.* London: Methuen, 1985.

Artaud, Antonin. *The Theater and Its Double.* New York: Grove, 1958.

Backer, John. *The Decision to Divide Germany.* Durham, N.C.: Duke University Press, 1978.

Baer, Harry. *Schlafen kann ich, wenn ich tot bin: Das atemlose Leben des Rainer Werner Fassbinder.* Darmstadt: Kiepenheuer and Witsch, 1982.

Balfour, Michael. *West Germany.* New York: Praeger, 1968.

———. *West Germany: A Contemporary History.* New York: St. Martin's, 1982.

Balio, Tino, ed. *The American Film Industry.* Madison: University of Wisconsin Press, 1976.

Barthes, Roland. "Authors and Writer." In *Critical Essays,* translated by R. Howard, 143–50. Evanston, Ill.: Northwestern University Press, 1972.

———. *Image-Music-Text.* Translated by S. Heath. New York: Hill and Wang, 1977.

Bathrick, David, and Mariam Hansen, eds. Special double issue on New German Cinema. *New German Critique* 24/25 (Fall/Winter 1981–82).

———. Special issue on *Heimat. New German Critique* 36 (Fall 1985).

Bausch, Hans. *Rundfunkpolitik nach 1945: Erster Teil 1945–1962.* Munich: Deutscher Taschenbuch, 1980.

Becker, Wolfgang. *Film und Herrschaft.* Berlin: Volker Spiess, 1973.

Bellour, Raymond. "Hitchcock: The Enunciator." *Camera Obscura* 2 (Fall 1977): 69–94.

Benjamin, Walter. *Illuminations.* New York: Schocken, 1978.

Bennett, Tony. *Formalism and Marxism.* New York: Methuen, 1979.

———. "Text and Social Process." *Screen Education* 41 (Winter/Spring 1983): 3–14.

Berg, Elisabeth. "Fernsehen als Wirtschaftpartner: Aufwendungen der deutscher Rundfunk-sansalten fuer filmwirtschaftliche Leitung." *Media Perspektiven* 11 (1975): 505–12.

―――. "Fernsehen—ökonomisches Standbein der Filmwirtschaft. Fernsehumsätze der Film-wirtschaft weiterhin steigend." *Media Perspektiven* 6 (1977): 330–37.

―――. "'Konkurrent' Fernsehen: gewichtiger Auftraggeber für die Filmwirtschaft." *Film-förderung 1974–1979*. 31–34.

――― and Bernward Frank. *Film und Fernsehen: Ergebnisse einer Represäntativerhebung 1978.* Mainz: Hase and Köhler, 1979.

Berling, Peter. *Die 13 Jahre des Rainer Werner Fassbinder: Seine Filme, seine freunde, seine Feinde.* Bergisch Gladbach: Lübbe, 1992.

Berman, Russell A. *The Rise of the Modern German Novel: Crisis and Charisma.* Cambridge, Mass.: Harvard University Press, 1986.

Bodex, Janusz. *Die Fassbinder-Kontroversen: Entstehung und Wirkung eines literarischen Textes: Zu Kontinuität und Wandel einiger Erscheinungsformen des Alltagsantisemitismus in Deutschland nach 1945, seinen künstlerischen Weihen und seiner öffentlichen Inszenierung.* Frankfurt: Peter Lang, 1991.

Bordwell, David. "The Art Cinema as a Mode of Film Practice." *Film Criticism* 4.1 (Fall 1979): 59–64.

―――. *The Films of Carl Theodor Dreyer.* Berkeley: University of California Press, 1981.

―――. *Narration in Fiction Film.* Madison: University of Wisconsin Press, 1986.

―――, Janet Staiger, and Kristin Thompson. *The Classical Hollywood Cinema: Film Style and Mode of Production.* New York: Columbia University Press, 1985.

―――, and Kristin Thompson. *Film Art: An Introduction.* 2d. ed. New York: Knopf, 1986.

Bourdieu, Pierre. *Distinction: A Social Critique of the Judgement of Taste.* Cambridge, Mass.: Harvard University Press, 1984.

Brecht, Bertolt. *Brecht on Theater: The Development of an Aesthetic.* Edited by John Willett. New York: Hill & Wang, 1964.

Briggs, Asa. *The Birth of Broadcasting: The History of Broadcasting in the United Kingdom,* Vol. 2. London: Oxford University Press, 1961.

Britton, Andrew. "Fox and His Friends: Foxed." *Jump Cut* 16 (November 1977): 22–23.

Bronnen, Barbara, and Corinna Brocher. *Die Filmemacher. Zur neuen deutschen Produktion nach Oberhausen 1962.* Munich: Bertelsmann, 1973.

Brooks, Peter. *The Melodramatic Imagination: Balzac, Henry James, Melodrama and Modes of Excess.* New Haven, Conn.: Yale University Press, 1976.

Budd, Michael. "Authorship as a Commodity: The Art Cinema and *The Cabinet of Dr. Cali-gari." Wide Angle* 6.1 (1984): 12–19.

Burgoyne, Robert. "Narration and Sexual Excess." *October* 21 (Summer 1982): 51–62.

Byars, Jackie. *All That Hollywood Allows: Re-reading Gender in 1950s Melodrama.* Chapel Hill: University of North Carolina Press, 1991.

Caughie, John. "Teaching through Authorship." *Screen Education* 17 (Autumn 1975): 3–13.

―――. Preface. *Theories of Authorship.* Edited by J. Caughie. London: British Film Institute, 1981.

Caves, Richard. *American Industry: Structure, Conduct, Performance.* Englewood Cliffs, N.J.: Prentice Hall, 1964.

Childs, David, and Jeffrey Johnson. *West Germany: Politics and Society.* London: Croom Helm, 1981.

Clay, Lucius D. *Decision in Germany.* Garden City, N.Y.: Doubleday, 1950.

Clayton, S., and J. Curling. "On Authorship." *Screen* 20.1 (Spring 1979): 35–61.

Collins, Richard. "West German Television: The Crisis of Public Service Broadcasting." *Sight and Sound,* Summer 1980: 172–77.

————. *Satellite Television in Western Europe*. London: John Libbey, 1992.

————, and Vincent Porter. *WDR and the Arbeiterfilm*. London: British Film Institute, 1981.

Combs, Richard. "*Chinese Roulette* and *Despair*." *Sight and Sound,* Autumn 1978: 258–59.

Corrigan, Timothy. *New German Film: The Displaced Image*. Austin: University of Texas Press, 1983.

————. *A Cinema without Walls*. New Brunswick, N.J.: Rutgers University Press, 1991.

————, ed. *Werner Herzog*. London and New York: Methuen, 1986.

Crofts, Stephen. "Authorship and Hollywood." *Wide Angle* 5.3 (1983): 16–23.

Culler, Jonathan. *Structuralist Poetics: Structuralism, Linguistics and the Study*. London: Routledge and Kegan Paul, 1975.

Cutler, Anthony, Barry Hindress, Paul Hirst, and Athar Hussain. *Marx's "Capital" and Capitalism Today*. London: Routledge and Kegan Paul, 1977.

Dahrendorf, Ralf. *Society and Democracy*. Garden City, N.Y.: Doubleday, 1967.

Dawson, Jan. "Germany in Autumn and Eine Kleine Godard." *Take One,* November 1978: 14–15, 44–55.

————. "Women—Present Tense." *Take One,* July 1979: 10–12.

————. "The Sacred Terror." *Sight and Sound,* Autumn 1979: 242–45.

————. "A Labyrinth of Subsidies: The Origins of the New German Cinema." *Sight and, Sound,* Winter 1980/81: 14–20.

Dennhardt, Jochim, and Daniela Hartmann, eds. *Schöne neue Fersehwelt. Utopien der Macher*. Munich: Kindler, 1984.

Diederich, Helmut H. "Märkte, Wüste, Oasen zur bundesdeutschen Kinosituation." *medium* 1978: 18–23.

Döblin, Alfred. *Berlin Alexanderplatz: Die Geschichte des Franz Biberkopf*. Oten: Walter, 1961.

————. *Berlin Alexanderplatz: The Story of Franz Biberkopf*. Translated by Eugene Jolas. New York: Ungar, 1983.

Dost, Michael, Florian Hopf, and Alexander Kluge. *Filmwirtschaft in der Bundesrepublik and Europa. Gotterdämmerung auf Raten*. Munich: Hanser, 1973.

Dreher, Burkhard. *Filmförderung in der Bundesrepublik Deutschland*. Berlin: Duncker and Humblot, 1976.

Dyer, Richard. *Stars*. London: British Film Institute, 1979.

————, ed. *Heavenly Bodies: Film Stars and Society*. London: St. Martin's, 1986.

————, and Ginette Vincendeau, eds. *Popular European Cinema*. London: Routledge, 1992.

Ebsworth, Raymond. *Restoring Democracy in Germany*. New York: Praeger, 1960.

Eckhardt, Bernd. *Rainer Werner Fassbinder: In 17 Jahren 42 Filme-Stationen eines Lebens für den deutschen Film*. Munich: Heyne, 1982.

Eidsvik, Charles. "The State as Movie Mogul." *Film Comment,* March–April 1979: 60–66.

Ellis, John. "Art, Culture and Quality—Terms for a Cinema in the Forties and Seventies." *Screen* 19.3 (Autumn 1978): 9–49.

————. *Visible Fictions*. London: Routledge and Kegan Paul, 1982.

————, and Sheila Johnston. "The Radical Film Funding of ZDF." *Screen* 24.4/5 (May/June 1982): 60–73.

Elsaesser, Thomas."Tales of Sound and Fury: Observations on the Family Melodrama." *Monogram* 4 (1972): 2–15. Reprinted in *Home Is Where the Heart Is: Studies in Melodrama and Woman's Film,* edited by Christine Gledhill, 43–69. London: British Film Institute, 1987.

————. "The Post-War German Cinema." In *Fassbinder,* edited by Tony Rayns, 1–16. London: British Film Institute, 1976.

————. "Primary Identification and the Historical Subject: Fassbinder and Germany." *Cinetracts* 11 (Fall 1980): 43–52.

———. "A Cinema of Vicious Circles." In *Fassbinder,* edited by Tony Rayns. London: British Film Institute, 1980.

———. "Fassbinder, Fascism, and Film Industry." *October* 21 (1982): 115–40.

———. "Film History and Visual Pleasure: Weimar Cinema." In *Cinema Histories/Cinema Practices,* edited by Patricia Mellencamp and Philip Rosen. Frederick, Md.: University Publications of America, 1984.

———. *New German Cinema: A History.* New Brunswick, N.J.: Rutgers University Press, 1989.

Farber, Manny, and Patricia Patterson. "Fassbinder." *Film Comment,* November–December 1975, 4–5.

Fassbinder, Rainer Werner. "Fassbinder on Sirk." *Film Comment,* November–December 1975: 22–24.

———. *Schatten der Engel.* Frankfurt: Zweitausendeins, 1976.

———. "Insects in a Glass Case: Random Thoughts on Claude Chabrol." *Sight and Sound* 45.4 (Autumn 1976): 205–6, 252.

———. "Klimmzug, Handstand, Salto mortale — sicher gestanden." *Frankfurter Rundschau,* February 24, 1979: 21.

———. *Querelle: The Film Book.* Edited by Dieter Schidor and Michael McLernon. Munich: Schirmer/Mosel, 1982.

———. *Filme befreien den Kopf: Essays und Arbeitsnotizen.* Edited by Michael Töteberg. Frankfurt: Fischer, 1984.

———. *Plays.* Edited and translated by Denis Calandra. New York: PAJ Publications, 1985.

———. *Die Anarchie der Phantasies.* Edited by Michael Töteberg. Frankfurt: Fischer, 1986.

———, and Harry Baer. *Der Film Berlin Alexanderplatz. Ein Arbeitsjournal.* Frankfurt: Zweitausendeins, 1980.

Feinstein, Howard. "BRD 1–2–3: Fassbinder's Postwar Trilogy and the Spectacle." *Cinema Journal* 23.1 (Fall 1983): 44–56.

Ferrario, Davide. *Rainer Werner Fassbinder.* Florence: Nuova Italia, 1982.

Feuer, Jane. "Melodrama, Serial Form and Television Today." *Screen* 25.1 (1984): 4–16.

Filmstatistische Taschenbücher. Wiesbaden: Spitzenorganisation der Filmwirtschaft, 1963–85.

Fischer, Robert, and Joe Hembus, eds. *Der deutsche Film 1960–1980.* Munich: Goldman, 1981.

Fish, Stanley. *"Is There a Text in This Classroom?" The Authority of the Interpretive Community.* Cambridge, Mass.: Harvard University Press, 1980.

Fisher, Peter. "Doing a Princely Sum — Structure and Subsidy." In *The German Theater: A Symposium,* edited by R. Hayman, 215–46. London: Oswald Wolff, 1975.

Fiske, John. *Television Culture.* London: Methuen, 1987.

Foss, Paul, ed. *Fassbinder in Review: An Appreciation of the Cinema of Rainer Werner Fassbinder.* Sydney: Australian Film Institute, 1983.

Foucault, Michel. *The Archeology of Knowledge.* Translated by A. M. Sheridan Smith. New York: Harper Colophon, 1972.

———. *The History of Sexuality.* Vol. 2, *An Introduction.* New York: Vintage, 1980.

———. "What Is an Author?" In *Theories of Authorship,* edited by John Caughie. London: British Film Institute, 1981.

Franklin, James. "Forms of Communication in Fassbinder's *Angst Essen Seele Auf.*" *Literature/Film Quarterly* 7 (Summer 1979): 182–200.

———. *New German Cinema: From Oberhausen to Hamburg.* Boston: Twayne, 1983.

Gaddis, John Lewis. *The United States and the Origins of the Cold War 1941–47.* New York: Columbia University Press, 1972.

Gay, John. "The Extraterritorial Life of Siegfried Kracauer." *Salmagundi* 31–32 (Fall 1975–Winter 1976): 49–106.

————. "Adorno and Kracauer: Notes on a Troubled Friendship." *Salmagundi* 40 (Winter 1978): 42–66.

Gimbel, John. *The American Occupation of Germany: Politics and Military 1945–1949*. Stanford, Calif.: Stanford University Press, 1968.

————. "Cold War: German Front." *Maryland Historian* 1971: 41–55.

Gledhill, Christine, ed. *Home Is Where the Heart Is: Studies in Melodrama and the Woman's Film*. London: British Film Institute, 1987.

Gorbman, Claudia. *Unheard Melodies: Narrative Film Music*. Bloomington: Indiana University Press, 1987.

Graf, Oskar Maria von. *Die Ehe des Herr Bolwiesers*. Munich: Feder, 1964.

Grafe, Frieda, and Enno Patalas. "Warum wir das beste Fernsehen und das schlechteste Kino haben." *Filmkritik* 12 (1970): 471–72.

Graham, Peter. *The New Wave*. London: Secker and Warburg, 1968.

Gray, Ronald. *Brecht: The Dramatist*. Cambridge: Cambridge University Press, 1976.

Gregor, Ulrich. "The German Film in 1964: Stuck at Zero." *Film Quarterly* 18.2 (Winter 1964): 7–21.

————. *Geschichte der Film ab 1960*. Munich: Bertelsmann, 1978.

————. *The German Experimental Films of the Seventies*. Munich: Goethe Institute, 1980.

Grosser, Alfred. *West Germany: From Defeat to Rearmament*. London: George Allen, 1955.

————. *The Federal Republic of Germany: A Concise History*. Translated by Nelson Aldrich. New York: Praeger, 1965.

————. "Federal Republic of Germany from Democratic Showcase to Party Domination." In *Television and Political Life*, edited by Anthony Smith. London: Macmillan, 1979.

Guback, Thomas. *The International Film Industry: Western Europe and America Since 1945*. Bloomington: Indiana University Press, 1969.

————. "Hollywood's International Market." In *The American Film Industry*, edited by Tino Balio. Madison: University of Wisconsin Press, 1976.

————. "Film as International Business: The Role of American Multinationals." In *The American Movie Industry: The Business of Motion Pictures*, edited by Gorham Kindem. Carbondale: Southern Illinois University Press, 1982.

Haag, Achim. *Deine Sehnsucht kann keiner stillen. Rainer Werner Fassbinders 'Berlin Alexanderplatz.' Selbstbildreflexion und Ich-Auflösung*. Munich: Trickster, 1992.

Hall, Stuart. "The State—Socialism's Old Caretaker." *Marxism Today*, November 1984: 24–27.

Halliday, Jon. *Sirk on Sirk: Interviews with Jon Halliday*. London: Secker and Warburg, 1971.

Hardach, Karl. *The Political Economy of Germany in the Twentieth Century*. Berkeley: University of California Press, 1965.

Harvey, Sylvia. "Whose Brecht? Memories for the Eighties—A Critical Recovery." *Screen* 23.1 (May/June 1982): 45–59.

Hayman, Ronald. *Fassbinder Filmmaker*. London: Weidenfeld and Nicolson, 1984.

Heath, Stephen. "Lessons from Brecht." *Screen* 15.2 (Summer 1974): 103–28.

Hebdige, Dick. *Subculture: The Meaning of Style*. London: Routledge, 1979.

————. *Hiding in the Light: On Images and Things*. London: Routledge, 1988.

Hembus, Joe. *Der deutsche Film kann gar nicht besser sein. Ein Pamphlet von gestern, eine Abrechnung von heute*. Munich: Rogner and Bernhard, 1981.

Hermand, Jost. *Pop Internationale*. Frankfurt: Athenäum, 1971.

Hess, John. "La politique des auteurs." *Jump Cut* 1 (May–June 1974): 19–22, and *Jump Cut* 2 (July–August 1974): 20–22.

Hickethier, Knut. *Das Fernsehspiel der Bundesrepublik: Themen, Form, Struktur, Theorie und Geschichte 1951–1977*. Stuttgart: Metzlersche, 1980.

Higson, Andrew, and Steve Neale. "Introduction: Components of the National Film Culture." *Screen* 26.1 (January/February 1985): 3–8.

Hohnstock, Manfred, and Alfons Bettermann, eds. *Der Deutshe Filmpreis, 1952–1980.* Bonn: Bundesministerium des Innern, 1980.

Hughes, John. "Fassbinder and Modernism." *Film Comment,* November–December 1975): 11–13.

Huyssen, Andreas. *After the Great Divide: Modernism, Mass Culture Postmodernism.* Bloomington: Indiana University Press, 1991.

Iden, Peter. "The Sensation Maker: Rainer Werner Fassbinder and the Theater." *Wide Angle* 2.1 (1977): 4–13.

Jameson, Fredric. "Ideology, Narrative Analysis, and Popular Culture." *Theory and Society* 4 (1977).

———. *The Political Unconscious.* Ithaca, N.Y.: Cornell University Press, 1981.

———. "Reading Hitchcock." *October* 23 (1982): 15–42.

Jansen, Peter. *The New German Film.* Munich: Goethe Institute, 1982.

——— and Wolfram Schütte, eds. *Rainer Werner Fassbinder.* Munich: Carl Hanser, 1983.

Joachim, Dierk, and Peter Nowotny. *Kommunale Kinos in der BRD.* Münster: Selbstverlag der Herausgeber, 1978.

Johnson, Catherine. "The Imaginary and *The Bitter Tears of Petra von Kant.*" *Wide Angle* 3.4 (1980): 20–25.

Johnston, Sheila. "The Author as Public Institution." *Screen* 32/33 (Autumn/Winter 1979–80): 67–78

———. "A Star Is Born: Fassbinder and the New German Cinema." *New German Critique* 24–25 (Fall/Winter 1981–82): 57–72.

Kaes, Anton. "Literary Intellectuals and the Cinema: Charting a Controversy (1909–1929)." *New German Critique* 40 (Winter 1987): 7–33.

———. *From Hitler to Heimat: The Return of History as Film.* Cambridge, Mass.: Harvard University Press, 1989.

Katz, Robert, and Peter Berling. *Love Is Colder Than Death: The Life and Times of Rainer Werner Fassbinder.* New York: Random House, 1987.

Kersten, Heinz. *Das Filmwesen in der soujetischen Besatzszone.* Bonn: Bundesministerium für gesamtdeutsche Fragen, 1955.

Kiderlen, Elisabeth, ed. *Deutsch-jüdische Normalität— Fassbinders Sprengsätze.* Frankfurt: Pflasterstrand, 1985.

Kluge, Alexander, ed. *Bestandsaufnahme: Utopie Film.* Frankfurt: Zweitausendeins, 1983.

Kracauer, Siegfried. *From Caligari to Hitler: A Psychological History of the German Film.* Princeton, N.J.: Princeton University Press, 1947.

Krasnova, G. "Rainer Werner Fassbinder— Anstoss und Anregung für den Westdeutschen Film." *Kunst und Literatur* 5 (1984): 679–85.

Kreimeier, Klaus. *Kino und Filmindustrie in der BRD. Ideologieproduction und Klassenwirklichkeit nach 1945.* Kronberg: Scriptor, 1973.

Kückelmann, Nobert, ed. *Kuratorium Junger Deutscher Film— Die ersten drei Jahre.* Wiesbaden: Kuratorium Junger Deutscher Film, 1968.

Landy, Marcia, ed. *Imitation of Life: A Reader on Film and Television.* Detroit: Wayne State University Press, 1991.

Lardeau, Yann. *Rainer Werner Fassbinder.* Paris: Etoile, 1990.

Lehman, Peter, ed. Special issue on New German Cinema. *Wide Angle* 3.4 (1980).

Lenman, Robin. "Mass Culture and the State in Germany, 1900–1926." In *Ideas into Politics: Aspects of European History 1880–1950,* edited by R. J. Bullen et al., 51–59. London: Croom Helm, 1984.

Lichtenstein, Heiner, ed. *Die Fassbinder Kontroverse, oder, Das Ende der Schönheit.* Königstein: Athenäum, 1986.

Limmer, Wolfgang. *Fassbinder.* Munich: Goethe Institute/Filmverlag der Autoren, 1973.

———. *Rainer Werner Fassbinder, Filmemacher.* Reinbek bei Hamburg: Spiegel, 1981.

MacCabe, Colin. "Realism and the Cinema: Notes on Brechtian Theses." In *Popular Television and Film,* edited by T. Bennett, Susan Boyd-Bowman, C. Mercer, and J. Woollacott, 216–35. London: British Film Institute/Open University, 1981.

MacKenzie, John M. *Propaganda and Empire: The Manipulation of British Public Opinion 1880–1960.* Manchester: Manchester University Press, 1984.

Mahle, Walter A., and Rolf Richter. *Communications Policies in the Federal Republic of Germany.* Paris: UNESCO Press, 1974.

Maier, Charles. *Recasting Bourgeois Europe.* Princeton, N.J.: Princeton University Press, 1975.

Manvell, Roger, and Heinrich Fraenkel. *The German Cinema.* New York: Praeger, 1971.

Märthesheimer, Peter, and Ivo Frenzel, eds. *Der Fernsehfilm Holocaust. Ein Nation ist betroffen.* Frankfurt: Fischer, 1979.

Mayne, Judith. "Fassbinder and Spectatorship." *New German Critique* 12 (Fall 1977): 61–75.

McCormick, Richard W. *Politics of Self: Feminism and the Postmodern in West German Literature and Film.* Princeton, N.J.: Princeton University Press, 1992.

McCormick, Ruth, ed. *Fassbinder.* New York: Tanam, 1981.

McGuigan, Jim. *Cultural Populism.* London: Routledge, 1992.

Mettler, Barbara. *Demokratisierung und Kalter Krieg: Zur amerikanischen Informations- und Rundfunkpolitik in Westdeutschland 1945–1949.* Berlin: Volker Spiess, 1975.

Meyer, Andreas. "Auf dem Weg zum Staatsfilm. Teile I-III," *medium* October/November/December 1977.

Miliband, Ralph. *The State in Capitalist Society.* London: Quartet, 1973.

Moeller, Hans-Bernhard. "Brecht and 'Epic' Film Medium: The Cineaste Playwright, Film Theoretican and His Influence." *Wide Angle* 3.4 (1980): 4–12.

———. "New German Film and Its Precarious Subsidy and Finance System." *Quarterly Review of Film Studies* 5.2 (Spring 1980): 157–68.

———. "Das destruktive Ideal? Fassbinder's Leinwand. National-charakterologie in *Die Ehe der Maria Braun.*" *German Studies Review* 5.1 (1982): 40–45.

Morris, George. "Fassbinder X 5." *Film Comment,* September/October 1981: 59–65.

Mulvey, Laura. "Notes on Sirk and Melodrama." *Movie* 25 (Winter 1977–78): 53–57.

———, and Jon Halliday, eds. *Douglas Sirk.* Edinburgh: Edinburgh Film Festival, 1972.

Neale, Steve. "The Art Cinema as Institution." *Screen* 22.1 (1981): 11–39.

Neumann, Hans-Joachim. *Der deutscher Film heute.* Frankfurt: Ullstein, 1986.

Norman, Albert. *Our German Policy: Propaganda and Culture.* New York: Vintage, 1956.

Nowell-Smith, Geoffrey. "Minnelli and Melodrama." *Screen* 2.28 (Summer 1977): 113–18.

October. Special issue on Fassbinder. *October* 21 (Summer 1982).

O'Kane, John. "Rainer Werner Fassbinder: Art Cinema and Politics of Culture." *Bennington Review* 15 (Summer 1983): 56–64.

Okun, Arthur M. *The Political Economy of Prosperity.* Washington, D.C.: Brookings Institution, 1970.

Parkes, Stuart. *Writers and Politics in West Germany.* New York: St. Martin's, 1986.

Patalas, Enno. "The Contemporary West German Film as a Social Symptom." *Film Culture* 1.4 (Summer 1955): 9–22.

———. "German Wasteland." *Sight and Sound* 26.1 (Summer 1956): 24–27.

Petley, Julian. *Capital and Culture: German Cinema 1933–1945.* London: British Film Institute, 1979.

Pflaum, Hans Günther. *Das bisschen Realität, das ich brauche: Wie Filme entstehen.* Munich: Hanser, 1976.

———, and Hans Helmut Prinzler. *Cinema in the Federal Republic of Germany.* Bonn: Inter Nationes, 1983.

Phillips, Joseph D. "Film Conglomerate Blockbusters: International Aspects and Product Homogenization." In *The American Movie Industry,* edited by Gorham Kindem. Carbondale: Southern Illinois University Press, 1982.

Phillips, Klaus, ed. *New German Filmmakers: From Oberhausen Through the 1970s.* New York: Frederick Ungar, 1984.

Pilgert, H. P. *Press, Radio and Film in West Germany 1945–53.* Bonn: Historical Division, Office of the U.S. High Commission, 1953.

Pleyer, Peter. *Deutscher Nachkriegsfilm 1945–1948.* Münster: Fahle, 1965.

Pollack, James, James H. Meisel, and Henry L. Bretton. *Germany under Occupation: Illustrative Materials and Documents.* Ann Arbor, Mich.: Wahr, 1947.

Poulantzas, Nicos. *Fascism and Dictatorship.* London: New Left Books, 1974.

Prinzler, Hans Helmut. *Satire, Irony, Humour in Federal German Films.* Munich: Goethe Institute, 1980.

Pronay, Nicholas, and Keith Wilson, eds. *The Political Re-education of Germany and Her Allies after World War II.* London: Croom Helm, 1985.

Raab, Kurt, and Karsten Peters. *Die Sehnsucht des Rainer Werner Fassbinder.* Munich: Goldmann, 1982.

Rayns, Tony. "Forms of Address. Tony Rayns Interviews Three German Filmmakers." *Sight and Sound* 44.1 (Winter 1974/75): 2–7.

———, ed. *Fassbinder.* 2d ed. London: British Film Institute, 1980.

Reiss, Curt. *Das gibt's nur einmal: Das Buch des deutschen Films nach 1945.* Hamburg: Nannen, 1958.

Rentschler, Eric. "American Friends and the New German Cinema." *New German Critique* 24/25 (Fall/Winter 1981–82): 7–35.

———. "Life with Fassbinder: The Politics of Fear and Pain." *Discourse* 6 (Fall 1983): 75–90.

———. *New German Film in the Course of Time.* Bedford Hills, N.Y.: Redgrave, 1984.

———. "The Elemental, the Ornamental, and the Instrumental: *Blue Light* and Nazi Aesthetics." In *The Other Perspective in Gender and Culture,* edited by Juliet McConnell, 161–88. New York: Columbia University Press, 1990.

———, ed. "New German Cinema Issue." *Quarterly Review of Film Studies,* Spring 1980.

———, ed. *German Film and Literature: Adaptations and Transformations.* London and New York: Methuen, 1986.

———, ed. *West German Filmmakers on Film.* New York: Holmes and Meier, 1988.

Rheuban, Joyce, ed. *The Marriage of Maria Braun: Rainer Fassbinder, Director.* New Brunswick, N.J.: Rutgers University Press, 1986.

Rohrbach, Günter. "Die verhängnisvolle Macht der Regisseure." *medium,* April 1983: 40–41.

Ross, Andrew. *No Respect: Intellectuals and Popular Culture.* London: Routledge, 1989.

Rugh, William A. "The Politics of Broadcasting in West Germany after World War Two." Dissertation, Columbia University, 1967.

Said, Edward. *The World, the Text, and the Critic.* Cambridge, Mass.: Harvard University Press, 1983.

Sammuelson, Paul. *Economics: An Introductory Analysis.* 7th ed. New York: McGraw-Hill, 1967.

Sandford, John. *The Mass Media of the German-Speaking Countries.* London: Oswald Wolff, 1976.

———. *The New German Cinema.* Totowa, N.J.: Barnes and Noble, 1980.

Sarris, Andrew. "Can Fassbinder Break the Box Office Barrier?" *Village Voice,* November 22, 1976: 57.

————. "Fassbinder and Sirk." *Village Voice,* September 3, 1980.

Schatz, Thomas. *Hollywood Genres: Formulas, Filmmaking and the Studio System.* New York: Random House, 1981.

Schidor, Dieter. *Rainer Werner Fassbinder dreht Querelle.* Munich: Heyne, 1982.

Schlunk, Jurgen L. "Images of America in German Literature and New German Cinema: Wim Wenders' *The American Friend.*" *Literature/Film Quarterly* 7.3 (1979): 215–16.

Schmid, Marion, and Herbert Gehr, eds. *Rainer Werner Fassbinder: Werkschau 28.5–19.7 1992.* Berlin: Aragon, 1992.

Schulberg, Stuart. "The German Film: Comeback or Setback?" *Quarterly Journal of Film, Radio and Television* 8.4 (Summer 1954): 400–4.

Seidl, Claudius. *Der deutsche Film der funfziger Jahre.* Munich: Heyne, 1986.

Seifert, Jürgen, ed. *Die Spiegel-Affäre.* 2 vols. Freiberg: Olten, 1966.

Shattuc, Jane M. "R. W. Fassbinder's Confessional Melodrama: Towards Historicizing Melodrama within the Art Cinema." *Wide Angle* 12.1 (1990): 44–59.

————. "Fassbinder as a Popular Auteur: The Making of a Legend." *Journal of Film and Video* 45.1 (Spring 1993).

————. "*Contra* Brecht: Fassbinder and Pop Culture in the Sixties," *Cinema Journal,* Fall 1993.

————, ed. "The Other Fassbinder," special issue. *Wide Angle* 12.1 (1989).

Silj, Alessandro, ed. *The New Television in Europe.* London: John Libbey, 1992.

Silverman, Kaja. *Male Subjectivity at the Margins.* London: Routledge, 1992.

Smith, Adam. *An Inquiry into the Wealth of Nations.* New York: Modern Library, 1937.

Smith, Anthony. *The Shadow in the Cave.* Urbana: University of Illinois Press, 1973.

Smith, Gordon. *Democracy in Western Germany: Parties and Politics in the Federal Republic.* New York: Holmes and Meier, 1979.

Sontag, Susan. *Against Interpretation.* New York: Farrar, Straus & Giroux, 1966.

Spaich, Herbert. *Rainer Werner Fassbinder: Leben und Werk.* Weinheim: Beltz, 1992.

Spiker, Jürgen. *Film und Capital.* Berlin: Volker Spiess, 1975.

Stolper, Gustav, Karl Hauser, and Knut Borchardt. *The German Economy 1870 to the Present.* Translated by Toni Stolper. New York: Harcourt, Brace, 1967.

Strang, Lord William. *Home and Abroad.* London: Deutsch, 1956.

Sweezy, Paul M. *The Theory of Capitalist Development.* New York: Monthly Review Press, 1942.

Text+Kritik. Special issue on Fassbinder. *Text+Kritik* 103 (1989).

Thomas, Paul. "Fassbinder: The Poetry of the Inarticulate." *Film Quarterly* 30.2 (Winter 1976–77): 2–17.

Thomsen, Christian Braad. "Fassbinder's *Holy Whore.*" *Take One* 4.6 (1974): 12–16.

Tracey, Michael. *A Variety of Lives: A Biography of Sir Hugh Greene.* London: Bodley Head, 1983.

Ungureit, Heinz. "Television Co-production—On the International Level and with the Cinema." *European Broadcasting Union Review* 29.3 (1978): 23–26.

Vernon, Raymond, ed. *Big Business and the State.* Cambridge, Mass.: Harvard University Press, 1974.

Welch, David. *Propaganda and the German Cinema 1933–1945.* Oxford: Clarendon, 1983.

Welsh, James, ed. *Literature/Film Quarterly* 7.3 (Fall 1979).

Willemen, Paul. "Sirk and Distanciation." *Screen* 12.2 (Summer 1971): 63–67.

Willett, John. *Art and Politics in the Weimar Period: The New Sobriety 1917–33.* New York: Pantheon, 1978.

Williams, Arthur. *Broadcasting and Democracy in West Germany.* Philadelphia: Temple University Press, 1976.

Williams, Raymond. *Television: Technology and Cultural Form.* New York: Schocken, 1975.
Wilson, David. "'Anti-Cinema': Rainer Werner Fassbinder." *Sight and Sound* (Spring 1972): 99–100, 113.
Zerges, Kristina. "Die TV-Series 'Berlin Alexanderplatz' von Rainer Werner Fassbinder. Dokumentation und Analyse eines Rezeptionsprocesses," *Spiel* 1 (1983): 137–81.
Zipes, Jack. "The Political Dimensions of *The Lost Honor of Katharina Blum.*" *New German Critique* 12 (Fall 1977): 75–84.
Zwerenz, Gerhard. *Der langsame Tod des Rainer Werner Fassbinder: Ein Bericht.* Munich: Knaur, 1982.

Newspapers and Periodicals

West German newspapers and periodicals read and/or cited in the text. For specific articles, consult the notes to each chapter.

Aachener Nachrichten
Abendszeitung
Allgemeine Zeitung
ARD Fernsehspiel
ARD Jahrbuch
Bayernkurier
Berlin Morgenspost
Berliner Zeitung
Bild am Sonntag
Bild+Funk
Bild Zeitung
Bonner Rundschau
Bunte Illustrierte
Darmstädter Echo
Deutsches Allgemeine Sonntagsblatt
epd
Erzeihung und Wissenschaft
Express
Fernseh Information
Fernseh und Bildung
Fernsehspiele
Fernsehspiele, Westdeutscher Rundfunk
Fernsehstudio
Film
Film Korrespondenz
Film und Fernsehen
Filmkritik
Frankfurter Allgemeine Zeitung
Frankfurter Neue Presse
Frankfurter Rundschau
frauen und film
Funk-Korrespondenz
Funk Uhr
General-Anzeiger
Gong

Handelsblatt
Hör zu
Kinemathek
Kirche und Rundfunk
Kölner Stadt-Anzeiger
Kölnische Rundschau
Konkret
Media Perspektiven
medium
Münchner Merkur
Neue Post
Neue Revue Aktuell
Neue Westfälische Zeitung
Nürnberger Nachrichten
Petra
Quick
Rhein Zeitung
Rheinische Post
Rufer und Hörer
Ruhrnachrichten
Saarbrücker Zeitung
Spiegel, Der
Stern
Stuttgarter Zeitung
Süddeutsche Zeitung
Tagesspiegel
Tageszeitung, Die
Theater heute
TV Courier/Documentation
TV Hören + Sehen
Twen
Variety
Vorwärts
WDR Jahrsbericht
WDR Print
Welt, Die
Welt am Sonntag
Westdeutsche Allgemeine
Westermanns Monatshefte
Westfälische Nachrichten
Westfälische Rundschau
ZDF Jahrbuch
Zeit, Die

Index

Brecht, Bertolt, 9, 43, 64, 66, 87–89, 91,
94–97, 99–104, 141, 195, 224n18,
237n15, 237n22, 237n23, 227n60
Bremen Freedom (*Bremer Freiheit* [Fassbinder
1972]), 46
British Broadcasting Corporation (BBC),
22, 24–28, 30–31, 35, 180, 197, 226n24
Bruckner, Ferdinand, 37, 65, 95, 221
Bruss, Elizabeth, 241n4
Brustellin, Alf, 55, 217
Büchner, Georg, 64

Cannes Film Festival, 71
capitalism, 8–13, 90, 102, 123, 190, 197
Catholic Church: and Fassbinder's *Berlin
Alexanderplatz,* 114–15, 170–73, 185,
189
Caughie, John, 16
CDU (Christian Democratic Party), 193,
235n67
Chabrol, Claude, 107, 126
Chinese Roulette (*Chinesisches Roulette*
[Fassbinder 1976]), 103, 107, 119,
127–33, 151, 157
classical narration, 107, 109, 111, 114–18,
139–45, 148, 151, 153–54
Cocaine, 127, 188
Coffeehouse, The (*Das Kaffeehaus* [Fassbinder
1970]), 46, 77
Collins, Richard, 193; and Vincent Porter,
35, 80, 235n65
Comolli, Jean-Luc, and Jean Narboni, 8
confession, 77, 98, 126–27, 190, 197, 199
confessional melodrama, 76, 105, 107,
119–33, 197, 240n30
coproduction, 52, 215–18
Corrigan, Timothy, 5, 191
counterculture, 84, 87, 89, 90, 94, 100, 103,
109, 160, 196, 198
critical melodrama, 40–45
cultural capital, 17, 165, 176, 196, 200
cultural competence, 17, 165, 197
cultural imperialism, 12, 100, 103, 197

dada, 67, 91, 96
democracy, 19–34, 89, 196
Despair (*Eine Reise ins Licht* [Fassbinder
1977]), 53, 58, 96
discourse, 63, 109, 196–97
distanciation (*Verfremdung*), 5, 9, 100–101

DKP (German Communist Party), 87–89
Döblin, Alfred, 1, 82, 108, 126, 135,
140–48, 155, 157–60, 162, 175, 178,
180–86, 195
docudrama, 33, 39, 50
Dreyer, Carl, 61, 138
Dyer, Richard, 63, 71–72, 103, 123; and
Ginette Vincendeau, 10, 15

Effi Briest (Fassbinder 1974), 45, 54, 108,
121
8 1/2 (Fellini 1963), 122, 125
Eight Hours Are Not a Day (*Acht Stunden sind
kein Tag* [Fassbinder 1972]), 2, 49, 78–81
Elsaesser, Thomas, 5–6, 16, 33, 99, 119,
136, 145, 223n14
Epic Theater, 93, 100
expressionism, 31, 93, 144

family TV series, 78–79
fascism, 13, 21, 25, 159, 197
Fear of Fear (*Angst vor der Angst* [Fassbinder
1975]), 50, 81, 112
Fernsehspiel (television film), 20, 34–41,
45–47, 49, 54, 57–58, 76, 81, 107, 114,
232n123
Feuer, Jane, 117
Film and Television Agreement (Film und
Fernsehen Abkommen), 51–56
Film Promotion Act (Filmförderungsgesetz),
45, 51, 231n109
Filmverlag der Autoren, 53–56, 113,
232n111
Fleisser, Marieluise, 77, 108, 113, 141,
221
Fontane, Henrich, 45
Foucault, Michel, 62, 126, 162, 165, 191
Fox and His Friends (*Faustrecht der Freiheit*
[Fassbinder 1975]), 70, 75, 99, 120–22,
126, 240n30
freelance workers, 45–46
French New Wave, 41–43, 179, 197
Freud, Sigmund, 32, 183

Garbage, the City, and the Dead, The (*Der
Müll, die Stadt und der Tod* [Fassbinder
play]), 82, 188, 196, 236n74, 245n8
gay camp, 100–101
gender, 7, 36, 144, 149–50
genre, 4–7, 76–78, 106–107, 117

Jane Shattuc is an assistant professor of film in the mass communication division of Emerson College in Boston. Previous to this appointment, she was a visiting assistant professor of film in the English department at the University of Vermont. She has published articles on Fassbinder in *Cinema Journal, Wide Angle,* and *Journal of Film and Video.* She was the guest editor of a *Wide Angle* issue devoted to Fassbinder (Winter 1989). Her two other notable articles have been devoted to feminism and popular aesthetics: "*Blue Velvet*: Postmodern Misogyny" for *Genders* and " 'Having a Good Cry' over *The Color Purple*: Affect and Imperialism in Feminist Theory" in *Melodrama* (a forthcoming British Film Institute anthology). The research for the Fassbinder manuscript was done on a two-year fellowship to the University of Bonn via the Deutscher Akademischer Austauschdienst.